SUBSTANCE ABUSE ASSESSMENT, INTERVENTIONS AND TREATMENT

INTEGRATED DYNAMIC RECOVERY FOR PEOPLE WITH SUBSTANCE ABUSE AND DRUG ADDICTION

INTERPRETATION AND INTERVENTION

SUBSTANCE ABUSE ASSESSMENT, INTERVENTIONS AND TREATMENT

Additional books in this series can be found on Nova's website under the Series tab.

Additional e-books in this series can be found on Nova's website under the e-book tab.

SUBSTANCE ABUSE ASSESSMENT, INTERVENTIONS AND TREATMENT

INTEGRATED DYNAMIC RECOVERY FOR PEOPLE WITH SUBSTANCE ABUSE AND DRUG ADDICTION

INTERPRETATION AND INTERVENTION

KAM-SHING YIP

nova publishers
New York

Library of Congress Cataloging-in-Publication Data

Integrated dynamic recovery for people with substance abuse and drug addiction : interpretation and intervention / Kam-shing Yip (Department of Applied Social Sciences, The Hong Kong Polytechnic University, Hong Kong, China), editor.
pages cm. -- (Substance abuse assessment, interventions and treatment)
Includes index.
ISBN 978-1-63483-425-4 (hardcover)
1. Substance abuse--Treatment. 2. Drug addiction--Treatment. 3. Psychodynamic psychotherapy. I. Yip, Kam-Shing.
RC564.I545 2015
362.29--dc23
2015026401

Published by Nova Science Publishers, Inc. † New York

CONTENTS

PREFACE

Substance abuse and drug addiction has long been a problem in our society. It represents a growing trend of emptiness and frustration in life, in which substance abuse and addiction seem to be the only substitute. In doing so, individuals' mental and physical health are severely deteriorated and damaged. The more the individual is addicted to drugs, the more one's physical and mental health are damaged and deteriorated. However, fear and worries towards deteriorating mental health further increase substance abuse and drug addiction. The individual needs addictive drugs to serve as an anesthetic to suppress his/her worries, anxiety, hopelessness and emptiness in life. It becomes a vicious circle in which the individual becomes more and more addicted to drugs and more and more empty, hopeless and anxious. Finally, substance abuse is an unresolved dilemma. On the one hand, individuals need drugs to sustain their sense of being in life. On the other hand, they clearly know that substance abuse and drug addiction eats up their mental and physical health; however, they have no way to get out of this vicious circle.

Throughout the years, there are many perspectives and theories in describing, explaining and intervening in the lives of persons with substance abuse. To name a few, they are psychodynamic perspective, cognitive perspective, biochemical perspective, existential perspective, sociological perspective and spiritual perspective. In fact, each perspective implies one dimension of an individual with substance abuse. It also implies one way of helping individuals to recover from substance abuse and addiction.

In this book, the writer, based on his profound clinical experiences in supervising and educating practitioners in working with clients with substance abuse suggests an integrated dynamic recovery model for clients. In doing so, a multi-dimensional model in re-anchoring of various humanistic dimensions persons with substance abuse and mental problems is articulated. By means of case vignettes and extracts of clients' self-narration, the whole book provides a humanistic, practical as well as reflective working guideline for related professionals, family members and other parties to understand and implement effective multi-dimensional interventions for people with drug addiction and substance abuse.

In introductory chapter, the writer begins with a comprehensive articulation of substance abuse and drug addiction. The differences among substance abuse, obsession and addiction are discussed. Their implications to services and interventions with persons with substance abuse are also mentioned.

Chapter One is a comprehensive review of different theoretical underpinnings of substance abuse. It includes biochemical, cognitive behavioral, psychodynamic, existential, sociological and phenomenological concepts. Different concepts and perspective outlines a multi-dimensional orientation in understanding persons with substance abuse. It represents different layers of a holistic and unique person with his/her own meaning of life, self-system, mind, morality, emotion, cognition, behaviors and roles in related social circles, community and society in understanding people with substance abuse.

Chapter Two is a discussion on integrated dynamic recovery for people with substance abuse. Recovery of substance abuse should be regarded as a personal journal of healing and transformation in achieving a meaningful life within individual own community in which the individual can fully exercise his/her potentials and ability. Within this theoretical foundation, the writer suggests a holistic integration with dynamic encouragement and facilitation. It should include a construction of a supportive environment and development of a meaningful and productive life for people with substance abuse.

Chapter Three is a discussion of stress and coping in substance abuse and its implications to integrated dynamic recovery. The chapter begins with a review of different types of coping mechanisms. People with substance abuse and drug addiction use drug addiction and substance abuse as the major coping mechanism when facing frustration in life. However, the more they do so, the weaker their coping mechanism becomes and the more they rely on substance abuse. Its implications to integrated dynamic recovery are discussed.

In Chapter Four is a comprehensive discussion on body and embodiment in substance abuse. People with substance abuse purposefully take drugs to induce intensive bodily experiences so to escape from their frustration and unresolved emotional complexes in life. Various concepts of embodiment are discussed in regard to effects of different drugs. Within the process of drug addiction, an individual's body, mind and consciousness are deeply affected. In fact, different types of drugs may have different effects on one's sense of body, mind and consciousness such dissociation, detachment from reality as well as out of body experiences. The more the clients are engaged in such bodily experiences, the more they are isolated from their reality and the more their social functioning are hindered. Finally, they may engage in a vicious circle of endless absorption in drug addiction so as to avoid consciousness of their deteriorating sense of reality and physical and mental condition. Within integrated recovery, related professionals should help clients to restore a healthy and holistic sense of body, mind and consciousness in the process of intervention.

Chapter Five is a comprehensive interpretation about the emotionality in substance abuse. Emotionality implies that emotions are related to interaction, interpretation and sharing of emotions among related actors within different social, physical, cultural and political contexts. Emotions composed of four crucial components, feeling, affect, mood and senses (Yip, 2012). Prolonged addiction may also result in the formation of several drug related addictive complexes. The first one is a drug-induced sense of superiority and shameful inferiority because of the addictive label. Another addictive complex is the craving and drug love and deep self-hate complex. As long as the individual engages in prolonged and chronic addiction, the individual also indulges in a drug related approach and avoidance of reality complex, in which the individual tries to approach or even adhere to abused substance on one hand, and tries to avoid facing the reality on the other hand. In the beginning of the substance abuse, the individual tends to abuse a substance as his/her own will. However, the more s/he becomes addicted to drug, the more s/he loses his/her sense of mastery to a degree that s/he fails to control himself/herself in taking drug. That means, s/he becomes the salve to the drug rather than the master of the drug that s/he abuse. Also, in the process of substance abuse, negative emotions such as senses of guilt, loneliness, inferiority and emptiness repeatedly **intrude** in the client's mind, making him/her feel highly uncomfortable. However, all these negative emotions are deeply *suppressed* by drug addiction. That means, it is hard for them to have sufficient *emotional attunement* with their significant others such as parents, family members, teachers, classmates, colleagues, or even with professionals who do not have experiences in substance abuse. On the one hand, persons with substance abuse are highly impulsive. On the other hand, they tend to *dissociate and repress* related negative emotion by means of the addicted drug. They incline to switch off and detach from emotions so that they can survive in everyday life. It seems that all negative emotions are *forcefully externalized* in sensual stimulation by drug addiction. In integrated recovery, related professionals should facilitate clients to deal with emotions in life frustration, emotion in relation to desires for drug, emotions induced by drug, emotions from a social and physical environment, as well as emotions before and after drug addiction.

Chapter Six is a full description about attachment and persons with substance abuse. Addiction and attachment can be related in many different ways. Firstly, addiction can be used as a means to deal with frustration in problematic attachment and bonding. Secondly, it is a substituted bonding and attachment. Thirdly, it is a means to gain bonding and attachment to related peers and social cycles such as drug related spouses and friends. Finally, addiction can be a means to punish related figures in problematic bonding. Each of this can be related to different forms of attachment such as deprivation from attachment, anxious attachment, attachment behaviors, compulsive self-reliance, compulsive self-reliance, compulsive caregiving, detachment and separation in childhood, adolescence and adulthood. Addiction and attachment may be a strong vicious cycle of addiction and attachment. Related implications to integrated recovery for persons with drug addiction are also discussed.

Chapter Seven is a comprehensive articulation of self-system for persons with substance abuse. Different perspectives of the self-system including Freud, Jung, Masterson, Horney, Hohway and Jaspsers are reviewed and their implications to people with drug addiction are also discussed. To regain an integrated and dynamic recovery, related professionals should facilitate clients with drug addiction to attain a good sense of self. Related stages of intervention is fully described in this chapter.

Chapter Eight is a full description about the meaning of life for people with substance abuse and drug addiction. The writer begins with a comprehensive articulation of various components of meaning of life. It includes a struggle for minimal survival; a constant search of meaning; a continuous sense of existence; ultimate insight and wisdom; a connection of the infinite; and a sense of ultimate and ontological existence. Frankl's (1962) description on meaning of life such as will to meaning, noogenic neurosis, 'noo-dynamics' meaning of love and meaning of suffering is mentioned. People with substance abuse and drug addiction certainly feel meaningless and empty in their lives. Facing endless frustration in life and loss of meaning of love and suffering, they use drug addiction as a constant search for meaning; a continuous sense of existence; ultimate insight and wisdom; a connection to the infinite; and a sense of ultimate and ontological existence. All these have strong implications to intervention in integrated dynamic recovery for clients with substance abuse and drug addiction.

Dr. Kam-shing Yip
Professor, Department of Applied Social Sciences
The Hong Kong Polytechnic University
ssksyip@inet.polyu.edu.hk

INTRODUCTION

Substance abuse is a common problem in modern society. People consume various types of substances, ranging from social acceptable substance such as alcohol and caffeine to illegal drug such as heroine, amphetamine, hallucinogens and tranquillizers. In the United States, the 12 month prevalence of alcohol use disorder is estimated to be 4.6% among 12- 17 years old and 8.5% among adults age 18 year and older in the United States. Also, more that 85% of adults and children in the United States regularly consumes caffeine. In addition, the cannabinoids, especially cannabis, are the most widely used illicit psychoactive substances in the United States. The 12 month prevalence of cannabis use disorder is approximately 3.4% among 12 to 17 year olds and 1.5% among adults aged 18 years and older. Similarly, the 12 month prevalence of sedative, hypnotic or anxiolytic use disorder are estimated to be 0.3 % among 12-17 year old and 0.2% among adults aged 18 years and older (American Psychiatric Association, 2012). Facing such an insurmountable social problem, in no way are services and interventions an easy task. The most difficult aspect of psychosocial intervention in dealing with clients with substance abuse and drug addiction was highly unmotivated and even resistant to professional help. Many of them only approach professionals only when they are in a tough situation. They lose their jobs, accommodations, families and mental and physical health when dealing with chronic substance abuse. They have no money, no peers and nowhere to go, and asking for professional help is their only way out in life. However, once professional help in terms of short accommodation, financial help, health services as well as employment are being given, they leave their professional workers and retain their previous drug related life again. Another difficulty is that substance abuse and drug addiction is a highly complicated psychosocial condition.

ABUSE, ADDICTION AND OBSESSION

The first challenge is that how should we distinguish three common terms used to describe clients' habit of drug use. They are abuse, addiction and obsession. In the DSM system, substance abuse is regarded as a more severe form than dependence.

In DSM IV, **substance dependence** should be defined as:

A maladaptive pattern of substance use, leading to clinically significant impairment or distress, as manifested by three (or more) of the following:

1. Tolerance, as defined by either of the following:
   a. A need for markedly increased amounts of the substance to achieve intoxication or desired effect.
   b. Markedly diminished effect with continued use of the same amount of the substance.
2. Withdrawal, as manifested by either of the following:
   a. The characteristic withdrawal syndrome for the substance (refer to Criteria A and B of the criteria sets for withdrawal from the specific substances)
   b. The same (or a closely related) substance is taken to relieve or avoid withdrawal symptoms.
3. The substance is often taken in larger amounts or over a longer period than was intended.
4. There is persistent desire or unsuccessful efforts to cut down or control substance use.
5. A great deal of time is spent in activities necessary to obtain the substance (e.g., visiting multiple doctors or driving long distances), use the substance (e.g., Chain-smoking), or recover from its effects.
6. Important social, occupational, or recreational activities are given up or reduced because of substance use.
7. The substance use is continued despite knowledge of having a persistent or recurrent physical or psychological problem that is likely to have been caused or exacerbated by the substance (e.g., Current cocaine use despite recognition of cocaine induced depression, or continued drinking despite recognition that an ulcer was made worse by alcohol consumption). (American Psychiatric Association, 1994: 181)

According to DSM IV description, substance dependence means that the individual is unable to control his/her use of substance, the amount of effect and frequency of using drug increase accordingly. The individual fails to cut down or control the amount of intake in order to create the desirable effect. At that same time, his/her occupational, recreational and social life is recurrently affected. Because of prolonged drug taking his/her physical and mental conditions are affected.

CRITERIA FOR SUBSTANCE ABUSE

A. A maladaptive pattern of substance abuse leading to clinically significant impairment of distress, as manifested by one (or more) of the following occurring within a 12 months period:
   1. recurrent substance use resulting in a failure to fulfill major role obligations at work, school, or home (e.g., Repeated absences or poor work performance related to substance use; substance related absences, suspensions, or expulsions from school; neglect of children or household)
   2. recurrent substance use in situation in which it is physically hazardous (e.g., Driving an automobile or operation a machine when impaired by substance abuse)

3. continued substance use despite having persistent or recurrent social or interpersonal problems caused or exacerbated by the effects of the substance (e.g., Argument with spouse about consequences of intoxication, physical fights)

B. The symptoms have never met the criteria for substance dependence for this class of substance. (American Psychiatric Association, 1994: 182-3)

For substance abuse, the situation is even worse than dependence. The adverse effects of drug increase accordingly. There are persistently or recurrent social problems caused by drug addiction. Individuals also take substance within a physically hazardous situation. Also, their major role obligations at work, school or home are deeply affected. That means, client's life become painful and uncontrollable.

However, in literal sense, the word abuse implies an active sense, in which the abusers take full control of something s/he abuses. For instance, an abusive father takes a full control how he abuse his children. The children are vulnerable to be beaten, attacked and oppressed by their father. They are powerless and cannot deter or fight back their father abusive behaviors.

In terms of substance abuse, literally, it should mean that clients abuse their own drug. The word abuser, according to Dictionary means:

> *'Use for bad effect or bad purpose'* (Oxford American Dictionary for Current English, Oxford University Press, 1999)

Clients are abusers of drug. In literal meaning, they possess a full control of psychoactive drugs they take it. That means they rationally and purposefully choose one or more than one type of drug to abuse. As the abusers are the subject and the abused drugs were the abused objects, they should bear a strong will, freedom or autonomy to take in or to stop using related drugs. This is particularly true for those clients who take the drug no longer than one or two months or just have tried the drugs for several times. Most clients harbor a belief that they are strong willed. They can quit substance abuse at any time they like. In actual reality, they are controlled by others, substance abuse is the only way for them to insert control and exercise their sense of agency and autonomy. From this sense of articulation, what described by DSM IV is not individuals abusing drug but rather individuals are being abused by substance.

The term addict, it means

> *'Devote or apply habitually or compulsively, make addicted'*. (Oxford American Dictionary for Current English, Oxford University Press, 1999).

The word 'devote' implies individual commits to or being totally connected with. That means individuals in drug addiction no longer have proper self-control. However, being devoted mean there should be something highly attractive or enjoyable so that the individual addict to it continuously. In addition, most regular users actually know about or have experiences of the adverse effects of drug on their mental and physical condition. They still addict to it simply because drug provides them an intensive and enjoyable bodily sense such as out of body experiences, euphoria, tranquillizing experiences or exciting hallucinations. All these intense bodily senses enable them to escape from their own painful sense of reality or life experiences. With all that, they addict to drug addiction. In other word, in terms of addiction, the pleasurable experiences actually outweigh their awareness of adverse effects of substance abuse making them addict to drug without self-control. In other words, within addiction, individuals are no longer 'subjects' to use, to control and to abuse drug. Instead, they are 'objects' being controlled, abused and manipulated by drug. The manipulative effects of drugs are further intensified by their withdrawal effects.

> 'A drug induced change in the physical state of an individual, such that she or he required the continued presence of the drug to functions normally. Further, upon abrupt termination of the drug, the addict would suffer through a physical crisis, of varying degree, known as a withdrawal syndrome (also termed abstinence syndrome). The withdrawal crisis could be ended at any time by re-administering the drug.' (Liska, 1990: 7)

In order to ensure constant and continuous drug addiction, many of them already sacrifice their social, physical and psychological wellbeing. For the sake of drug induced 'physical stimulation' and 'exciting escape from painful reality', they offer their health, their self-esteem, their mental stability, their family and their spirit to their 'drug master'. They are slaves from their drug masters. The longer they commit in drug addiction, the more slavery they become and they sacrifice to drug addiction. In no way, they can escape from this addictive and slavery vicious circle. In terms of all these, the definition of 'substance abuse' suggested by DSM IV can actually means 'drug addiction' in which the individual has already lost his/her subjectivity and self-control in the use of drug.

In terms of 'obsessions', it also means a continuous and non-stopping process in the use of substance. However, it differs from addiction, in which the individual does not feel happy or enjoyable in doing so. For example, an individual who has an obsession of hand cleaning, in fact, does not feel happy or enjoyable in doing so. Instead, s/he feels that s/he is unable to stop doing that. It is driven by a compulsive thought that s/he has to do for the sake for security. In DSM IV, obsession is defined as:

> 'Obsession as defined by 1, 2, 3 and 4.
>
> 1. Recurrent and persistent thought, impulses, or images that are experienced, at some time during the disturbance, as intrusive and inappropriate and that cause marked anxiety or distress.
> 2. The thoughts, impulses, or images are not simply excessive worries about real life problems.
> 3. The person attempts to ignore or suppress such thoughts, impulses, or images, or to neutralize them with some other thoughts or action.
> 4. The persons recognize that the obsessional, thought, impulses, or images are a product of his/her own mind (not imposed from without as in thought insertion).
>
> Compulsions are defined by 1 or 2.

1. Repetitive behaviors (e.g., hand washing, ordering, checking) or mental acts (e.g., praying, counting repeating words silently) that the person feels driven to perform in response to an obsession, or according to rules that must be applied rigidly.
2. The behaviors or mental acts are aimed at preventing or reducing distress or preventing or reducing distress or preventing some dreaded event or situation; however these behaviors or mental acts either are not connected in a realistic way with what they are designed to neutralize or prevent or are clearly excessive. (American Psychiatric Association, 1994: 423).

Within these definitions, obsessions are performed to ease out distress and anxiety or to avoid improper images, thought and impulses. That means, while addiction is a pleasurable experiences, obsession involve a repeated act or thought to avoid unhappy triggers and experiences. In related psychodynamic literature, underlying obsession is a prevailing sense of guilt and frustration in which the individual use obsessive thought or compulsive behaviors to cover all these. In other words, substance abuse as an obsession is a different state. People with substance abuse, in the state of obsession, are even more chronic and complicated than in the state of addiction. On one hand, they take the drug continuously without stopping. On the other hand, they know that continuous drug addiction is their own way for them to avoid unhappy experiences and frustration reality. On the other hand, they deeply beware that they will finally end up with severe deterioration in physical and mental condition. In some case, people with chronic drug addiction when they take drug they cry bitterly. In their mind, they feel deeply frustrated, guilty, helpless and worthless. That means, their

All these happen together in the process of drug intake making the individual feels highly ambivalent, conflicting and uncomfortable.

Liska (1990) reflected similar view in the development of involvement and addiction in the use of drug. He described this in the following stages within a continuum of involvement with drug use.

1. Occasional use
2. Frequent use
3. Physiological dependence (habituation mild to severe)
4. Compulsive drug use (pre-occupation)
5. Addiction (overwhelming involvement).

As a summary of above mentioned argument, and based on Liska's model, in terms of severity, drug addiction or substance abuse can be developed into the following stages:

Stage 1: Initial causal user (The user takes full control of himself/herself. S/he only aims at trying to use the drug because of others' influence or sense of curiosity.)

Stage 2: Occasional user (The user formulates a habit of using drug when s/he needs it for psychosocial purpose within certain social occasion. The drug serves certain functions in enhancing social relationship or alleviating stress and negative emotions. In doing so, the individual still maintain good control of himself/herself. S/he is partially dependent on drug. S/he abuses drug but his/her sense of subjectivity is still maintained. In literal terms, s/he is an abuser in drug uses. S/he believes and thinks s/he can take full control of his/her life.)

Stage 3: Regular user (The individual uses drug regularly. S/he may take drug daily. The intensity, frequency and dosage of drug taking may be various according daily stress and related negative emotions. This stage can be divided into two sub-stages.)

Stage 3A: Substance Dependence: In this sub-stage, the individual is fully dependent on drug on his/her daily life. Without drug, s/he may not able to have full social functioning in encountering daily stress and negative emotions.)

Stage 3B: Substance Abuse: In this sub-stage, the individual begins to loss his subjectivity and control on taking drug. Drug taking not only formulates his/her unavoidable daily habit. It gradually becomes part of his/her meaning of life. Without drug, s/he could not pass his/her daily life. In that situation, the harmful effect of drug begins to appear with explicit hindrance on his/her social functioning. In literal terms, s/he is not abusive user of drug. Instead, s/he begins to be abused by drug.

Stage 4: Chronic user (The individual merely losses his/her self-control in drug taking. S/he usually has a long history such as more than several years in drug use. S/he may come from a regular user and gradually becomes more and more addicted in drug taking. Or s/he may be occasional user for a long period of time and suddenly become a heavy user for quite a long period time. There should be both internal and external factors in intensifying his/her drug usage. It can be frustrating life events such as loss of spouses, employment, or being spontaneously humiliated or bullied by their significant others. Facing all that, drug addiction seems to be the only way the individual to deal with his/her life frustration. However, the more s/he engages in this, the more s/he is trapped within drug addiction induced traumas and the more frustrated his/her life becomes. In this vicious circle, there should be two sub-stages, drug addiction and chronic drug addiction with painful obsession and conflict.)

Stage 4A: Drug Addiction: In this stage, individual engages in this endless vicious circle. Drug addiction becomes his/her ways of life. In fact, in that situation, because of deteriorating mental and physical conditions, clients with chronic drug addiction may have severe impairment in their social functioning. They may be unable to fulfill their normal social roles as family and in work. Many of them may have already been expelled out by their family members. Similarly, they are sacked by their employers. They are employed, lonely, isolated and even emotionally, financially and socially deprived. Drug addiction is their only way in life.

Stage 4B: Chronic drug addiction with painful obsession and conflict: In this sub-stage, individual on one hand is entirely dependent on the stimulated physical effects from drug to rid of their drug induced deteriorating mental, physical and social conditions. On the other hand, they fully know that drug can finally end up their own life. In that dilemmas, in no way they enjoy the stimulating effects of drug. Instead, they feel highly painful and avoidably obsessive in taking drug. Many clients, in this sub-stage, cry bitterly in the process of chronic drug addiction. This should be the rough bottom of the client in chronic drug addiction. Many clients, despite they are highly resisting and reluctant, they tend to seek help from professional workers. If they fail to do and there is no one can help them to get away from their rough bottom, some may even commit suicide by taking an intensive or high dosage of drug.

CONCLUSION

In the introductory chapter, the writer fully describes the differences among substance abuse, obsession and addiction. In terms of clients' subjectivity, as an abuser actually means that the individual still maintain a sense of control in the drug use. Addiction means that that sort of self-control is being replaced by a strong sense of adherence and sticking to the use of substance and drug. That means in addictive users, they do not abuse drug. Instead, they are abused by drug. The sense of highly stimulated bodily sense is an enjoyable experience that is far more comfortable than the frustrating outside world. Finally, in obsession, they harbor a highly uncomfortable feeling that they are fully alert of the harmful effects of drug addiction, but they still have to take it as the only way to face the frustrating world. In terms of this, the writer describes four stages of drug users. They are initial users (stage 1); casual users (stage 2), regular users (stage 3) and finally chronic users (stage 4). In regular users, according to DSM IV classification, they can be substance dependence (stage 3A) and substance abuse (stage 3B). In chronic users, there are two sub-stages, drug addiction (stage 4A) and chronic drug addiction with painful obsession and conflict (stage 4B).

REFERENCES

American Association of Psychiatric Association (1994) *Diagnostic Systematic Manual (4th Edition)*, Washington D.C. American Psychiatric Association.

Liska, K. (1990) *Drug and the Human Body: With Implication for Society*, (4th Edition) New York; Macmillan Publishing Company.

Chapter 1

SUBSTANCE ABUSE: A MULTI-DIMENSIONAL CONCEPTUAL REVIEW

INTRODUCTION

Chapter one is a comprehensive review of different theoretical underpinnings of substance abuse. It includes biochemical, cognitive behavioral, psychodynamic, existential, sociological and phenomenological concepts. The biochemical perspective describes the neurocognitive process in substance abuse. The cognitive behavioral perspective assumes the individual harbors a cognitive schema in which the individual include substance abuse and physical stimulation as a way to deal with his/her misbelieve.

Psychodynamic perspective asserts that individuals with substance abuse suffer from unresolved suppression of sexual desires. They may also harbor difficulties, problems or even traumas in childhood attachment, mother child relationship as well as inner psychic complex. Existential perspective assumes that individuals with substance abuse suffered from intensive senses of frustration, meaninglessness and ontological emptiness. Substance abuse is only a mean to fill out all these internal emptiness and frustration. Sociological perspectives imply persons with substance abuse are outcasts in the society. They are being oppressed, excluded and rejected by the dominant society.

Substance abuse tends to be the only means for the face the frustration in facing all these. It also provides a common substance abuse related subculture for them to group together, to regain a sense of belonging and a sense of identity.

All these different concepts and perspective outlines a multi-dimensional orientation in understanding persons with substance abuse. It represents different layers of a holistic and unique person with his/her own meaning of life, self-system, mind, morality, emotion, cognition, behaviors and roles in related social circles, community and society. All these help related parties to understand persons with substance abuse as a normal person with different dimensions.

DISEASE AND BIOCHEMICAL CONCEPTS OF SUBSTANCE ABUSE AND RELATED INTERVENTION

Disease Model

Starting from E. M. Jellinek (1960), the disease model was used to describe the problem of substance model. Before that, the World Health Organization acknowledged alcoholism was a medical problem. In 1956, American Medical Association declared that alcoholism was a treatable illness in 1956. Following Jellinek's work, the American Psychiatric Association began to use the term disease to describe alcoholism is 1965.

Jellinek (1952) wrote:

> 'The aggressive, feeling of guilt, remorse, resentments, withdrawal, etc., which develop in the phases of alcohol addiction, are largely consequences of the excessive drinking... these reactions to excessive drinking – which have quite a neurotic appearance-give the impression of an 'alcoholic personality.'... (Jellinek, 1952: 682)

The greatest advantage of the disease model is to remove related social stigma attached to people with drug addiction and substance abuse. However, the disadvantage of this model is that people with substance abuse and addiction are regarded as weak, inadequate and poor that needs to be hospitalized, detoxified and medicated. The disease model also encourages a tight social control model in which clients with substance abuse should be institutionalized and fully controlled by detoxification centre.

Biochemical Model

Biochemical model and disease model are still the dominant ones in the society. While the disease model stresses classification, diagnosis and detoxification, the biochemical model described the harmful effects of various types of drug on human bodies. According to their pharmacological effects on human bodies, addictive drugs can be divided into the following types:

1. Pain killers
2. Stimulants
3. Tranquilizers
4. Marijuana
5. Hallucinogens

Liska (1994) briefly describe the biochemical effects of these five types of drug as follows:

> For ***pain killers,*** the most common ones are morphine and heroin. Narcosis is defined as the depression of the central nervous system (brain and spinal cord) leading to analgesia, drowsiness, changes in mood, mental clouding, apathy, lethargy and ultimately

unconsciousness….. Morphine ability to relieve severe pain without causing loss of consciousness …. Heroin…is an excellent pain reliever, long considered by some to more effective than morphine…. (Liska, 1994: 147)

'For **cocaine**, it blocks reuptake of NE from synaptic junctions and stimulators release of dopamine. For **amphetamines**, it blocks catecholamine, reuptake, promote release of dopamine, and directly stimulate receptors (Liska, 1994: 127)'

Cocaine has two main pharmacological actions. It is a powerful CNS stimulant, and it is effective local anesthetic with its own vasoconstrictive action…. Modern users describe cocaine's central effects as the 'perfect illusion'. They think they are more competent, smarter, sexier, vigilant, masterful, confident, productive and full of energy (Liska, 1994: 174)

In low to moderate oral doses (1-50 mg) ***amphetamines*** generally have the following effects:

1. Sensation of the CNS
2. Delay the onset of fatigue and the need for sleep
3. Increase blood pressure
4. Increase respiration rate
5. Raise blood or sugar level
6. Dilate the bronchi
7. Divert blood flow from internal organs to skeletal muscle
8. Constrict nasal mucous membranes
9. Depress the appetite
10. Improve athletic performance. (Liska, 1994: 185)

'When we refer to **minor tranquillizers**, we mean primarily the benzodiazepines. I constitute the main group of drugs for the control of anxiety neuroses. They are also prescribed for tension, muscle spasm, skin rashes, alcohol withdrawal, alcoholism, agitation, hallucinations and convulsions and frequency for insomnia. Benzodiazepine receptors are located predominantly-if not exclusively- in the brain, which explains why benzodiazepines have no action on other tissues such as heart and skeletal muscle. The brain receptors are in the limbic region (the part that deals with emotional regulation and control) and are quite specific; no other drugs bind to these receptors. Benzodiazepines probably act as anti-anxiety, anti-insomnia and anti-convulsing agent by virtue of their ability to facilitate GABA function. (Liska, 1994: 256)

'The word, hallucinogen, described drug in small doses could alter perception, thought, and mood, creating illusions in the mind of the user.' (Liska, 1994: 289)

The common types are LSD, PCP, Methaqualone, and Hallucinogenic Amphetamine Derivates (Liska, 1994)

Biochemical model is a crucial model in substance abuse and drug addiction, in which it enables related professionals to understand the physical effects of different drug being imposed on clients with drug addiction and substance abuse. Together with this is also knowledge of long term harmful effects on various kinds of drugs on human bodies in particular on one's mental and physical conditions. For instance, many types of drug such as physical stimulants and hallucinogens may create long term damage on central nervous system. Prolonged intake of Ketamine may result in kidney and bladder damage. Being equipped with all these biochemical knowledge, related professionals may have a sense of 'professionalism' assuming that knowing the effects, in particular the long term harmful effects of various kinds of drug can serve as a valid mean to enable clients to abstain from long term and chronic drug addiction. In doing so, related professionals tend to assume that clients did not know or have no knowledge on harmful effects on clients. They presume that once clients know about the prolonged harmful effects of drug on their mind and body, they are then highly motivated to quit their substance abuse and drug addiction. Many professional, in particular those young and inexperienced ones, may incline to a highly simplified intervention process of introducing the immediate effects and long term harmful effects of various kind of popular to clients and their significant others and different kind of detoxification and abstinence programs. However, in actual practice, many experienced professionals frankly reveal that only some initial or causal users may not beware of long term harmful effects of various kinds of drugs. Most regular users and chronic users are; in fact, fully beware these harmful effects on their body and mind. They still cling to drug addiction because of unresolved lifelong traumas and frustrating effects in current and past life.

Harm Reduction Model in Drug Addiction

Harm Reduction Model

In parallel with the biochemical model of drug addiction is that the harm reduction approach in which that assume that the most important thing to do is to eradicate or to minimize the harmful effects of drug on human bodies. As the effects of the drug on human bodies can both be immediate and long term. Harm reduction should also be immediate effect and long term effects. Blume and Logan (2013) have summarized several harm reduction approaches. They defined it as

> 'Harm reduction approaches are strategies that are used to reduce the harmful consequences of addictive behaviors. Harm reduction often includes multiple approaches including pharmacological, psychological and environmental interventions, designed to reduce risky behaviors and their consequences.' (Blume and Logan, 2013: 633)

Harm Reduction by Prescribed Controlled Substance

In fact, the traditional disease model treatment also use harm reduction approaches for many years during the detoxification process. For many years, prescribed controlled substances, usually benzodiazepines, has been to reduce the discomfort of withdrawal symptoms. Blume and Logan (2013) described that there are several main strategies in individualized harm strategies. The first strategy is modern pharmacological approach.

> 'Recent pharmacological advanced have been used successfully to reduce potential harm from substance abuse. Opiate agents such as naltrexone, as well other types of substances (such as acamprosate); have been used to successfully reduce substance-related cravings in many patients. Certain depressant drugs …have been used similarly to control mood-triggered substance sued with anxiety and depression in addiction. Recently vaccinations have been used with some success to interfere with psychoactive properties (inhibiting the high) of certain substance of abuse to dissuage further use.' (Blume and Logan, 2013: 634-5)

Pharmacological harm reduction approach is a less evil strategy in which the individual use another substituted less harmful substance/drug to replace the harmful drug s/he addicts. In doing so, the replaced substance is still harmful. That means the physical dependence of addicted drug is eased out. However, the psychological need of taking drug is still there in which once the substituted drug is stopped, the individual's urge and former pattern of drug addiction still prevails.

Behavioral Harm Reduction Strategies

Apart from pharmacological approaches, behavioral approaches such as check and count of times of addiction, alternating addictive behaviors to other behaviors, and switching to one type of high risk addiction to low risk addiction as well as tapering to reduced drug addiction to certain goals and target in drug addiction (Blume and Logan, 2013).

Behavioral strategy assumes that individual's drug addiction has a strong internal self-control mechanism to control his/her drug addiction. Once, his/her insight of harmful effect of drug addiction is acknowledged or with other's help, this internal self-control mechanism can be developed simply by various kinds of behavioral methods such as check and count to times of addiction. This assumption may be valid and true for client with substance abuse in the initial stage. However, for those regular and chronic users of drugs, most of them embrace deep frustration and suffering in time, for them, drug addiction is the only way to escape from painful reality. Unless, their life frustration and negative emotions can be thoroughly resolved, otherwise, behavioral management strategies harm reduction strategies suggested above are far too simple and superficial for them.

Cognitive Harm Reduction Strategies

Apart from behavioral approach, harm reduction approach also include cognitive approach. The most common cognitive strategy is to challenge the client's positive expectation about the positive effect and outcome of substance abuse.

> Positive expectancies are the beliefs that clients have about the positive effects or outcomes related to the addictive behavior. Common positive expectancies involve beliefs that the addictive behavior will contribute to increased socialization, power, sexuality, and euphoria.' (Blume and Logan, 2013)

All this positive expectation can be modified with the use of cognitive therapy intervention such as thought disrupting in terms helping clients to set up his/her hypothesis in drug addiction and detoxification. Within the help of the therapist, the client challenges his irrational beliefs of positive experiences in drug addiction accordingly. Cognitive based harm reduction strategies, similar to behavioral ones assume that clients with substance abuse possess enough ego strength or self-control to regulate their own cognitive expectation on substance abuse. It also assumes positive expectation such as increased socialization, courage to initiate courtship and euphoria are inadequately experienced by the clients. In fact, many people drug addiction, in particular those chronic ones narrate that they are not addict to the drug itself but rather the drug induced positive inner experiences such as euphoria, out of body experiences, excitement and tranquillizing peacefulness. For them all these drug induced inner experiences are not only positive expectation but rather actual valid subjective experiences that helps to escape from the oppressive and apathetic outside world. If the external oppressive environment cannot be removed or if they cannot find a supportive social environment to involve and engage in, why they should abstain from such wonderful drug induced positive but delusive feelings. In other words, the cognitive harm reduction strategies can help only those with positive and supportive social environment and with good self-control mechanism. For those chronic drug users, such strategies are entirely meaningless.

Lifestyle Balance Activities

Lifestyle balance activity is also a harm reduction approach in recent decade. It assumes that substance abuse and drug addiction is in fact, originate from problems in time management and unbalance life style. Once, a regular life style is restored, individuals are able to maintain a life free from drug addiction and substance abuse. In this approach, related worker or life coach examine the life style of clients in terms of their time management in everyday life. A lifestyle balance assessment is introduced to check whether the individual spend appropriate time in different domains in life such as family life, physical self-care, emotional self-care, spirituality, recreation and social life. Personal distress is originated from spending too much time in one domain and neglecting the others. Together with time management is one's habits is examined whether or not the individual is able to have good nutrition, healthy eating, sleeping and exercise as well as medical care. Adjustment is needed to improve one's balanced life style. It presumes that individuals abuse drugs because of poor life habit or unbalance life style. Thus, once all these healthy life habits are restored, the individual mental and physical health improve, the substance abuse and drug addiction can thus be restored. This approach of harm reduction, similar to behavioral and cognitive ones, is effective for those clients with good self-control mechanism, good ego strengths and good sense of reality. Once, they know that substance abuse is no good for their physical and mental health; they can change their living habit, adjust their positive expectation and reduce their behavior of substance abuse accordingly. For change of life style, this sort of logic and thinking may be appropriate for those clients who abuse sleeping bills or minor tranquillizers in life. They may have very unbalance life style such as highly busy work life, with no time to exercise and harbor a high level of anxiety. They may have habitual insomnia in which they abuse sleeping bills and minor tranquillizers so. For them, a balance life style with more time in recreation, social activities and good food certainly low their anxiety level and improve their sleeping condition. As a consequence, their addiction to sleep pills can be gradually alleviated. However, for those who abuse ketamine, amphetamine regularly, a balance life style may not be appealing to them.

EXISTENTIAL PERSPECTIVE IN DRUG ADDICTION

The Need of Existential Perspective

While the cognitive behavioral perspective assume that substance abuse is merely a problematic cognitive schema in facing stress and frustration in life, the behavioral perspective tend to assume physical senses induced by related drug is a valid and powerful reinforcement in avoiding frustration and difficulties in actual life situations. However, including the disease and biochemical models fail to address the complexity of human life. They merely assume human thinking and action can be articulated in a highly reductionistic simplified measurement and controlled physical and mental mechanism. They fail to acknowledge human being is continuously strives for profound meaning and sense of existence in life. Most clients with severe substance abuse or chronic drug addiction are empty and meaningless in their life endeavor.

There seems to be a strong need of employing an existential perspective in understanding and perceiving addiction.

> There is a clear demand from existentialists to examine the concept of addiction. They point out that much addiction research already highlights existential issues even though the author may use other terms to describe them. However, these 'givens' are unlikely to be assessed during evaluation of treatment if the treatment modalities are based on narrow, reductionistic models of alcohol use and human behavior.' (Wright, 2013: 1)

EXISTENTIAL PERSPECTIVE IMPLIES CHOICE AND MEANING

In existentialism, people in drug addiction are regarded as having choice. They are not 'dependence' and 'addiction'. The choice of drug addiction is a way to ease out their pain, anxiety, meaninglessness and frustration in life (Wurm, 2003). It is a humanistic perspective in regarding people as not drug addicts or abusers. Instead, they are people with value and responsibility. Frankl (1997) affirmed that everyone harbors a strong will to meaning. Everyone urges for meaning of suffering and love. For clients with drug addiction and substance abuse, they are actually deprived for meaning in life. They deprive of love and their sufferings are lack of meaning. Thus, drug addiction becomes their immediate and preferable choice in escaping from the sense of meaninglessness and existential frustration. Related studies show that people with a better meaning of life decreased their frequency and amount of drug addiction and substance abuse at (Waisburg & Porter, 1994; Wright, 2013)

PSYCHODYNAMIC PERSPECTIVE ON DRUG ADDICTION

Psychodynamic approaches are well developed school of thought with many prominent scholars such as Freud, Klein, Bowlby, Winnicott, Sullivan, Kohut and many others. However, among these prominent figures, their prime interest does not concern substance abuse and drug addiction. Related scholars tried to apply related theories from these prominent figures in understanding and intervention of substance abuse.

Self Psychology in Drug Addiction and Treatment: Narcissism and Narcosis

Based on Kohut's self-psychology, Ulman and Paul (2006) construct a Narcissus' model in interpretation of addiction and treatment. Their model consists of four components:

1. A phenomenology of addiction of what is addiction.
2. An etiology and pathogenesis of addiction or when are the origins and where are the developmental pathways leading to addiction.
3. A typology of addiction or who are the various types of addiction.
4. A therapeutics of addiction or how does a psychotherapist work psychotherapeutically with an addiction pattern. (Ulman and Paul, 2006: xiv)

Ulman and Paul (2006) further compared similarities of narcissism and narcosis as follows:

> 'Narcissism and narcosis may be compared like this: in case of narcissism an archaic form of self-love function like a narcotic drug that induces a state of enraptured self-absorption: whereas in the case of narcosis, a drug or other substance produces a narcissistic state of bliss characterized by an ecstatic trance and euphoric obliviousness. (Ulman and Paul, 2006: 4)
>
> Ulman and Paul (2006) 'employ an empathetic introspective stance from Kohut as a means to gaining access to the unconscious fantasy lives of our addicted patients. We discover that unconsciously they are organized in terms of a specific type of archaic does not reinvest the narcissistic capital, which is originally derived from early caregivers, back into nonhuman being things or activities (that is transitional object) as well as later human caregivers (Ulman and Paul, 2006: xiv)

Khantzian's Self Medication Articulation in Drug Addiction

Khantzian (1980, 1981) based on self-pathology; asserted substance abuse and drug addiction is actually a matter of self-choice. Different persons because of various types of personality and unfulfilled psychological needs generated from self-pathology, they tend to choose their own types of drug.

'Most substance dependent individual prefers and self-selects a particular drug. This preference and selection is the result of the drug of choice and its distinctive psychopharmacologic effects interacting with the unique personality organization and reactive patterns of an individual that predisposes a person to dependency on a particular drug...... I have been particularly interested in the narcotic addict's preference for opiates... heroin addicts led me to conclude that the compelling nature of opiates for many narcotic addicts resides in a specific anti-aggression action of narcotics, namely to relieve and countered regressed, disorganized, and dysphoric ego states related to overwhelming feelings of rage, anger and elated depression. (Khantzian, 1980: 32)

Compulsiveness of Drug Addiction

Wurmser (1978) affirmed drug addiction is not a kind of dependency. Instead, it is a psychological compulsion. Based on Glasscote and others (1971) stressed the following:

'By contrast to the term psychological dependence, compulsion is a more specific term that connotes one of the greatest obstacles successfully treating people who have abused drugs. Compulsivity can be manifested in practically any aspect of behavior....

Compulsivity is believed to commonly underlie any number of widespread behavior problems, such as overeating, heavy use of alcohol, gambling, and so on. It seems certain that some portion of those who use illegal drugs do so out of compulsion. This significance is this: compulsions are notably resistant to presently known methods of treatment; the long term success rate is low, the relapse rate is high. (Glasscote and Others, 1972: 55 & Wurmser, 1979: 345)

In the life history and the direct experience of every patient dependent upon physically addicting drugs, we may discern three layers of compulsion:

a) Acute Withdrawal

The compulsiveness of physical dependency based on entirely on processes on the level of the cells. (The compulsive need to continue with drug to avoid the very uncomfortable feeling of acute withdrawal. This is a strictly physical problem)

b) Protracted Withdrawal

The compulsiveness of protracted withdrawal, a gray area in theory (Addict who have been withdrawn and are not physically dependent anymore, typically show a persistent longing to return to the drug. This urge or desire is known to endure years, even decades, of enforced abstinence.)

c) Emotional Need

The emotional compulsiveness leading first to start drug use and then to continue the search of effect. Only this third form will be encountered in compulsive users of drugs which are not also physically addictive, like psychedelics or stimulants.

(Every neurotic compulsion is viewed as outcomes of a conflict of several incompatible wishes and fears, a conflict which is forcibly pushed out, and kept out, of consciousness. It is characteristic of such compulsions that the more they are lived out in outer reality, the more insatiable they become; it is as if they were continually searching

for their real, though unconscious, aim without ever being able to attain it- precisely because the real aim of the wish is buried.

Under any psychological or physiological stress the compulsion to take drug (or to show other forms of symptoms) increases. In turn it can be observed that the emotional dependency on the drug is overcome if the psychological dependency and commitment is displaced onto other objects, e.g., to a concrete community, to a cause, or to a therapist. In other words, potent meaning giving factors can replace in highly motivated individuals the compelling role the drug exerts (Wurmser, 1978:78)

Wurmser (1978) affirmed that drug addiction and substance abuse is, in fact, a kind of compulsiveness. This included three types of compulsiveness. The first type is actual physical compulsiveness in which the individual suffer intensively form acute withdrawal. S/he has to take the drug immediately to ease up the intensive physical tension and withdrawn symptoms. The second type is protracted withdrawal. It is a kind of delayed sense of compulsiveness in which the individual has a lengthened sense of physical withdrawal. It is a longing sense to return to the drug. The third type is emotional need. It is a kind a mixing of fear, wishes, desires and internal frustration. The sense of compulsiveness is, theoretically, opposite to Khantzian's self-medication. In self-medication, drug addiction is a kind self-choice. That means, the individual is the subject in choosing related drug to abuse. However, in Wurmser's (1978) compulsiveness, related individuals are compulsive objects being controlled by their drug addiction. Because of acute withdrawal and protracted withdrawal symptoms and emotional needs, they are controlled by their own drug addiction. That means, in Khantzian' self-medication concepts, drug addiction is an entirely voluntary individual's choice. In Wurmser (1978) drug addiction is a voluntary compulsion in which the individual cannot control himself/herself. Instead, s/he is controlled by drug. The compulsion is short term and intensive (acute withdrawal) and long term attraction (protracted withdrawal) as well as an emotional and psychological adhesiveness.

Drug Addiction as Attachment and Love

Drug Addiction and Love

Within Bowlby's attachment concepts, drug addiction is regarded as a substituted object for attachment. Peele in his book 'Love and Drug Addiction' affirmed that in many ways, love and addiction have similar natures.

'The addict is a person who never learns to come to grip with his world, and who therefore seeks stability and reassurance through some repeated, ritualized activity. This activity is reinforced in two ways-first, by a comforting sensation of well induced by the drug or other addictive object; second, by the atrophy of the addict's other interests and abilities and the general deterioration of his situation while he is preoccupied with the addiction. As alternatives grow smaller, the addiction grows larger, until it is all there is. A true addict progresses into a monomania, whether the object of addiction is a drug or a lover. Vicky and Bruce's sheltered childhoods denied them the self-confidence and the well-formed enthusiasms that a complete life is built on. As a result, they fastened out each other as a daily habit, and this habit became the raison detre of their existence.' (Peele, 1975: 27)

Peele (1975) affirmed that the person with drug addiction gradually absorb in worsening his degree of addiction because his/her ability to seek pleasure in other normal activities and hobbies gradually deteriorate accordingly. S/he may be thus regarded drug as his/her lover. In other words, in his/her daily life, s/he is totally attached to drug. The habit of drug addiction finally becomes the aim of existence of the individual.

> There is a fundamental similarity between opiate addiction and love. In both cases, a person repeatedly seeks out a kind of stimulation which is intensely pleasurable. But as time goes on, he finds that he needs it more even as he enjoys it less. The heroin addict gets less and less of a positive kick from the drug, yet he must return to it to counteract the insistent pain caused by its absence. The lover is no longer so excited by his or her partner, but is more and more dependent on the comfort of the partner's continued presence, and is less able to handle a separation. Here the negative aftereffect overcomes initially positive stimulation. (Peele, 1975: 53)

Peele (1975) further affirmed that drug addiction is similar to love affairs in which the person seeks pleasure in it. However, as the time goes by, the pleasure in the lovable or addictive objects becomes less and less. Thus, the individual needs this more and more so as to maintain the degree of pleasure s/he initially has. That means, the addictive objects and the drug occupied most of his/her time. In other words, the individual becomes more and more dependent on the addictive or lovable objects. The separation and absence of addictive and lovable object becomes more and more intolerable for the individual.

Addiction to Experience

> 'People become addicted to experiences. The addictive experiences is the totality of effect produced by an involvement, it stems from pharmacological and physiological sources but takes its ultimate form from cultural and individual construction of experience. The most recognized from of addiction is an extreme, dysfunctional attachment to an experience that is acutely harmful to a person, but that is an essential part of the person's ecology and that the person cannot relinquish. This state is the result of a dynamic social learning process in which the person finds an experience rewarding because it ameliorates urgently felt needs, while in the long run it damages the persons' capacity to cope and ability to generate stable sources of environmental gratification. (Peele, 1985: 97)

Peele (1985) firmly asserted that people with drug addiction are, in fact, addictive to experiences. The subjective experience in drug addiction becomes their involvement shield as well as their personal ecology. They become more and more attached to the addictive experiences in which is highly rewarding and can satisfy their unfulfilled needs but in the long run creates harm and damages to them. The addictive experiences are highly comprehensive and deeply engaged within human phenomenon. The addictive individuals earnestly and eagerly urge for rewarding addictive experiences in his/her daily life. It may become his/her most important involvement to an extent that penetrates into his/her social and situational context and finally becomes part of his/her personality.

> Because addiction is finally a human phenomenon, it engages every aspect of a person's functioning, starting with the rewards (as interpreted by the individual) that an involvement provides and the individual's need for these rewards. The motivation to pursue the involvement, as compared with other alternatives, is a function of an additional layer of social, situational and personality variables. ... (Peele, 1985: 97)

Peele (1985) has formulated an addictive formula. It is a matching of addictive experiences and addictive needs in which the addictive experiences are influenced by different types of drug intake as well as beliefs in power, controllability and legal and moral interpretation of related experiences. Addictive needs are reflected in related social milieu, individual traits and needs as well as individual's values and needs.

E: Addictive experience includes:

E1: Natures of experiences
E1a: Psychoactive or experience modifying power
E1b: Substance use versus nondrug activity
E1c: Stimulant versus depression

E2: Socially Mediated Effects
E2a: Belief in efficacy and power of experience
E2b: Belief in uncontrollability of experiences
E2c: Legal versus illicit, socially approved versus disapproved
E2d: Traditions of excessive, magical, or unhealthy involvement

Addictive Experiences is a process of maturational, life span, and situational variation

N: Addictive need includes:

N1: Social Milieu
N1a: Uncontrollable, stressful
N1b: Prescribes values that are difficult to attain
N1c: Inhospitable to enterprise

N2: Individual Traits and Need
N2a: Low achievement need, high fear of failure
N2b: Need for immediate gratification, intolerance of uncertainty
N2c: Low self-efficiency, high dependence needs, low self esteem
N2d: Need for personal dominance, aggression

N3: Values and Outlook
N3a: Negativistic, avoidant
N3b: Excessive, immediate, lacking values towards health, sobriety

N3c: Antisocial, alienated
N3d: Belief in magical solution

Addictive Needs are a Temporal Dimension

In other words, Peele (1985) advocated for a multi-dimensional perspective, in which addictive needs are related to personal, interpersonal and social variables. Addictive experiences and addictive needs interact with one another making the individual fully engages or attaches to drug addiction.

Addiction and Attachment

People with attachment problems usually have insecure attachment. They always harbored negative emotions such as anxiety and fear of being abandoned by others. Furthermore, they also have fear of intimacy in relating to others (Bowen, 1976, 1978, Hazen and Shaver, 1987). Facing all these negative emotions, they are more vulnerable to seek other means to deal with their negative emotions as well as they attach to addictive experiences instead of attachment to others (Cooper, et al., 1998; Dotten, et al., 2003). Hoefler and Kooyman (1996) proposed that drug abuse can reflect a delayed maladaptive attachment transition in young adults and associated fear of intimacy. Similarly, Descutner and Thelen (1991) found that fear of intimacy served as a risk factor for emotional problems and substance abuse. Finally, Thorberg and Lyvers (2006) found out that subjects with drug addiction (alcoholism, heroin addiction, amphetamine/cocaine addiction or cannabis abuse) reported higher levels of insecure attachment and fear of intimacy, and lower levels of secure attachment and differentiation of self, compared to controls. Insecure attachment, high fear of intimacy and low self-differentiation appear to characterize clients enrolled in addiction treatment programs (Thorberg & Lyvers, 2006: 723).

Motivational Interviewing

Apart from above mentioned perspectives in interpretation and intervention for people with drug addiction, in recent years, a new model, motivational interviewing was suggested by Miller & Butler (2008). This model was originated from clinical work with adults with alcoholic problems and later extended to other types of addiction.

Motivational interviewing tries to focus on clarifying the myth that clients with substance abuse are resisting to change and unmotivated for recovery. Rollnick, Miller & Butler (2008) suggested four guiding principles. Principle one is resisting the righting reflex. Principle two is understanding the client's motivation. Principle three is listening to your clients. Principle four is empowering your clients. Regarding the change of clients in the process of recovery, six stages are suggested. They are pre-contemplation stage, contemplation stage, determination stage, action, maintenance, and relapse (Miller & Rollnick, 1991; Prochasks, & Diclemente,1982). Within these six stages of changes, related professionals should have continuous patience, accepting, encouragement and appreciation of clients' efforts in their process of recovery. Motivational interviewing tends to be a breakthrough within the dominant deficit oriented model of detoxification. However, its applicability to the full recovery to persons in various types of substance abuse, in particular with adolescents is still subjected to its constraints and limitations. Furthermore, motivational interviewing fails to address the important influences of environmental contexts, especially oppression and difficulties in life that initiate and provoke substance abuse. In fact, persons with substance abuse are not unmotivated to quit drug addiction. They need drug substance to cope with their senses of emptiness, inferiority, loneliness and fear in facing hardships and trauma in current and previous life encounter.

Conclusion: A Multi-Dimensional View

Drug addiction is not a problematic behaviors, it affects the whole person including meaning of life, self-system, mind, body and social functioning. Any one of the above mentioned perspectives can be regarded as focusing on any one of the dimension of a human being. It can be shown in the following tables:

Table. Different Dimension of a Person and Drug Addiction Theories

Related Dimension in Human Being	Related Figures and Scholars
Existential Dimension: Meaning of Life	The choice of drug addiction is a way to ease out their pain, anxiety, meaninglessness and frustration in life (Wurm, 2003)
Self-system (Self-identity, Self-image and Self-boundary)	Narcissus' model in interpretation of addiction and treatment Khantzian (1980, 1981) based on self-pathology, asserted substance abuse and drug addiction is actually a matter of self-choice. Different persons because of various types of personality and unfulfilled psychological needs generated from self-pathology, they tend to choose their own types of drug.
Mind: Cognition	Cognitive harm reduction approach
Mind: Emotion	Khantizian model, Peele model, Wurmser model and Khantzian model also concern of emotions.
Mind: Experiences and Memories	Peel's addiction to experience
Body	Pharmacological harm reduction approach Physiological effects of different kind of drug
Behaviors: Social functioning, Roles and Interpersonal relationship	Wurmser (1978) affirmed that drug addiction and substance abuse is, in fact, a kind of compulsiveness Attachment and drug addiction Love and addiction

In other words, any one of the above perspective may only mean focusing one dimension of a human being. In addition to this, there can be three foci among all these perspectives.

1. Focus on deficit and destructive power of drug addiction (e.g., harm reduction approach).
2. Focus on unfulfilled need of any one dimension of human being that needs to be pathologically coped with drug addiction and substance abuse.
3. Focus on addiction of drug induced experiences, stimulated physiological and psychological effects rather than the drug itself.

Thus, to have a holistic, humanistic and multi-dimensional understanding of clients with drug addiction and abuse, instead of focus on any one of the above mentioned perspectives, it is better to focus our attention in narrating and discussing different dimensions including, body, emotionality, stress and coping, attachment, self-system as well as meaning of life in being influenced by drug addiction and substance abuse. In doing so, the above mentioned three foci will be further elaborated.

References

Bean. M. H. & Zinberg, N.E. (1981) (Edited) Dynamic Approaches to the Understanding and Treatment of Alcoholism, New York: Free Press.

Blume, A. W. & Logan, D. (2013) Harm reduction approaches, *Interventions for Addiction*, 3: 633-642.

Bowen,M. (1976). Theory in the practice of psychotherapy. In P. J. Guerin (Ed.), Family *therapy: Theory and practice* (pp. 42–90). New York: Gardner Press.

Bowen, M. (1978). Family therapy in clinical practice. New York: Jason Aronson.

Brennan, K. A., & Shaver, P. R. (1995). Dimensions of adult attachment, affect regulation, and romantic relationship functioning. Personality and Social Psychology Bulletin, 21, 267–283.

Cooper, M. L., Shaver, P. R., & Collins, N. L. (1998). Attachment styles, emotion regulation, and adjustment in adolescence. *Journal of Personality and Social Psychology*, 74, 1380–1397.

Descutner, C. J., & Thelen, M. H. (1991). Development and validation of a fear-of-intimacy scale. *Journal of Consulting and Clinical Psychology,* 3(2), 218–225.

Dottan, R. F., Cohen, O., Iwaniec, D., Sapir, Y., & Weizman, A. (2003). The drug-user husband and his wife: Attachment styles, family cohesion and adaptability. *Journal of Substance Use and Misuse,* 38(2), 271–292.

Frankl, V. (1997). *Man's Search for Ultimate Meaning*. New York: Plenum.

Glasscote, R., Sussex, J. N., Jaffe, J. H., Ball, J., and Brill, J. (1972) *The Treatment of Drug Abuse: Programs, Problems, Prospects.* Washington, D. C.: Joint Information Service, APA and NIMH.

Hazan, C., & Shaver, P. (1987). Romantic love conceptualised as an attachment process. *Journal of Personality and Social Psychology*, 52: 511–524.

Hoefler, D. Z., & Kooyman, M. (1996). Attachment transition, addiction and therapeutic bonding—An integrative approach. *Journal of Substance Abuse Treatment*, 13(6): 511–519.

Jellinek, E. M. (1960) *The Disease Concept of Alcoholism*, New Haven, Hillhouse Press.

Jellinek, E. M. (1952) Phases of alcohol addition, *Quarterly Journal of Studies in Alcohol*, 13: 673-684.

Khantzian, E. J. (1980) An ego/self theory of substance dependence: A contemporary psychoanalytic perspective, *Theories of Drug Abuse: Selected Contemporary Perspective,* pp. 29-33. U.S.: National Institute on Drug Abuse.

Khantzian, E. J. (1981) Some treatment implication of the ego and self disturbances in alcoholism', in Bean. M. H. & Zinberg, N.E. (1981) (Edited) *Dynamic Approaches to the Understanding and Treatment of Alcoholism,* New York: Free Press.

Liska, K. (1990) *Drug and the Human Body: With Implication for Society*, (4th Edition) New York; Macmillan Publishing Company.

Miller, W.R. & Rollnick, S. (1991) *Motivational Intervention: Preparing People to Change Addictive Behaviors,* New York: The Guildford Press.

Peele, S. (1975) *Love and Addiction*, New York: Taplinger Publishing Company.

Peele, S. (1985) *The Meaning of Addiction*, Toronto: Lexington Books.

Prochasks, J.O., & Diclemente, C.C. (1982) Trans-theoretical therapy: Towards a more integrative model of change; Psychotherapy, *Theory, Research and Practice*, 19:276-288.

Rollnick, S., Miller, W.R. & Butler, C.C. (2008) Motivational Interviewing in Health Care, New York: The Guildford Press.

Siegel, A. M. (1996) *Heinz Khout and the Psychology of the Self*, New York: Routledge.

Thorberg, F. A., Lyvers, M. T. (2006) Attachment, fear of intimacy and differentiation of self among clients in substance disorder treatment facilities, Addictive Behaviors, 31: 732–73.

Ulman, R. B. & Paul, H. (2006) The Self Psychology of Addiction and Its Treatment: Narcissus in Wonderland, New York: Routledge.

Waisburg, J., & Porter, J. (1994). Purpose in life and outcomes of treatment for alcohol dependence. *British Journal of Clinical Psychology*, 33:49-63.

Weegmann, M & Choen, R. (2002) (Edited) *The Psychodynamics of Addiction*, London: Whure Publishers.

Wright, S. (2013) An Existential view of Alcohol Dependence and the Search for Meaning.

Wurm, C. (2003). Is 'Addiction' a helpful concept? *An existential view. European Psychotherapy,* 4(1): 175-182.

Wurmser, L. (1978) *The Hidden Dimension: Psychodynamics in Compulsive Drug Use*, New York: Jason Aronson.

Wurmser, L (1987) Flight from conscience: experiences with the psychoanalytic treatment of compulsive drug abusers, *Journal of Substance Abuse Treatment*, 4: 157-179.

Chapter 2

INTEGRATED DYNAMIC RECOVERY OF PERSONS WITH SUBSTANCE ABUSE

INTRODUCTION

In this chapter, the integrated dynamic recovery model (IDR) is introduced. In this model, individuals with substance abuse are regarded as persons rather than patients with addiction. As other normal persons in the society, they have their own unique personality, experiences, potentials and ability. They engage in substance abuse merely because of various difficulties, hardships and traumas in life experiences. Thus, related parties should facilitate them to change from substance abuse to healthy life. In doing so, persons with substance abuse should not be institutionalized or medicalized with hospitals and institution. Instead, their own potentials and resilience in life should be fully developed so that they can be recovered in their own pace. Furthermore, related parties should help individuals to integrate back into their own community and live a normal life with constructive and meaningful activities and interaction with others.

INTEGRATED DYNAMIC RECOVERY

A Holistic Integration

Within this model of practice, there are three important elements, multidimensional integration, dynamic facilitation and encouragement as well as holistic recovery in substance abuse. Multidimensional integration implies integration of mind and body, social integration within various social circles.

Regarding the sense of mind, substance abuse harbors and nurtures distorted emotions and perception of reality. Individuals always substance abuse to repress and dissociated their negative emotions. It is important for related professionals to help persons with substance abuse to express and share their fixated or repressed negative emotions as well as related unpleasant or even traumatic experiences. Once all these are fully shared and ventilated, individual with substance abuse should develop self-image and competence through meaningful and constructive interaction and activities with others. All these can be arranged by their significant others with the support of related professionals. Then, with good and substantial ego strengths and competent self-image, related professionals should help individuals to resolve their unresolved frustrating past experiences, in particular those traumatic and complicated ones. Finally, individuals should re-build positive emotion and relationships with others. With all that, they can live a normal life with full abstinence from substance abuse.

Regarding sense of body, individuals with substance abuse are used to use drug induced intensive sense of body to compensate frustrated sense of mind in terms of emptiness, insecurity, loneliness, inferiority and anger. Gradually, as the body conditions and functioning are severely impaired by the harmful effects of abused substance, the individual is then kept with an unresolved dilemma. On one hand, the individual's sense of mind and sense of body is getting worse and worse as his/her substance abuse increase and his/her body functioning and condition deteriorated. On the other hand, the individual has no way out. The only way they can deal with all these frustrating senses of body and mind is to be continuously involved in increasing dosage of substance abuse. Gradually, this becomes an unresolved vicious circle of poor senses of mind and body and increasing substance abuse. Thus, in the recovery process, it is important for the individual to regain positive senses of mind and body. First, individuals should be facilitated to beware of impaired senses of body in particular the deteriorating body conditions. In doing so, related medical assessments and treatments should be delivered to help the individual to regain better health conditions. Second, instead of relying unhealthy means to induce an intensive sense of healthy body, the individual should be facilitated to use healthy means such as enjoying physical exercise, having a good rest, eating good food, dressing oneself up and having a good physical appearance. All these enable one to have good sense of body as well as good sense of self-image. Coupled with the above mentioned, it means in developing good sense of mind by normal and constructive means, individuals can finally attain a natural and smooth integration of mind and body without relying on substance abuse to deal with intensive sense of emptiness and frustration in life.

Integration should also implies social integration with individuals' significant others within various social circles, including peers, family, community, school and working environments. Related parties should facilitate individuals with substance abuse to establish meaningful and healthy interactions with key members in these social circles. They should be facilitated to accept, include, support and forgive individuals with substance abuse. That means, inclusive peer system, school system, family system and community should be restored or established by related professionals in help persons with substance abuse in the process of recovery. In doing so, related professionals should be patient and negotiate with related parties so that a gradual inclusion process can be done to include persons with substance abuse with their own social circles in everyday life. In many cases, individuals with substance abuse may still cling to substance abuse and their previous addiction related peers, especially when they face various difficulties and frustration in life. In fact, it is a pull and push force for individuals with substance abuse in the recovery process. If significant others in various social circles are able to accept them, then their inclination to adhere to substance abuse and addiction related peers will gradually decline. However, if not, they properly turn back to substance abuse and related peers. Thus, professionals should on one hand, prepare clients to include in various social circles. On the other hand, they should negotiate with different parties to include persons with substance abuse. This should be a dual interacting process within which the right of persons with substance abuse to be integrated and included is seriously advocated. Also, integration should be regarded as an inherent human urge to relate with others; a way to detach from absorption/addiction in substance abuse. It is the duty and responsibility of related professionals and social welfare and medial organization to facilitate social integration for persons with substance abuse.

FACILITATE SOCIAL INTEGRATION FOR PERSONS WITH SUBSTANCE ABUSE

Dynamic Encouragement and Facilitation

Dynamic encouragement and facilitation means that individuals with substance abuse should not be forced or pushed to involve in the recovery process. Instead, they are should encouraged and facilitated to do so. In doing so, related professionals should be highly patient and enduring as clients with substance abuse or drug addiction are highly fluctuating in their process of recovery. Firstly, according to Prochasks & Diclemente (1982) and Miller & Rollinick (1991), the process of changes is not a linear process.

It consists of the following stages:

Stage 1: Pre-contemplation (The individual does not aware that a problem exists and would generally be surprised to learn that others perceive a problem).

Stage 2: Contemplation (The individual becomes aware that others perceive a problem and vacillates between considering change and rejecting it (Ambivalence about change).

Stage 3: Determination (The client is determined to change).

Stage 4: Action (The client intentionally acts, with or without assistance, tolerating about change).

Stage 5: Maintenance (Help the client to identify and use strategies to prevent relapse).

Stage 6: Relapse (Client may cycle among stages of determination, action, maintenance, and relapse until long term maintenance occurs. (Prochasks & Diclemente, 1982; Miller & Rollinick, 1991)

Related professionals, in helping persons with substance abuse, should remind clearly that the recovery process is an up and down process. Many professionals are used to expect clients' changes in terms of concrete behavioural and attitude changes. However, for clients with substance abuse, they usually have a lot of personal struggle in the pre-contemplation and contemplation stages. Even if they do not make any concrete changes, they are still preparing to do so. It is crucial that related professionals be considerate, empathic and patient in tolerating motivational and emotional fluctuation. Second, it is important that for people with substance abuse to connect their will and determination to change with their life aspiration and meaning of life. In clinical practice, it is common to see a young woman is determined to quit from substance abuse for the benefit of her new born baby. An adult male is prepared to be free from drug simply because he wants to gratify the unfulfilled wishes of his deceased parents. All these should be done within a natural and supportive environment in which individuals' significant others should be facilitated to accept, to support and develop individuals' will power for recovery. Dynamic encouragement and facilitation means that related professionals should relate clients' will to get well and abstinence from drug addiction to their different dimensions in life such as clients' meaning of life, unfulfilled wish, aspiration in life, self-identity, self-image, sense of morality, unresolved emotions as well as sense of body and mind. In fact, the whole process should be highly dynamic, flexible and caring so that people with drug addiction can be nurtured, developed and asserted in a natural, gradually and smooth process of recovery.

A Full Mental Health Recovery

Recovery implies a full mental health recovery. It is a personal journey of the individual to live his/her full potentials. It is also a healing and transformational process so that the individual can live a meaningful life within his/her community (U.S. Department of Health and Human Services, 2004).

> 'Mental health recovery is a journey of healing and transformation enabling a person with a mental health problem to live a meaningful life in a community of his or her choice while striving to achieve his or her full potential. (U.S. Department of Health and Human Services, 2004)

That means, recovery of substance abuse should be regarded as a personal journal of healing and transformation in achieving a meaningful life within individual own community in which the individual can fully exercise his/her potentials and ability.

In 2004, US Department of Health and Human Service and related parties have affirmed ten components in mental health recovery. They are self-direction, individualized and person-centered; empowerment; holistic; non-linear; strengths-based; peer support; respect; responsibility and hope (U.S. Department of Health and Human Services, 2004). Within these ten component, recovery of substance abuse should be an up and down process (non-linear), within which individuals with substance abuse should be self-initiated to plan and implement their own recovery path (self-directedness). It is not a public label of their deficits and impairment in substance abuse, rather than it is a search and development of their own strengths and potentials (strengths based) as well as empowerment their own rights (empowerment) to be treated as persons with dignity, respect and support within their own communities (respect and peer support). Every individual with substance abuse is unique and special in his/her own needs, aspirations, unfulfilled wishes and experiences (individualized and person centered). His/her physical, psychological, social and spiritual aspects should be fully articulated so that their recovery is a holistic and multi-dimensional one (holistic). S/he should restore their hope to restore normal social functioning and daily life within his/her own community (hope and responsibility).

Recovery of People with Substance Abuse and Drug Addiction

Within this articulation, the full recovery of persons with substance abuse should not be a detoxification of substance abuse and a forced hospitalization of intake of psychiatric drug. It should be a development of the individuals' full potentials, a healing and transformation from his/her addiction related life pattern, a meaningful personal journey in re-establishing his/her meaning of life and a return to his/her own community with good support from his/her significant others. In other words, individuals no longer need substance abuse to fill up their loneliness, boredom, frustration and difficulties in life. Instead, they are complete persons with dignity, respect, competent self-images and assertiveness to have meaningful contribution to the society. White (2007) defined recovery as:

> 'A voluntarily maintained lifestyle composed of sobriety, personal health and citizenship'. Recovery is a lived experience. It enables the individual to be away from related addiction/temptation. It is a connectedness with families and community. In many ways, it is also a mission, a goal and commitment to live a better life within an integrated community. In the process of recovery, related parties are accountable to the betterment of persons with substance abuse. (White, 2007: 231)

> *'Recovery is the experience (a process and a sustained status) through which individuals, families, and communities impacted by severe alcohol and other drug problems utilize internal and external resources to voluntarily resolve these problems, actively manage their continued vulnerability to such problems, and develop a healthy, productive and meaningful life. (White, 2007: 241)*

From this definition, it is clear that recovery for people with substance abuse includes the following elements:

1. Constructing a supportive environmental factor by family and communities.
2. Cultivating external resources (service, community support, related policies and legislation).
3. Cultivating internal resources (individual coping and resilience in facing difficulties and frustration in life).
4. Developing clients' will power to abstain from drugs.
5. Facilitating clients to develop a meaningful and productive life.

Within these five important components, there should be three foci, clients' own subjective experiences, a gradual process and an affirmative status in the recovery.

White affirmed that recovery in people with substance abuse should be as an experience, a process and a sustained status.

> Recovery is an experience, we reinforce that recovery is deeply personal and filtered through other dimensions of self-age, gender, ethnicity, sexual orientation, cultural affiliation, degree of religiosity and particular life shaping experiences (e.g., Personal or historical trauma). Defining recovery as an experience is inclusive of change processes that can be either a clinical, healthy inducing event. ……Recovery can be achieved with

> or without professional treatment or participation in peer based recovery mutual aid groups, although the potential necessity of treatment and mutual aid participation increases as problem severity and complexity increases and recovery asset decrease. (White, 2007: 239)

As an experience, recovery of people with drug addiction should be a highly personal and subjective encounter that is unique and specific for people with different age, sex, gender, ethnicity, sexual orientation and cultural difference. Recovery as an experience also mean people with drug addiction can have their own process and interpretation of recovery. While one person regards it as a complete abstinence from drug, another one may regard it simply as occasional usage as a recovery. It also means the recovery is a unique personal experience in which the person with drug addiction should be the focus rather than related professionals, methods of detoxification or intervention models. In some cases, individual can be fully recovered even without the help of the professionals.

> Acknowledging that recovery is a process conveys that resolving severe addiction problems is more than a point in time decision and that the achievement of long term recovery requires that recovery initiation and recovery maintenance are qualitatively different process (White, 2007: 239)

Recovery of people with drug addiction should also be regarded as a process. It means that the abstinence of drug should not only be a timely decision. It should be regarded as a long term process in which consists of *an initiation, a continuation, and a maintenance.* Initiation may mean, under what conditions, the individual is willing to or ready to abstain or lessen his/her dependence on drug. For people with drug addiction, in particular those long term or chronic users, the initiation is a process of ups and downs, initial abstinence and retaking of drug again, or making a decision to quit but disregard this decision when facing drug. In some cases, the decision or the determination to abstain from drug is only an external coping mechanism to gain the trust and help from significant others or it is only an internal self-soothing means in facing the deteriorating mental, physical, social and financial conditions because of prolonger drug addiction. That means, once the situation changes or the deteriorating conditions become stabilized, the will or the decision to abstain from drug simply vanish or is taken over by the 'excitement or stimulating effects' of drug taking.

A continuation means that recovery should be a long term continuation in which individuals with drug addiction should have various degree of recovery or various stages of recovery. For those initial users, their recovery may be a complete abstinence from drug. For those occasional users, their recovery may be a process of becoming less and less dependent on drug until complete abstinence. For those regular users, their recovery may first becoming an occasional users in particular in facing stress before they can finally reduce their dosage, frequency and dependence on drug. For chronic users, their recovery may first start with becoming a self-controlled regular users, later become occasional users before they can finally abstinence from drug. In the whole process, the decrease of intake of drug should be a highly unique with lots of ups and downs according the impact of related personal and environmental factors. Recovery as a process of maintenance means that abstinence from drug could be maintained for a long period of time. The individual not only abstains from drug, but s/he does not need to drug to suppress or escape from the deep frustration in life.

Instead, s/he finds new meaning in life, has a new and good self-identity, and has good morality and positive emotion in life.

> 'Acknowledging recovery as a sustained status confirms the ability of recovery to alter personal identity and engender meaning from having survived a potentially life-threatening condition. The phase also suggests that recovery requires external validations.... Recovery of severe drug problem is a status that must stand the test of external validation. (White, 2007: 236)

'An affirmative status' implies that people with drug addiction should be regarded as having frustration in real life in which they are being depowered, oppressed, neglected or even abused. Facing all these traumas in life, their own unique position and status in various social circles such as family, work and community are deeply diffused. They no longer feel that they are complete or unique human beings. Instead, their sense of inadequacy, inferiority and even worthlessness prevail. That is why they engage in drug addiction to ease out or escape from these frustrating senses or exercise their own sense of manipulation and agency in choosing and taking their own drugs at their own pace and own time. Thus, in the recovery process, it should a re-affirmation of clients' status in their home, family, work, and other social circles. That means professionals should cultivate a supportive social environment that related parties can lend a helping hand for the recovery for people with drug addiction.

Putting all these together, a good recovery should have three important elements intermingling together. Recovery in terms of 'personal experience' implies that recovery should be a personal recovery. Recovery in terms of a process of initiation, continuation and maintenance, implies that a multi-level and multi-dimensional process in which the individual have a full recovery in meaning of life, self-system, inner world, roles and social functioning. Recovery in terms of 'a sustained status' implies that a full recovery should include a highly supportive and nurturing social environment in which the client can be supported to regain and restore his/her self-identity, self-competence and opportunities in living a normal and integrated. In doing so, the inner frustration and traumas in life is gradually resolved within the normal respect, integrity and dignity. In doing so, s/he is a complete and integrated person living a normal and respectable life. S/he does not only abstain from drug but rather s/he needs drug addiction any more.

In other words, an integrated dynamic recovery should be a personal and subjective experience, with multi-dimensional anchoring and changes in clients' meaning of life, self-system, mind and body, a gradual and natural process within a highly supportive and caring social environment. The clients are integrated in multi-dimensional levels including peer system, school system, work organization, family system, community and society.

References

Miller, W.R. & Rollnick, S. (1991) *Motivational Intervention: Preparing People to Change Addictive Behaviors,* New York: The Guildford Press.

Prochasks, J.O., & Diclemente, C.C. (1982) Trans-theoretical therapy: Towards a more integrative model of change; *Psychotherapy, Theory, Research and Practice*, 19:276-288.

The Betty Ford Institute Consensus Panel (2007) What is recovery? A working definition from the Betty Ford Institute, *Journal of Substance Abuse Treatment*, 33: 221- 228.

United States Department of Health and Health Sciences (2004) National Consensus Statement on Mental Health Recovery, Washington, DC: United States Department of Health and Health Sciences.

White, W. L. (2007) Addiction recovery: Its definition and conceptual boundaries. *Journal of Substance Abuse Treatment,* 33: 239-241.

Chapter 3

STRESS AND COPING IN SUBSTANCE ABUSE AND DRUG ADDICTION: AN INTEGRATED DYNAMIC RECOVERY

INTRODUCTION

For persons with substance abuse, most of them have problems in stress and coping. They may experience traumas and abuse in their childhood and adolescence. They may have severe and prolonged stress and unpleasant experiences in a way they cannot express freely. They may also have problems and difficulties in asking for help. As a result, their stress level may reach an intolerable limit that substance abuse tends to be the only way to reduce their inner pain and frustration.

As a coping mechanism, substance abuse seems to be an effective to facilitate one to dissociate from intolerable inner pain, frustration, unresolved emotional complexes and chronic boredom. It is also a substitute for attachment hunger as well as a compensation for introjected guilt and shame. It is a pathological coping for hardships, sufferings and traumas in life. However, prolonged substance abuse can create further additional stress and frustration because of drug induced physical and mental deterioration.

Very often, chronic addiction also nurtures social isolation, public labeling as well as self-isolation. All these intensify individuals' senses of loneliness, boredom, ontological emptiness. In other words, the more the individual uses substance abuse to cope with unresolved negative emotional complexes, the more s/he individual feels hopelessness, emptiness and ontologically boring and the more s/he relies on substance abuse. As a consequence, it becomes a vicious circle in which the individual gets more and more addictive as well as more and more stressful and frustrating they are. In many ways, substance abuse paradoxically becomes both a source of stress as well as the only coping mechanism. In this chapter, the writer will articulate all these in full details.

STRESS AND COPING: A THEORETICAL REVIEW

Stress and coping has long been a concern for scholars in recent decades. Related scholars discovered that stress may come from adverse events or important occasion in life. In facing stress in life, one may be accustomed to a tense and aggressive behavioral pattern that can lead to poor physical and mental conditions. Even in workplace, prolonged stress may lead to burnout and fatigue. In fact, individuals may have different ways in coping with stress in life.

Stress in Life Event

Human life is full of life stress. In facing stressful life event, the individual's mental health is being deeply threatened. Lazarus and his colleagues (1982) affirmed that both stressful life events and minor stressors such as annoying, minor stressors, and daily hassles are predictors of mental illness. Holmes and Rahe (1967) have constructed a life event stress scale as follows.

Table. Homes and Rahe's Life Event Stress Scale

Related Life Event	The Value of Stress Level
Death of spouse	100
Divorce	73
Marital separation	65
Jail term	63
Death of close family member	63
Personal injury &illness	53
Marriage	50
Fired from job	47
Marital reconciliation	45
Retirement	45
Change in family member's health	44
Pregnancy	40
Sexual difficulties	39
Addition to family	39
Business readjustment	39
Change in financial status	38
Death of close friend	37
Career change	36
Change in number of marital arguments	35
Mortgage or loan over $10,000	31
Change in work hours, conditions	20
Change in residence	20
Change in schools	20
Change in recreational habits	19
Change in church activities	19
Change in social activities	18
Mortgage or loan under $10,000	17
Change in sleeping habits	16
Change in number of family gatherings	15
Change in eating habits	15
Vacation	13
Christmas season	12

According to Holmes and Rahe (1967), if the total score is more than 150, one should find ways to reduce stress in daily life.

Type A and Type B Behaviors

In 1974, Friedman and Rosenman (1974) discovered that individuals with Type A behaviors were more vulnerable than those with Type B behaviors to have heart attack and heart diseases. Characteristics of Type A behaviors are as follows:

1. sense of time urgency
2. excessive competitiveness and achievement striving
3. hostility
4. aggressiveness
5. tense, preoccupied with deadline
6. work oriented
7. impatient
8. control oriented (Smith, Sulsky & Uggeersley, 2002)

It was found that Type A behaviors are correlated with the following pathological conditions:

1. high cholesterol levels,
2. higher triglyceride levels,
3. greater blood clotting tendencies,
4. greater sympathetic nervous system arousal (Lovallo & Pishkin, 1980),
5. higher stress levels (Gamble & Matteson, 1992),
6. increase physical health problems (Kirkcaldy & Martin, 2000),
7. increase smoking and decrease exercise behaviors. (Howard, Cunningham & Rechnitzer, 1976)

Burnout Inventory

Maslash and Jackson (1986) had constructed the Maslach Burnout Inventory (MBI) in measuring the burnout situation in workplace. It consists of three dimensions including, emotional exhaustion, depersonalization and reduce accomplishment. An individual suffering from burnout symptoms in work actually feels that s/he has used up their psychic and physical energy to deal with frustration, heavy work load and demand in the work setting. S/he feels physically, emotionally and mentally exhausted in facing, issues, persons, events and demand in work. S/he does not have any competence in work. S/he losses his/her endurance and confidence to perform his/her roles, actualize his/her commitment as well as fulfill his/her responsibility in work. In doing so, his/her actual attainment in work decreases drastically.

Biochemical Articulation of Stress

Naughton (1997) defined stress in a biochemical way as follows:

Threat or challenge that an individual perceives in the environment triggers a chain of neuro-endocrine events (Naughton, 1997:5)

In facing external stress, the individual embraces the following biochemical response

1. sympathetic/adrenal response, with the secretion of catecholamines (epinephrine, norepinephrine): heart rate quickens and the blood pressure rises
2. the pituitary/adrenal response, with the secretion of corticosteroids
3. But since cortisol is a potent hormone, the prolonged secretion of it will lead to health problems such as the breakdown of cardiovascular system, digestive system, musculoskeletal system, and the recently established immune system
4. Also when the organism does not have a chance for recovery, it will lead to both catecholamine and cortisol depletion and result in the third stage of the General Adaptation Syndrome of exhaustion (Naughton, 1997: 56)

Cognitive Appraisal in Stress and Coping

Within a cognitive perspective, in facing stress, the individual is under a mental process in appraising the situation, where the level of appraisal determines the level of stress and the unique coping strategies that the individual takes. (Lazarus & Folkman, 1984). The process and related components of appraisal can be listed as follows:

1. A primary appraisal: conscious evaluation of harm or loss, threat or challenge.
2. Secondary appraisal individual asks him/herself "What can I do?" by evaluating the coping resources around him/her.
3. These resources include, physical resources, social resources, and material resources.
4. Personal control (an individual will find themselves feeling more stressful in uncontrollable situations).
5. The more one has a sense of personal control, the better his/her coping ability is.
6. An individual perceives most control where the situations are internal, transient, and specific. At the opposite end is external, stable, and global where the person will perceive lack of control.
7. Other ways: Constructive and destructive thinking and levels self-efficacy and self-esteem have a crucial impact on one's coping to stress. (Naughton, 1997:56)

Different Types of Coping and Related Conditions

According to related literatures and perspectives, there should four different type so of coping. The first type of coping is coping by avoidance. That means, individuals cope with prevailing stress by avoidance in facing persons, issues, objects, contexts and tasks relating to the sources of stress. For instance, if a person has severe stress in facing his job, *s/he tries* to shift to another job so that s/he can avoid in facing that stressful job again.

The second type is *coping by resources*. That means, an individual tries to cope his/her stress by finding extra resources in dealing with this stress. This can be finding suitable persons, time, space, information, guidance and experts to resolve his/her stressful situation. For example, in facing a difficult assignment, a female college student may ask her boyfriend to do the assignment for her. Or she may try to find related references, information as well as samples of assignment done by students in the same subjects in last year. All these enable her to increase her available resources in coping with the stress in facing her home assignment.

The third type should be *coping by problem solving*. That means, individuals tries to cope with related stress by performing appropriate actions to resolve problems, stress and frustration in life. For example, a student may concentrate his/her effort in finishing his/her assignment. A worker may try all mean to accomplish the task or duties assigned by his/her bosses. A merchant may explore new market and customers to increase his income so to pay back the debt of his company. In problem solving coping, the most common strategy may be appropriate time management, prioritization of issues, appropriate input of effort and concentration, creative thinking of means in resolving related stress.

The fourth one should be *coping by cognitive re-appraisal.* It is an assurance of one's resources and ability to overcome the stress. It is also a cognitive focus on one's capacity and strengths to deal with the stress. Finally, it can be a positive thinking about the stress such as bringing challenges to oneself and having a good consequence after conquering the stress.

The fifth coping mechanism should be *coping by meaning.* The individual does not do anything in eliminating or resolving difficulties, challenges and frustration relating with the stress. Instead, s/he simply absorbs the stress as an irreplaceable event in his/her life. In doing so, s/he finds new meaning in facing the stress. For example, a worker faces severe stress in his working company. Instead of change his job to another company (coping by avoidance), thinking and trying different ways to cope with various challenges in his job (coping by problem solving) and finding someone to help (coping by resources), he simply absorbs his stress by convincing himself that work is demanding and salary is low in every company. He tells himself that his children, his wife and his whole family need this job to survive. He is not working for his company but working for his own family. Working hard is far better than being unemployed. By means of this, he can face his job stress smoothly and quietly.

All these types of coping mechanism can be summarized as follows:

Level 1: coping by avoidance
Level 2: coping by resources
Level 3: coping by problem solving
Level 4: coping by cognitive appraisal
Level 5: coping by meaning

Within these five types of coping, it seems that different levels of coping may imply different type of pre-requisites and conditions. For type 1, the individual avoids the source of stress. On one hand, s/he immediately avoids stress by avoiding related persons, task and contexts. On the other hand, the sources of stress may finally accumulate and intensify later. In some case, the individual avoids one source of stress but have to face another new source of stress. For example, an individual because of job stress quits his/her current job and finds another new one. Immediately, s/he has to face the stress in coping with the new job. That means, individuals using type 1 coping mechanism has to embrace the courage and adaptation ability to face new source of stress as well as with psychological preparation to face accumulated and more intensive stress in the future.

For individuals using type 2 coping, they are very eager in finding suitable resources in resolving their stress and difficulties. Usually, they are quite competent in social interaction.

Or they should have their own ways to attract others to lend a helping hand. Furthermore, they are very resourceful. If they can find someone to help, they should have a strong and comprehensive social network. If they can find some useful information or means, they must have knowledge and accessibility to related information, facilities. Most of them are quite outgoing, extroversive and resourceful. They are assertive in asking for help or presenting and transforming their stressful situation to others without feeling of shame or inferiority. Most of them are quite experiences in dealing with certain types of stress of difficulties. Comparing individuals with type 1 coping, they are more resourceful, more realistic to face and resolve the challenges of stress and difficulties in life. But they are less courageous to meet new challenges, new job, new persons and new source of stress. They prefer to stay within their acquainted social networks, resources and experiences in life.

Individuals using type 3 coping by problem solving are courageous enough to face the stress, challenges and difficulties in life squarely. They neither escape nor find someone to help. They try all means to alleviate their stress. They may be quite rational in assessing pros and cons in using various means to face the stress and challenges. For severe stress and difficulties, apart from rationality in assessing and choosing the right way, they need to be creative in thinking and trying new means to alleviate stress and resolve difficulties.

Comparing individuals using other types of coping, individuals engaging in problem solving coping are mostly diligent, courageous as well as creative. They are the actual front line practitioners.

They should be persistent, diligent and patients. In fact, to have an appropriate problem solving strategy in resolving stress and difficulties, individuals may need to try and testify various means until they can find the suitable one. In doing so, they need to be patient and persistent.

Comparing with individuals using type 1 and type 2 coping mechanism, individuals with type 3 coping are practitioners and front line workers. They are not powerful and resourceful as those in type 2. They do not have to courage to change new job, new place, and meet new challenges in new source of stress. But they are persistent and enduring in facing stress and difficulties in life. They are more introversive than those with type 1 and type 2 coping. Because of their persistence and endurance, they finally can turn their dream into reality gradually. They became expertise in solving life problems within their own social contexts. They possess substantial practice wisdom in meeting daily challenges. Individuals involves in the fourth type of coping by cognitive re-appraisal. They develop cognitive schema and positive thinking affirming they actually possess ability to resolve related stress and difficulties in life. Individuals may not be resourceful as individuals with type 2 coping. They may not be experienced and creative as individuals with type 3 coping. But they are courageous and self-assertive assuming that they can deal with the prevailing stress in their own ways. They regard stress as challenges and difficulties to test their own ability. They usually possess strong self-identity and capacity to work independently. They like to do things in their own ways and means. They are not practitioners as those using type 3 coping. They are not resourceful and sociable persons as those using type 2 coping. They are not unstable and changeable persons as those using type 1 coping. But they are courageous and self-assertive presuming that they can get over their stress and challenges in life.

For clients accustomed to type 5 of coping by meaning, they are usually mature and sophisticated. They have experienced various kinds of hardships and sufferings in life. Comparing with individuals with other types of coping mechanism, they may not have the courage to avoid stress as they know that stress in life is unavoidable. Even you avoid one source of stress, there may have other sources of stress in life.

They do not think that using resources and problem solving means are necessary. As there are also stress in exploring resources and means in resolving difficulties and stress. It is better to be still rather than going around and wasting one's psychic and physical energy. Also, as they have experienced various kinds of sufferings, hardship and torture in life, they conclude stress at the present is tolerable and endurable. It is better to remain in the same situation and be inert.

Any movement may have a possible risk of having a far more stressful situation in the future. They usually have a rich life experience and have a full articulation of meaning of life. They may tolerate the stress for others. Some may be for their beloved family members. Some may be for their good will of their profession, countries and communities.

Stress and Coping and Drug Addiction

Drug as Coping in Facing Life Stress

There are quite a number of literatures and studies show that drug addiction is a coping mechanism to different types of stress in life. Vargas and Trujillo's (2012) study show that drug addiction was used by female students as a coping mechanism for the stress in college life.

> 'The consumption of cannabis has increased in the female population. The risk and protection factors associated with an increase or decrease in its consumption may differ as a function of gender, age and substance consumed. The objectives of the present study were to examine the relevance to cannabis consumption by female students of legal drugs consumed by the university students and family members, the consumption of legal and illicit drugs by friends, sociodemographic factors and, psychological variables in terms of perceived stress and different coping strategies). Three questionnaires were administered to 465 female students studying for Psychology degrees. The prevalence of cannabis consumption was 36.3%. The variables predicting its consumption were: a) consumption of illicit drugs and cocaine by friends; b) consumption of tobacco by the students and; c) emotion-oriented coping. (Vargas & Trujillo, 2012: 119)

Vargas and Trujillo (2012) showed that students with more stress in college life were more vulnerable to drug addiction. Interestingly, their use of drug addiction as a coping mechanism was influenced by their peers. Those consume illicit drug such as cocaine were actually provided or influenced by their peers. The findings showed that students with poor emotional coping were more vulnerable in using drug to cope with life stress. Similar results were found in Lopez-Torrecillas', (et al., 2000) study in which individuals taking alcohol were less assertive, with poor self-control and less self-efficiency. Interestingly, individuals with low consumption of drug and high consumption of drug make no difference in using drug addiction to cope with life stress.

Sinha (2001) has done a rich literature review on related stress and drug addiction. He concluded it stress in life include two main groups.

Group 1: Genetic and Individual Vulnerability Factors

1. Family and Social Influence
2. Genetic and Family History
3. Individual Difference in Initial Response to Substance abuse
4. Specific Personal Traits
5. Family Life Events and Chronic Distress
6. Low Frontal Executive Function

Group 2: Maladaptive Stress Response

1. High/Low Reactivity and Sensitivity to Stress/Stimuli
2. Slow Recovery to Baseline
3. Poor Behavioral/Cognitive Coping

Group 1 factors enable the individual to have experimental drug use. It makes the individual becomes highly vulnerable to further stress exposure in which the individual. It increased individuals' frequency of drug use. Finally, it brings along Group 2: Maladaptive Stress Response in which the individual's substance abuse pattern gradually consolidates to become regular and chronic users. In doing so, individual's neuro-adaption in brain waves and response.

Type of Coping and Substance Abuse and Drug Addiction

As mentioned above, there are five types of coping mechanism for one in facing life stress. It seems that drug addiction is used by the individual in facing the failure of each type of coping mechanism. For those engaging in level 1 coping by avoidance, drug addiction is an effective means to let the individual avoids in facing the stress. For many individuals, in facing life stress, in particular those unavoidable ones, drug addiction seems to be most effective way for them to be mentally isolated from stressful sources even though they are still within a stressful environment. For example, a student has to face a stressful examination in which s/he fully aware of his/her poor performance and result. S/he has no way out. S/he cannot avoid in facing the stressful examination. S/he cannot avoid in facing the poor performance in the future. Thus, the only way can lessen his/her frustration, stress and worry is immediate drug addiction and substance abuse. Drug addiction becomes the only mean for them to be mentally isolated and avoiding from the pressing and frustrating reality- the stressful examination and painful future of poor academic performance.

For those with type 2 coping by resources, if they have enough resources, they properly can face and resolve their stress in an easy manner. However, if they do not possess enough resources, their stress level may increase accordingly, in particular when the source of stress is familiar. As they may not have sufficient human resources or experiences in facing the stressful situation, their stress level may be intolerable. In some cases, when familiar resources such related friends, information and experiences are not currently available, their stress level may become intolerable. Under this condition, because of availability of drug, or because of being surrounded by drug related peers, individual in type 2 coping may finally use drug to resolve their stress that cannot be resolved by type 2 coping.

For those individuals using type 3 coping, they are usually with good expertise and experiences in working through stress and difficulties. They are also hard working individual with courage to try new things and new ways to solve the source of stress. In doing so, they actually consume a huge sum of psychic, mental and physical energy. Some of them can finally find out appropriate ways to solve the source of stress. Some of them can accumulate related experiences in solving this source or another source of stress. However, as times goes by, some new or difficult sources of stress or within some highly demanding environment full of constraints, individuals may finally consume most of their psychic, mental and physical energy. In that occasion, they are no longer able to use their usual coping mechanism in problem solving. As their usual coping mechanism fails, they may feel highly stressful. If they can use other types of coping such as coping by resources or coping by avoidance, their stress can be successfully reduced. In some cases, they cannot do so. When the accumulated stress reaches an intolerable level, they may consider use other unhealthy means to alleviate their stress. Under this condition, if they are exposed to any type of drug, they may incline to use drug addiction as a way to cope with their stress.

For those who use level 4 coping by cognitive appraisal, they are usually assertive and confident individuals. They are able to affirm their self-confidence and assertiveness in facing stressful life. However, if the stressful events and sources are really too demanding and too challenging, they may finally fail to face these constructively. Instead, prolonged unresolved stress challenges their self-identity and confidence. They may finally become depressive, anxious and inferior. Under these conditions, drug addiction may be as effective mean to lessen their intolerable and uncomfortable feelings of inferiority, anxiety and depression.

For people accustomed to type 5 of coping by meaning, they are usually mature and sophisticated. Comparing with individuals with other types of coping mechanism, they do not avoid stress as they know that stress in life is unavoidable. Even you avoid this source of stress; there may be other sources of stress in life. They do not think that exploring resources and problem solving means are necessary. As there are also stress in doing so. It is better to be still rather than going around and wasting one's psychic and physical energy. Also, as they have experienced various kinds of sufferings, hardship and torture in life, they conclude that stress at the present is tolerable and endurable. It is better to remain the same situation and be inert rather than facing a possible risk that inappropriate movement may imply far more stressful situation in the future. They have a full articulation of meaning of life. Many of them have a higher level of meaning in his life. They may tolerate the stress for others. Some may be for their beloved family members. Some may be for their good will of their profession, countries, religions, ideals and communities.

In some cases, even if they have sacrificed, tolerated and accepted all these internalized hardship, torture and suffering, they are finally betrayed, rejected and expelled by their family members, profession, religion and countries. They may lose their meaning of life, meaning of suffering and meaning of love. They may collapse mentally, physically and psychologically. If drug addiction is available, they easily use it as a way to dissociate them from this painful and intolerable reality.

All in all, it seems that drug addiction is a mean for individuals to cope with intolerable stress, in particular when individuals' normal habitual coping mechanism fails. The failure may be due to the following conditions.

1. The sources and types of stress are vastly different from usual one encountered by the individual.
2. They are entirely out of clients' previous coping experience.
3. The coping mechanism used by the individual is inappropriate or ineffective in facing the new sources of stress.
4. Because of various reasons, the individual may not have sufficient mental, physical energy in using his/her normal coping mechanism.

The failure of one's coping mechanism, in fact, does not directly relate to the use of drug addiction for coping. Instead, it needs other inter-dependent variables and factors such as the following:

1. Encouragement from friends and peers.
2. Availability and exposure to drugs.
3. Intolerable and unbearable family stress or life frustration.

According to Sinha's (2001) literature review, the failure of the coping mechanism is only the group 2 factors: maladaptive stress response, it needs the individual vulnerability factors to make the individual engage in drug addiction. There may be the environmental factors such as availability of drug, peer influence and social stress, difficulties, oppression and frustration from family, work and other social circles.

Pathological Coping in Substance Abuse and Drug Addiction

Because of above mentioned situations and factors, individual may finally enter into a pathological coping process. In the first stage, there is a severe or new source of stress that is out of the clients' normal coping mechanism. In the second stage, the individual feels highly stressful and become intolerable to incoming stress. In stage 3, there is availability and exposure of drug as well as seduction or encouragement from related peer in using drug to alleviate stress and frustration. In stage 4, the individual begins to use substance abuse to alleviate his/her unbearable stress in daily life. In stage 5, the individual gradually accustoms to use drug addiction in alleviating his/her daily life. S/he becomes a regular user of drug. In doing so, his/her normal coping mechanism is dreadfully deteriorated. In stage 6, the drug addiction not only deteriorates the individual's coping mechanism, it also adds into new sources of stress including being labeled and isolated by others as drug addict, unemployment, and poor physical and mental health due to harmful effects of drug. In facing all that, as the individual losses his/her normal coping mechanism, s/he can only use drug addiction to face all these insurmountable stress. As a consequence, the individual engages in a vicious circle of the more s/he feels frustrated in daily life, the more s/he engages in using drug to cope with his/her stress in life, and the more his/her mental and bodily conditions deteriorates because of prolonged severe drug addiction. In stage 7, the vicious circle intensifies with a result of endless chronic intake of drug. The individual becomes a chronic drug user. Despite s/he knows and suffers from the adverse effects of drug addiction, s/he still depends on drug as the only and most important meaning, goal and activity in life. The vicious circle and adverse effects goes on until the individual losses his/her career, family, fortune, and even his/her life.

Integrated Dynamic Recovery in Stress and Coping in Substance Abuse and Drug Addiction

In an integrated recovery, related professionals have to motivate clients to quit the vicious cycle of pathological coping. They should integrate clients to normal and health coping. They should facilitate clients to restore their normal life before his/her substance abuse. Related strategies in psychosocial intervention can be listed in the following:

1. Related professionals should totally accept clients' pathological coping and their heavy dependence on drug addiction in facing life stress and trauma.
2. Enable clients' significant others to accept clients' pathological coping and dependence on drug addiction in facing life stress.
3. Facilitate clients and their significant others to induce hope in their recovery.
4. Enable clients and their significant others to have a holistic understanding of clients' stress and coping before, during and after the drug addiction.
5. Enhance clients and their significant others to restore clients' normal coping mechanisms before the onset of their drug addiction.
6. Facilitate clients and their significant others to improve clients' coping mechanism. Apart from their usual coping mechanism, they should also learn and develop other types of coping mechanisms in facing stress and difficulties in life.
7. Enable clients and their significant other to regularize and stabilize clients' multi-dimension coping mechanism in facing stress, difficulties and frustration in life.

All these can be demonstrated by the following case illustration. Related parties' consensus in using their stories for academic purpose was sought. For the sake of confidentiality, their personal information and stories were properly disguised.

S: The Stressful and Anxious Young Man

S had been engaged in substance abuse for five years. He was born in a low class family in which his father was a manual labor in a construction site. His mother was a housewife taking care of S and his three younger brothers and one younger sister. As the eldest brother, S was responsible to take care of his younger brothers and sister. His parents also wanted him to have good education and good career path so that he could take good care of the whole family. S certainly felt highly stressful in his life.

In facing all these stress, S was accustomed to cope by problem solving. He tried very best to resolve any problems he encountered in daily life. He worked very hard to finish the household chore imposed by his mother. Apart from cooking breakfast and dinner, he was also responsible to look after his younger brothers and sisters. Despite all that, he had to attend school every day. After school, he tried his best to finish his home assignment.

He was busy, responsible and hard working. However, as he did not have sufficient time to do his home assignment, his academic performance was just fair. Gradually, he was a bit lagging behind in his class. This made S was very frustrated as his father always reminded him to have good academic performance so that he could have a better future in supporting him and his whole family. S worked hard to finish his primary school education with a fair result. His academic performance declined in his secondary school. In Year Eight, S even failed in two subjects, English and Mathematics. He needed to repeat this year.

For him, this a year full of frustration and difficulties. He felt inferior in comparing with other classmates. He was also bullied by his classmates as silly and stupid. S had no way to face all these difficulties. He tried to argue and negotiate with his classmates, saying he worked hard and everyone should give him a second chance. However, his classmates did not concern about that. They simply laughed and teased him and went away. His teacher also criticized him as he was so poor in English and Mathematics.

At home, his father always compared his academic results with his first younger brother who was the top student in his class. As a consequence, S's sense of inferiority and worthlessness prevailed. Although he was the eldest brother in the family but he was not respected by his younger brothers and sister. Instead, they regarded the second elder brother as the model of sibling.

Under that condition, S felt really dreadfully. At that moment, some of his classmates seduced S to take ketamine to ease out his sense of frustration in life. S began a regular user of ketamine. He dared not to disclose this to his parent. He secretly took up part time employment in McDonald Restaurant to earn money for his drug addiction. Gradually, his mental and physical condition deteriorated. Following this was poor academic performance. He failed four subjects even in the repeated year of study. One day, he felt sick and fainted in a lesson. He was sent to a nearby hospital for a medical check. The result showed that his body, in particular his bladder was seriously hurt by prolonged intake of ketamine. S's parents were totally shocked by the bad news that their son was a chronic drug addict. They felt guilty, helpless and hopeless.

They sought help from a social welfare agency in which the writer was the professional consultant. Under the supervision of the writer, related social worker, G induced the following interventions for the rehabilitation and recovery of S.

Total Acceptance by Others

First, in motivating clients to quit the vicious cycle of pathological coping, related professionals and significant others have to avoid judging, condemning and confronting and excluding clients with pathological coping. They have to help clients to acknowledge the vicious cycle of pathological coping. They should listen to frustration and life traumas behind pathological coping. Finally, they should provide immediate measures to protect clients from intensive social and self-isolation, oppression and traumas. All these can be demonstrated in related interventions to S by the social worker G.

'S was admitted in a residential unit for rehabilitation of drug addiction. He was required to stay there for six months under the care of a social worker G there. Under the supervision of the writer, G encouraged S's parents to accept S's pathological coping by drug addiction. He helped them to understand S's feeling of failure in both school and at home. They gradually understood S's stress in his childhood and adolescence. Instead of blaming S for his prolonged drug addiction, they tried to ensure they had total acceptance and unconditional love towards S. Every Saturday, they visited the residential unit and had a long chat with S. Three months later, S was allowed to have a home leave on Saturday and Sunday. With good acceptance from his parents, they no longer put a strong expectation on S. Instead, they tended to regard S as a child that needed to embrace with love, care and forgiveness. S felt being loved and cared. With this total acceptance, S began to harbor a strong determination to get well and recovery.

A Holistic Understanding of Clients' Stress and Coping

Secondly, related professionals have to integrate clients to normal and healthy coping. That means they should integrate clients to good social support, resources in ventilating their frustration, asking for help and developing their own problem solving skills as well as adaptation to various challenges and difficulties in real life situations. They should recognize clients' stress and frustration in life behind drug addiction. They should facilitate clients and their significant other to develop a secure and accepting atmosphere to face previous sufferings, hardship and traumas in life. They should enable clients to develop good social support and peer groups in facing adversity in life. Finally, they should enhance clients' resources, ability and problem solving skills in facing life stress. All these can be shown in the intervention induced by G towards S.

'In a home leave, G accompanied S and visited his parents. They had a good sharing of S' stress and frustration in life. S frankly disclosed that he deeply worried about his father expectation on him. He felt deeply shameful in being unable to fulfill his father's expectation. He also showed deep sorrow of poor academic performance. He cried bitterly before his parents. At that moment, his parents embraced him and his father said sorry for his past unreasonable demand on S. Being embraced by his father's prevailing love, he began to harbor a strong determination to get well. In the home leave, his parents purposefully displayed a number of family photos in which S was a happy young kid being embraced and loved by his parents. From all these photos, S fully recalled his sweet past childhood memories with his family. He was no longer lonely and stressful in his life endeavor. Under this condition, the social worker S enabled them to have a full discussion about S' future. In fact, before the onset of the substance abuse, S was hard working, diligent and keen to handle his own problems. He firmly asserted that he should continue his secondary school education and tried his best to have a satisfactory academic result. He was motivated to do well not because of his parental unreasonable and stressful demand but merely because deep love by them.

Restoration and Strengthening of Clients' Normal Coping Mechanism

Thirdly, related professionals should facilitate clients' recovery from their previous life stress and traumas. They should provide a safe and secure intervention context so that clients can share their traumatic childhood, adolescence and/or adulthood at their own pace. They should also help clients to live with and resolve their life-long traumatic experiences in restoring their normal coping in life. Their resilience in facing difficulties, hardship and traumas should be gradually nurtured by rebuilding their meaning in life and normal life patterns. Finally, they can face and cope with hardship, problem and stress in normal and constructive ways rather than regarding substance abuse is the only coping mean. All these can be shown in S case illustration.

> 'With his parents' encouragement and total acceptance, S returned to his former school for study. As his previous coping mechanism, he worked hard and tried to solve problems by himself. However with the help from G, he learnt to use other coping mechanism such as using of resources. Instead of isolating himself from others, he tried to study and play with his classmates. Within the arrangement of the school social worker, S was under the care of two schoolmates as his mentors. They helped S to catch up with his school work. Apart from that, they also encouraged S to join in the school football team. As a consequence, S learnt how to cope with his stress by use of supportive network and resources. He also learnt how to release his stress by means of vigorous exercise. By mean of all that, S was no longer use drug addiction to release his stress and cope with life frustration. Instead, he was a normal, diligent, motivated and healthy young man with regular exercise, good support network and academic performed. He was loved by his parents and his school mates.

CONCLUSION

As a conclusion, this chapter is a discussion about stress and coping of people with substance abuse. For people with substance abuse, before onset of substance abuse they also use different kind of coping mechanism in facing their stress and frustration in life. However, as the stress and frustration is too difficult or the individuals' coping mechanism is inappropriate, they tend to engage in drug addiction and substance abuse to ease out their plight in life. In doing so, their normal coping mechanism is also weakened. Gradually, they become more and more dependent on drug. Prolonged drug addiction can also lead to various kind of stress in life such as social exclusion, unemployment, financial difficulties, as well as poor physical and mental health. Finally, it is a vicious circle in which drug addiction becomes the only available mean to cope with stress and frustration that come from drug addiction. To break this vicious circle, related professionals should totally accept clients' pathological coping and their heavy dependence on drug addiction in facing life stress and trauma. Furthermore, with the support from clients' significant others, related professionals to induce hope on their recovery. In doing so, they should have a holistic understanding on their stress and coping before, during and after drug addiction. Clients should be helped to restore, enhance and stabilize their normal coping mechanism before the onset of drug addiction.

REFERENCES

Epstein, S., & Meier, P. (1989). Constructive thinking: A broad coping variable with specific coping components. *Journal of Personality and Social Psychology*, 57:332-350.

Eysenck, H. J. (1988). Personality and stress as causal factors in cancer and coronary heart disease. *In*: M. P. Jaisse, ed. *Individual Differences, Stress, and Health Psychology*. New York: Springer-Verlag.

Holmes, T. & Rahe, R. (1967) "Holmes-Rahe Social Readjustment Rating Scale", *Journal of Psychosomatic Research*, 2: 45-86.

Holmes, D., & Rahe, R. (1967). The Social Readjustment Rating Scale. *Journal of Psychosomatic Research*, 11:213-218.

Lazarus, R. S., & Folkman, S. (1984). *Stress, Appraisal, and Coping*. New York: Springer

Lopez-Torrecillas, F., Garcia, J., Garcia, M. P., Izquierdo, D. G., Sanchez-Barrera, M. B. (2000) Variable modulating stress and coping that discriminate drug consumers from low or non-drug consumers, *Addictive Behaviors*, 25(1): 161–165.

Smith. C., S & Sulsky. L.M., (2002) Effects of job stress on mental and physical health, in J.C. Thomas & M. Hersen (Edited) *Handbook of Mental Health in the Workplace*, pp.61-82. London: Sage.

Sinha, R. (2001) How does stress increase risk of drug abuse and relapse, *Psychopharmacology*, 158: 343-3.

Southerland, V.J., & Cooper, C.L., (2002) 'Models of stress' in J.C. Thomas & M. Hersen (Edited) *Handbook of Mental Health in the Workplace*, pp.33- 60. London: Sage.

Vargas, C. Trujillo, H.M. (2012) Psychology students: The influence of perceived stress, coping and consumption of drugs in their social environment, *University Psychology*, 11(1): 119-130.

Chapter 4

BODY AND EMBODIMENT IN SUBSTANCE ABUSE AND DRUG ADDICTION: AN INTEGRATED RECOVERY

INTRODUCTION: BODY AND EMBODIMENT

Addiction can be regarded as a self-induced bodily experience. The individual voluntarily and purposefully induces various forms of substance abuse so that they can induce intensive bodily experiences so cover or to escape from their frustration and unresolved emotional complexes in life. In fact, within the concept of embodiment, body can also include body condition and functioning, desires, appearance, and senses of perception of reality. That means, body can be interpreted as senses of being, consciousness, relation to other, visibility to environment as well as related expression and communication. Also, body can also represent frustration in life including the sick body, isolated body, frustrated body, fatigue body, oppressed body and inferior body. That means, the body and mind are fully related to one another. It manifests various inner psychic conditions such as traumatisation, repression, suppression, dissociation, derealisation, humiliation in various forms of body condition, function, desires and appearance. For example, after the experience of a severe traumatic experience such as accidents and disasters, individual may appear as inert, numbed and totally fatigue in terms of his/her senses of perception, body condition, appearance. Also, in facing highly humiliating experience, the individual feels angry, with tightening body and muscle, and the whole body with the secretion of adrenaline, s/he is prepared to fight back. In this chapter, the writer tries to articulate the sense of body in people with substance abuse and drug addiction.

BODY, MIND AND REALITY

Every human being has a living body in which it contains mind with spontaneous interaction with related objects, issues and persons within the physical and social reality. The interaction among body, mind and reality starts on the first day when one is born. It moves on until, the individual's body deteriorates and the mind declines in a detached reality. The spontaneous interaction among body, mind and reality is influenced by three important components. They are listed as follows:

1. Different states of consciousness (being conscious, sub-conscious or unconscious);
2. Demand and support from related objects, persons and issues in the physical environment and social environment (Whether the environment is tough, demanding and/or oppressive or it is caring, supportive, and/or nurturing);
3. Health conditions of the body (Whether the body is healthy or sick, weak or strong, young or old, tense or relaxed, and/or beautiful or ugly);
4. These three components interact with individuals' body, mind and reality. They can be conceptualized as the following:
   1. *State of Mind (Related perception, cognition, emotions and sense of self)*
      1A: Consciousness
      1B: Sub-consciousness
      1C: Unconsciousness
   2. *State of Reality (Connection, reception, interpretation and response to related objects, issues and persons in immediate social and physical environment)*
      2A: Demand from the reality (Demanding, Oppressive and Abusive)
      2B: Support from the reality (Accepting, Supportive and Nurturing)
      2C: Connection with the reality (Detached, Connected, and Involved)
   3. *State of Body (Health, movement, appearance, energy level and desires)*
      3A: Healthy Body
      3B: Sick Body
      3C: Impaired and Disabled Body

According to Stam (1995) and Ralley (1995), the body, mind and reality are united together in a form of embodiment. It is an integration of psychological, social and phenomenological bodies.

> The language of bodies can takes on a highly individualized and ethereal, being at one remove from both the social and the psychological. In this language, bodies are no longer seem as constituted in social relations, or, rather, the sensuous existence of the body cannot be seen as the primary prerequisites of all that emerges from persons. Whereas psychology splits and compartmentalizes the body into functions that deny the embodied nature of psychological life and experience, so can an individualistic language of bodies in discourse deny the crucial manner in which the body is already and always social in its expressions and impressions. (Stam, 1995:5)

Stam (1995) asserted that embodiment is a combination, integration and spontaneous experiencing ones' existence, relation with others, impression and sensation. Apart from that, Ralley (1995) suggested that the concept of embodiment should also include the ground of being, in relation to each other and mutual visibility.

> The concept of display is useful because it highlights the fact the embodiment not only provides the ground of being, but places us in relations to each other in our mutual visibility. (Ralley, 1995: 15)

The full integration of body, mind and reality are within a spontaneous interaction with others in which related parties in the spontaneous interaction are fully aware of one and other. This is a kind of complete and continuous sense of being and existence.

Without this, the body is just a kind of object. Sampson (1995) descried a kind of 'object body' as follows:

> The body that a third person observer can know. It is the corpse that is the subject of medical scrutiny in contrast to the body which we live. (Sampson, 1995: 30)

That mean, a body without proper connection with mind and reality is an object body. With proper connection and integration with mind and reality, it is a phenomenological body (Sampson, 1995:30) in which it is continuously responding to issues, objects and persons within the reality. A phenomenological body is a spontaneous sense of body with connection with others senses of mind, sense of self and sense of environment. All these senses combine together to form the continuous sense of existence. In other words, the sense of existence consists the following senses:

1. Sense of self
2. Sense of mind
3. Sense of body
4. Sense of environment. (Yip, 2012)

All these senses can be positive and negative. One can have a positive sense of self of being respected by others. However, one can also have a negative sense of self if s/he is being neglected, humiliated and neglected by others. One can have a positive sense of mind if s/he engages in mental stimulating experiences. S/he has a negative sense of mind if s/he has boring and stagnant mental experiences. A positive sense of body implies one is healthy and strong. A negative sense of body means one is weak, sick and even disabled. Finally, a positive sense of environment means that related social and physical environment is pleasant and supportive. A negative sense of environment should be just the opposite.

In terms of state of mind, state of body and state of reality, a present state of existence should be good consciousness (2A), good health condition (3A) and supportive reality (2B) in which the individual embraces a good sense of body, sense of mind, sense of environment and sense of self. Within a painful sense of existence, the individual may embraces a sick or tortured body (3B), very oppressive or even abusive social environment (2A) as well as a highly conscious mind (1A) in which the individual is highly conscious about the pain and oppression in the social environment. In terms of sense, the highly oppressive social environment makes the individual embraces a highly negative sense of environment, his/her sense of self, sense of body and sense of self are deeply and negatively affected.

In extreme torture and painful reality, the more the individual is conscious of the reality, the more painful s/he is. Thus, individuals have a tendency to cloud or numb his/her consciousness, his/her senses of mind and self so that the pain from the immediate social environment can be enlightened. One of quickest way to do so is by immediate effects of drug taken on the body. It is common or acceptable that when we feel frustrated in life, we incline to intake alcohol so that we can detach or numb our painful sense of mind, self and environment. However, as the painful reality cannot be alleviated, alcohol taking may finally become habitual and the intake dosage can gradually be increased to become alcoholic addiction. In doing so, the individual actually uses a heightened sense of body to overcome the painful sense of mind, body and environment.

Drug Addiction and Bodily Sense

In the process of drug addiction, the sense of body is highly stimulated so that a dreadful sense of mind or a highly painful or oppressive reality can be repressed and detached. Within the process of drug addiction, the sense of body is a completely new experience. It is not a sick body, and is not a healthy boy. In no way, it is an impaired or disabled body. Instead, it is a drug induced body (3D). Together with this a drug induced mind (1D) as well as a drug induced reality.

Within the drug induced body, the physical stimulation effects of the body can both be immediate and long lasting. The immediate effects make the individual feels being tranquillized, elated or relaxed. The lost lasting effect is harm and damage to related organs including lung, heart, kidney, liver and bladder as well as the central nervous system. Before the drug taking, because of a frustrating mind and a highly oppressive reality, the body of the individual may be fatigue and nervous (3Da) which is intolerable for the individual. To ease out this frustrating body, the individual inclines to take drug. The addicted drug, on one hand, creates a powerful body (3Db) (excited, tranquillized and relaxed body) immediately after the drug. On the other hand, in the long run, it weakens the whole body and the body finally becomes a drug induced sick body (3Dc). As a weak body is very frustrating for the individual, it makes the individual to take a higher dosage of drug to stimulate the weak body to become strong and powerful. It finally turns into a vicious circle in which the body becomes weaker and weaker because of the harmful effects of the drug and s/he needs more and more drug to stimulate the weakening body.

Similarly, the drug induced mind (1D) is actually a drug induced subconscious state. Before the drug taking, the individual is highly conscious of his/her painful existence (1Da) within a highly oppressive environment. To avoids being conscious of his/her painful existence, s/he engages in this drug induced sub-consciousness (1Db) so that s/he can be temporarily free from uncomfortable emotions such as inferiority, loneliness, anger, fear and emptiness. However, when the effect of drug is over, the individual regains his/her consciousness (1Dc). Under this condition, the individual's negative emotions return in a more intensive way. His/her life problems and difficulties do not resolve. Instead, it is even worse than before. In addition to psychosocial problems, s/he has addiction problem.

Regarding the state of reality, the individual, before the intake of drug, s/he may encounter a highly demanding, oppressive and exploitative reality (2Da) in which her mind and body are seriously affect. To escape from this exploitative and harmful reality, the individual engages in drug addiction in which drug induced bodily senses help the individual to temporarily detach from this demanding reality (2Db). However, when the drug effects vanish, the individual has to face the demanding, oppressive and exploitative reality again. Gradually, individual's ability to face and connect with exploitative, abusive and oppressive reality declines as his/her functioning of body and mind are deteriorated by the harmful effects of the drug. S/he becomes more and more intolerable to the threatening reality (2Dc). In other words, it becomes a vicious circle that s/he becomes more and more dependent on drug addiction to detach from highly threatening reality.

In actual practice, 1D, 2D and 3D interrelate to one another in the process of drug addiction. Before the drug intake, 1Da, 2Da and 3Da work together. During the drug intake, 1Db, 2Db and 3Db all happen together. When the effect of drug declines, 1Dc, 2Dc and 3Dc occur together. As a consequence, the individual's body and mind becomes more and more dependent on the drug to detach or disconnect himself/herself from the oppressive and threatening reality.

As the drug addiction becomes prolonged and chronic, the individual's state of mind and condition of body are deteriorated. His state of consciousness is gradually eroded. Even without drug taking, the individual's consciousness becomes diffused and confused. His/her attention and concentration on related affairs in daily life is deeply affected. Even in daily activities, the individual is in a state of sub-consciousness. His body condition is a sick body. Apart from strong withdrawal effects, their body is deteriorated. The functioning of internal organs such as central nervous system, liver and kidney is deeply impaired by the poisonous effects of drugs. Because of weakening body and mind, his resilience towards related difficulties, hardships in life were much weakened. S/he become quite detached and alienated from related persons, issues and objects in related psychosocial environment. His/her urge to have a total drug induced escape (detachment) from substantial reality becomes stronger and stronger.

Different Types of Drugs and Impacts on Body, Mind and Reality

Within all these different inner psychic conditions, the sense of body as being, consciousness, relation, expression and visibility, is also deeply affected. The integration among mind, body and reality is also affected. In fact, within drug addiction and substance abuse, individuals' senses of body are deeply affected by the addicted drug. Different types of drugs induced different experiences of body, mind and perception reality. By means of taking stimulants such as amphetamines, cocaine, methamphetamines, individuals are able to induce an intensive sense of stimulated body. In taking depressants such as sedatives (barbiturates, alcohol, minor tranquilizers, GHB), individuals indulge in a strong sense of tranquilized body. Similarly, after abusing hallucinogens such as LSD and 'Give Me Five', individuals absorb in drug induced hallucinations and delusion. All these are a heightened sense of delusive body. In abusing pain killers and anesthetics such as opiates, heroin, morphine and ketamine, individuals enjoy the state of sub-consciousness as well as the out of body experiences (Liska, 1990). In many ways, persons with chronic substance abuse may use mixed drugs. They may mix stimulants with depressants, stimulants with hallucinogens, anesthetics with stimulants and depressants with anesthetics and many other forms. In doing so, individuals try to switch from one type of intensive sense of body to another one.

There may be several types of drug in substance abuse serving different needs of the individual in attaining various senses of addicted body, mind and perceptions of reality.

The primary drug is the individual most preferable type of drug in meeting his/her need to stimulate, tranquilize, hallucinate or anesthetize his/ her body so as to conceal and escape from the intolerable sense of a frustrating mind. **The functional drug** means that the individual uses this type of drug to serve certain functions such as to fall into sleep, to keep fit, to stay awake and to feel energetic. **Auxiliary drug** means the individual only uses this type of drug for social togetherness with his/her drug related peers. **Gateway drug** implies individuals take this type of drug as a mean to take other type of drug.

Body, Mind, Consciousness and Desire in Substance Abuse

Dissociation and Re-Association Complex

With the process of drug addiction, individual's body, mind and consciousness are deeply affected. The first process is the dissociation and re-association complex. In fact, different types of drug may have different effect on one's sense of body, mind and consciousness. It can be a substance induced subconscious state in which the individual is neither being conscious or unconscious. Detachment from consciousness means that s/he can avoid the painful and frustrating reality. Without becoming unconscious implies that s/he can still gain a sense of self control and self-directedness.

Euphoria and Dyshoria

Some substances, in particular stimulants can induce a sense of euphoria. That is a state of extreme excitement, individuals not only feel fully energetic, but also highly self-competent, with a strong sense of self mastery. It certainly enables the individual to cover up his/her senses of boredom, inadequacy, inert and passivity. Under the influence of the stimulant, a passive and timid individual becomes talkative and courageous enough to do anything that s/he rarely dare to do in normal state of life.

As an opposite, certain drugs especially tranquillizers create a state of dysphoria in which the individual's mind feel peaceful, relaxed and secure. All these substance induced senses of mind and body facilitate the individual to escape from the highly stressful and anxious reality in which s/he is being pushed to his/her physical and mental maximum. In actual conditions, the addictive state of mind is an altered state of consciousness. It is a distorted sense of time and space in which the individual tries to free himself/herself from confused and traumatic experiences. If the individual experiences continuous depersonalization in the actual environment, then the state of an addictive mind is a personalized experience. In the substance induced altered state of consciousness, it can be a quick state of change of mind, some even make the individual experiences a sense of near death experience and follows by a sudden release or out of body experience. All these altered states of consciousness become a habitual involvement shield for the individual to escape from the unacceptable apathetic reality.

Within all these intensive but distorted substance induced sense of body, mind and consciousness the individual's body image and self-care are gradually deteriorated. S/he may deteriorate form care of body image to ignorance of body figure and appearance; from good embodiment of body and mind to poor and un-embodiment; from good personal hygiene to poor self-care; from good consciousness of gender identity to ambivalence of gender identity.

Furthermore, as the individual becomes more and more involved in intensive but highly distorted substance induced sense of body, mind and consciousness, his/her normal sense of perception and consciousness gradually shift from good heightened, relaxed and new sense of perception to retarded sense of perception after addiction. S/he also has a prolonged and gradual alienation from reality. S/he has progressive increase in his/her own subjectivity but has decrease in objectivity in reality perception. There are also inter-relationship among dissociation and re-association complex. That means, the individual's negative feelings and consciousness of terrible reality are being dissociated because of substance abuse. However, at the same time, his normal and spontaneous sense of mind, sense of body, sense of environment, sense of growth and consciousness are being retarded. That means, his/her social functioning is also deeply affected. Apart from interacting with drug related peers, the individual's social circle becomes more and more restricted. Self-isolated life may nurture intensive senses of boredom and frustration. As a consequence, it further increases individual's urge for addicted drug induced body stimulation to cover all these senses of boredom and frustration.

Addiction and Sex

Regarding the sense of body, addiction is also correlated to sex. At first, the individual uses drug to gratify his/her unfulfilled sex desires, demand and need. That means, substance abuse is closely related to sex drive and urge, thoughts and thinking, behaviours and performance, pleasure and feeling. The drug is used as a mean for intensification, maximizing one's courage and remove burden and embarrassment in attaining all these sex related activities and emotions. However, as long as the substance abuse and psychological dependence on drug increases, the individual tunes into the second stage with confusion of sex and addiction. That means, s/he becomes more and more dependent on senses of body induced by substance rather than the sex related gratification and emotions. His/her attention shifts from sex to drug. As the abused substances have prolonged deteriorating effect on his/her body function. His/her sex functioning is also deeply affected. Gradually, s/he enters into the third stage in which s/he increases his/her attachment to substance but his/her needs and interests in sex decrease. In this stage, the individual turns his/her focus on the intake of the drug. The psychological and psychological dependence of the drug increases. His health and life conditions are continuously shaped by the substance abuse. Not only the dosage and frequency of the abuse increase but also his/her social circles and daily life are restricted. Furthermore, his/her body function and health conditions deteriorate accordingly. As a consequence, his/her sex drive, functioning, drive, demand and needs also decrease drastically. In some case, the sex needs are totally suppressed by the drug addiction. Finally, the individual tends to be on the fourth stage. It is a focus on addiction and substance abuse with a loss of interest, need and ability on sex. In chronic drug addiction, individuals' attachment to the addicted drug is even stronger than their attachment to their significant others.

Integrated Dynamic Recovery of Addicted Body and Mind

Facing all these confused sense of body, mind and perception of reality in substance abuse and drug addiction, the process of recovery should focus on body and mind integration; motivating clients to constructive new and healthy body experience; and facilitating clients to have a holistic recovery on his sense of body.

Regarding integrating the sense of body experiences, it should be an integration of body and mind including integration of consciousness and sub-consciousness; self and other perception; reality and addictive experiences, sex, desire and relation; as well as aspiration of aspiration and reality. Related professionals should help clients to recognize the importance of all these integration, facilitate them to express, to communicate all these deep seated needs of integration of body mind. They should help clients to reconstruct healthy experiences in body mind integration. All these experiences should be a re-connection, re-association, and re-embodiment of body experiences. They should also create and nurture good social environment and peer support for the clients to re-anchor healthy body experiences.

Related professionals should also motivate clients to engage in constructive, meaningful and healthy body experiences. They can be regular physical exercises, ball games, dancing, swimming, making up and relaxing exercises. All these enable the individual to have a stimulating sense of body by healthy and constructive means rather than relying on substance abuse. At first, clients may be highly reluctant to all these normal and healthy body experiences. It is important that related parties should persistently encourage and facilitate clients to engage in all these experiences by group activities, interesting competition, learning class, as well as volunteer services. In doing so, related professionals should help clients to resolve the following unresolved complexes and difficulties in substance abuse.

1. Fixation of Dissociation and Re-association.
2. Absorption in Egocentric Trip in Addiction.
3. Confinement in Sensational oriented Peers.
4. Alienation from Professional Intervention and service.
5. Assess the clients' degree of absorption in these addictive body experience and peers.
6. Understand clients' previous traumatic experience in childhood and adolescence.
7. Facilitating and preparing clients to disclose their conditions.

In the first unresolved complex, related professional should help persons with substance abuse and drug addiction to re-association of their dissociated senses of body and mind by proper ventilation of unpleasant past experience in life as well as in drug addiction. Furthermore, they should also facilitate them to use healthy means to suppress frustration, difficulties, and negative emotions in life. In many ways, all these prolonged suppressed feelings, traumatic experiences, and painful recall should be properly shared, accepted and even forgiven by clients significant others. Regarding absorption in egocentric trip in addiction, related professional should help clients with substance abuse to engage in meaningful outside activities. In doing so, they should also help clients with substance abuse to build a safe and secure social environment, so that they feel supportive and caring by others. Only by means of that, they can come out from their absorption in their egocentric trip in addiction.

In terms of holistic recovery, related professionals should help persons with substance abuse to have a good recovery of related conditions, image, appearance, visibility, experiences and consciousness of their body. That means, they should facilitate individuals to develop health means such as body movement, physical exercise, healthy daily habits, physical treatment, constructive and meaningful activities *to deal with their frustrated, sick, immoral, traumatic and humiliated body*. Finally, for persons with substance abuse and drug addiction, a holistic dynamic integrated recovery on their sense of body means that they begin to learn to love, care, and develop their body. Even though they encounter a frustrated, boring, lonely and angry mind, they still know how to engage in healthy body activities. With good food, good rest, good exercise, good activities, good body appearance, their frustrated mind can be energized and revitalized.

CONCLUSION

As a conclusion, this chapter is a discussion about body and drug addiction as well as substance abuse. In fact, drug addiction and substance abuse have a strong negative impact on state of mind (consciousness, sub-consciousness and unconsciousness), state of reality (connection, reception and response to related objects and issues in immediate environment) and state of body (health, movement, appearance, energy level and desires). Within the process of drug addiction, the sense of body is a drug induced body. Together with this a drug induced mind as well as a drug induced reality. After prolonged drug addiction, clients have a firm fixation of dissociation and a total absorption in physical stimulation induced by drug with an alienation from reality. Related professionals should properly deal with all these in psychosocial intervention. They should assess and understand clients' absorption in drug addiction as well as their traumatic experiences. They should facilitated and prepare clients to free from all these. Finally, they should enhance clients to build up their sense of body by healthy activities and interaction.

REFERENCES

Liska, K. (1990) *Drug and the Human Body: With Implication for Society*, (4th Edition) New York; Macmillan Publishing Company.

Ralley, A. (1995) Display and fragments: Embodiment and the configuration of social worlds, H. J. Stam (Edited) *The Body and Psychology*, pp. 13-29, London: Sage.

Sampson, E. E. (1995) Establishing embodiment in psychology, H. J. Stam (Edited) *The Body and Psychology*, pp. 30-54 London: Sage.

Stam, H. J. (1995) The body psychology and psychology's body: disciplinary and extra-disciplinary examination, H. J. Stam (Edited) *The Body and Psychology*, pp. 1-10 London: Sage.

Yip, K.S. (2012) *Emotionality and Mental Illness: A Multi-dimensional Model.* New York: Nova Science Publishers.

Chapter 5

EMOTIONALITY IN SUBSTANCE ABUSE AND DRUG ADDICTION: AN INTEGRATED DYNAMIC RECOVERY

INTRODUCTION: EMOTIONALITY

Feeling, Mood, Affect and Sense

Emotionality implies that emotions are related to interaction, interpretation and sharing of emotion among related actors within different social, physical, cultural and political contexts. Emotions composed of four crucial components, feeling, affect, mood and senses (Yip, 2012). Feelings is implies internalized of emotions with a focus of self. It includes different layers, natures and complexity. Mood is an externalization of internalized emotions. It includes different intensity, duration and frequency. Affect is a response others' emotion. It can be direct or indirect response; continuous or delayed response, straight or crooked responses. Sense is the continuous perception of external stimuli in related physical and social environment. It includes sense of mind, sense of body, sense of self, sense of growth and sense of being and existence.

Primary and Secondary Emotions

Emotion can also have primary and secondary. Primary emotions are inherent and cannot be further reduced. Secondary emotions are combined by one or more than one type of emotions. Primary positive emotions are senses of security and content, trust and being connected, love and being loved, feeling of excited and involved, and confidence and actualization.

Primary negative emotions are senses of inferiority, loneliness, anger, fear and emptiness. Secondary negative emotions are combined primary feelings. For example, envy is a combination of anger and inferiority. Hate is a combination of inferiority and anger.

Emotional Complexes and Emotional Processing

There are also various forms of emotional complex such as superior and inferior complex, approach and avoidance complex, love and hate complex, autonomy and dependency complex, and respect and fear complex. All these unresolved complexes play a crucial role in describing the plight and difficulties of human being in their lives. Within cognitive behavioral perspective, emotion can also be regarded as emotional processing and control. Emotional process is regarded as ‘A process whereby emotional disturbances are absorbed and declined to the extent that other experiences and behaviors can proceed without disturbance’ and ‘If emotional experiences were incompletely absorbed or proceeded, then certain direct signs of this failure would appear’ (Baker, et al., 2007: 45). In terms of control, emotion can be regarded as an input of current and past events, memories, schema, experience, appraisal and expression. That means if the emotional processing is completed, then new emotion and new experiences can proceed without disturbance. If not, individuals may have problems in absorbing and responding to new emotions and new experiences. It also implies, if emotional process is completed, individual may have better control of his/her emotion. If not, s/he may have problem in control his/her emotion. S/he has difficulties in controlling, regulating, and adjusting input of current and past events, memories, schema, experiences and expression in relation to his/her emotion.

EMOTIONALITY, SUBSTANCE ABUSE AND DRUG ADDICTION

Complexity and Conflicts

For persons with substance abuse, their emotions are complicated and full of related conflicts. Firstly, in the process of addiction, like highly stimulated bodily senses such as euphoria and pleasure, dysphoria and withdrawal all contain intensive emotions. Craving, tolerance, bodily dependence and belief dependence on abused substance and addicted drug all consists strong emotions like being angry at anyone who deter them for continuous addiction; being totally loss and empty in failure to get related drug for addiction; and being highly resistant to change and recovery. Denial, body harm, relapse social isolation and inability to quit all arouse intensive senses of worthlessness, inferiority and meaninglessness in life. All positive emotions within addiction such as happiness, excitement, togetherness with addicted peers, peace and powerfulness are all substance abuse related. Once, drug addiction and substance abuse still continue, the individual still needs them to pull up their negative emotions in life, in particular in facing difficulties and hardship. The more they engage in drug addiction, the more they rely on drug to suppress their sense of frustration, fear, loneliness, fear and inferiority in life. All these emotions can be further interpreted in terms of feelings (how these emotions are being internalized), mood (how these emotions are being expressed and externalized), affect (how these emotions are responded to external stimulation), and sense (how these emotions are being stimulated. They also have unresolved emotional complexes such as love and hate complex, approach and avoidance of their abused substance and related peers. In the process of detoxification, they can also have autonomy and dependency complex. On one hand, they want to abstain from drug. On the other hand, they depend on drug in times of frustration and difficulties. All these negative feelings may be complicated by the focus towards oneself and/or others, the past and/or the present, as well as the external and/or internal.

Emotionality in Process of Drug Addiction and Substance Abuse

Within the process of addiction, involved emotions are also different. Before the addiction, individual may feel deeply frustrated and annoyed by difficulties, emptiness and boredom in life. Individuals harbor a strong urge to release, to attach and to crave for drug. After taking related substance, individuals enter into a state of extreme bodily related emotions such as euphoria and pleasure, dysphoria and withdrawal, out of body experiences as well as a deep sense of release or anesthesia. Together with these may also be a strong sense of warmth, genuineness in being together with other peers who abuse substance with their peers intensively. After the addiction, persons with substance abuse harbor intensive senses of regret, emptiness, guilt, shame and worthlessness as s/he feels that s/she cannot control his/her own desires for further addiction. S/he always feels highly regretted for his/her wrong doing especially in craving for drug in severe and chronic addiction. S/he also feels deeply conflicting and ambivalent in being sorry to his/her family members and friends. S/he feels hopeless and worthless and s/he cannot ease from her continuation of drug addiction. Her life is entirely massed up with physical and mental problems related substance abuse.

Mood, Feeling, Affect and Sense in Drug Addiction and Substance Abuse

Regarding emotion in addiction as mood, in drug addiction, it is usually fluctuating. There is a drastic change of mood before, during and after addiction. Mood of euphoria and dysphoria and withdrawal is always intensive and fluctuating. It makes the individual engage and absorb in a state of sub-consciousness as well as a certain degree of detachment of reality. That sort of intensive mood, in many ways on one hand is purposefully searched by the individual in the process of substance abuse. On the other hand, they may incline to take over-dosage of drug in a way that drug induced may be too intensive to tolerate. In that sense, individuals may take another drug to counteract the over stimulated and intensive. As a consequence, individuals may incline to take physical stimulants to counteract the effect of tranquillizers or to take tranquillizers to counteract the effect of physical stimulants. In other words, the mixture of drugs may finally result in deep fluctuation of mood in various forms and degrees.

In terms of feeling, feelings in addiction is highly subjective and only shared by people with similar substance abuse. In the process of substance abuse, there seems to be a form of pseudo-ventilation of deeply internalized unpleasant feelings. All deeply internalized feelings are either repressed by drug addiction or intensively burst out by substance abuse. The negative consequence of substance abuse may intensify all these deeply internalized unpleasant feelings. The longer and more chronic of the addiction, there may be the deeper the unpleasant feelings being intensified and internalized from environment, to recent period of time, to ego system to meaning of life.

Regarding substance abuse as an affect, the individual may gradually absorb in their substance abuse and be inert and withdrawn to others' feeling and emotions. Prolonged drug addiction and substance abuse tends to stir up problem affect such as paranoia, fear and confusion, or over-excitement in responding to others' emotions. The continuity and spontaneity of normal senses of self, mind, body, environment and being are burdened and suffocated. Individuals in taking drug, they are more inclined to their peers who take drug together. Among them, they may become less defensive, more open up to others, and empathetic and highly excited to other emotions. The common affects shared by collective addiction may be an intensive senses of togetherness, sharing similar senses of mind, self and body in the process of additions. All these substituted senses enabled individuals to shelter from frustrating emotions generated from external social and physical environments. In fact, intake of abused substances alters individual's visual, audio, touch, taste and smell perception. Prolonged stimulation of senses and perceptions by chronic addiction may result in impairment of sense perception. The individual becomes more and more inert to physical stimulation as well as external perceptions. As a consequence, the individual is more and more detached from the actual reality as well as more and more inclined to higher and higher dosage of drugs to stimulate related senses. That means, the tolerance effects of abused substance decrease individual's senses of perceptions and effects of drug. Also, the dependence effects on the drug make the individual's urge for drug intensifies to a degree that s/he craves for drug earnestly. In doing so, the burning need of drug taking may even slow down or even paralyze his/her normal senses of body, self, environment, mind, growth and being.

Addictive Emotional Complexes

Superiority and Inferiority Complex

Prolonged addiction may also result in the formation of several drug related addictive complexes. The first one is drug induced sense of superiority and shameful inferiority because of addictive label. The individual feels superior, detached and alienated from the reality and the society after taking drugs and substance. S/he may gain a sense of mastery in controlling the dosage and types of drug and substance for addiction. The effects of abuse substance makes him/her embrace a feeling that s/he is superior than other people as s/he can be free from the painful reality and present frustration in any time s/he likes. However, beyond the time of drug addiction and substance abuse, s/he clearly aware that s/he is totally depends on the addictive drug and abusive substance. S/he is a poor substance abusers and drug addict. His/her body and mind are deteriorating and eroding by the drug and substance. S/he is being excluded and labeled by others in every social circle except with his/her drug related peers. All these make him/her feels deeply inferior. The more s/he feels inferior and shameful, the more s/he needs to pull up himself/herself by drug and substance. As a result, the complex continues and gets worse and worse.

Love and Hate Complex

Another addictive complex is the craving and drug love and deep self-hate complex. Persons with prolonged substance abuse tend to crave for drug. Because of tolerance and dependence effects of drug, individuals tend to crave for drug especially in times of deep frustration and difficulties in life. In craving for drug, they may even commit illegal and immoral acts. They may steal and hurt their most beloved relative and friends. In extreme situations, drug is even more important than their own life. In order to continue their addiction, they can sacrifice everything. Nevertheless, deep down in their mind, they know that the more they crave for drug, the more inferior and shameful they become. Thus, on one hand, they crave for drug regardless their own dignity and respect. On the other hand, they hate themselves knowing that they are inferior, shameless and worthless because of prolonged addiction. This is an endless and dynamic unresolved complex driving the individual to a self-deteriorating life.

Approach and Avoidance Complex

As long as the individual engages in prolonged and chronic addiction, the individual also indulges in a drug related approach and avoidance of reality complex in which the individual tries to approach or even adhere to abused substance on one hand, and tries to avoid in facing the reality on the other hand. In many cases, even though individuals are addicted to drug, deep down in their heart, they still urge to avoid or even quit from drug. For him/her, there is an endless internal struggle; s/he fully acknowledges the physical and mental deteriorating of substance abuse. However, s/he cannot or fails to resist the temptation of substance abuse, as s/he is full engaged within social exclusion, self-rejection, self-isolation as well as senses of chronic loneliness, boredom, helplessness, fear and inferiority in the reality because of substance abuse. Substance abuse seems to be his/her only way for the individual to escape from all these negative emotions. As a consequence, his/her drug addiction and substance abuse becomes more and more serious and his/her alienation from reality becomes more and more intensive. Drug addiction and substance abuse tends to become his/her own focus in everyday life.

Autonomy and Dependence Complex

Coupling with this complex is also the autonomy in choosing drug and dependency on addictive experience complex. In the beginning of the substance abuse, individual tends to abuse substance as his/her own will. S/he exercises his/her sense of mastery in taking drug thinking that s/he can abuse drug accordingly to his/her own will. In every day, they usually feel frustrated and loss of his/her own sense of agency and autonomy. Thus, abusing substance seems to be the only way or the quickest way to regain a sense of mastery by controlling the time, the frequency, the dosage and the effects of drug accordingly to his/her own will. However, the more s/he addicts to drug, the more s/he loses his/her sense of mastery to a degree that s/he fails to control himself/herself in taking drug. That means, s/he becomes the salve to the drug rather than the master of the drug that s/he abuse. At the same time, s/he also becomes inert, passive, alienated and detached from everyday life. His/her urge to regain senses of mastery and autonomy increases accordingly. Increase in dosage, frequency and duration of substance abuse tends to be only alternative for the individual to regain the 'pseudo' sense of mastery and autonomy. As a consequence, the individual finally traps within a vicious circle of substance abuse as well as abused by substance.

Finally, individuals with substance abuse can also engage in a respect of drug related issues, objects and people and fear of loss of accessibility of drug complex. In the process of addiction, the individual is deeply interested in drug related issues, object (the effects, availability, ingredient and harmful consequences of drug) and people (drug related peers, drug dealers), s/he becomes more and more experienced in all these areas. S/he also knows how to conceal and hide his/her addiction in front of others. As s/he becomes more and more dependent on drug, s/he harbors an intense fear that sooner or later s/he may not able to be accessible. Thus, s/he may try every mean to ensure the proper accessibility of drug in his/her daily life, including knowing every detail about where and when to get and take drug, how to avoid being discovered by family members, teachers and classmates at school, and the police in public place.

Emotional Processing and Substance Abuse

Regarding problems in emotional processing, in the process of substance abuse, negative emotions such as senses of guilt, loneliness, inferiority and emptiness repeatedly **intrude** in the client's mind, making him/her feel highly uncomfortable. However, all these negative emotions are deeply **suppressed** by drug addiction. The individual cannot find anyone s/he trusts to express all these negative emotions. Even s/he finds someone, according to his/her own experiences, s/he still fear that others may reject him/her or simply saying that all these negative emotions are entirely meaningless due to unnecessary substance abuse. Once, s/he quits the drug, all these negative emotions can vanish immediately. Thus, instead of ventilating or sharing all these negative emotions with others, s/he prefer to bottle up them and appears as inert, detached and alienated from normal social interaction. Furthermore, as the experiences of substance abuse are quite unique and distinct among persons with substance abuse, it is a bit hard for them to share related experiences and emotions in process of substance abuse with those who do not engaged in substance abuse. That means, it is hard for them to have sufficient **emotional attunement** with their significant others such as parents, family members, teachers, classmates, colleagues, or even with professionals who do not have experiences in substance abuse. Apart from their drug related abused, it is easy for them to feel being alienated and isolated from their normal social circles. As a consequence, the more they suppress all these negative emotions, the more they feel isolated, rejected, detached from others, and the more they are disturbed by all these negative emotions. As a consequence, they may become highly impulsive in emotional control. They may be highly dependent on substance abuse and drug addiction as a release or further suppression of all the re-bounce of these negative emotions. On one hand, persons with substance abuse are highly impulsive. On the other hand, they tend to **dissociate and repress** related negative emotion by means of addicted drug. They incline to switch off and detach from emotions so that they can survive in everyday life. Gradually, addicted drug and abused substance becomes their only way to escape from painful life traumas, **avoid** recalling hardship and suffering in craving for drug, suppress plights in facing social isolation, labeling and rejection, as well as detach from intensive sense of hopelessness in facing their future. By means of frequent addiction in high dosage of drug, their emotions are discordant. They are blank in feeling as emotions are not belonging to themselves. It seems that all negative emotions are **forcefully externalized** in sensual stimulation by drug addiction.

Integrated Dynamic Recovery of Addictive Emotions

As a conclusion, substance abuse and drug addiction can be regarded as a way to block the occurrence of negative emotions, to ventilate suppressed feelings, to develop emotional attunement with other persons with substance abuse, to moralize the uncontrolled emotions, to re-associate detached body and mind, to shift away from unpleasant emotions, and to revitalize related senses of self and mastery.

All these have important implications to integrated recovery of persons with substance abuse and drug addiction. There are various levels of appropriate intervention.

Level 1: Dealing with emotions in life frustration.
Level 2: Dealing with emotions and Desires for Drug.
Level 3: Dealing with Emotions Induced by Drug.
Level 4: Dealing with Emotions from related social and physical environments in drug taking.
Level 5: Dealing with Emotions after substance abuse.

In the first level, related professionals should assist clients to deal with negative emotions in frustration in life including past and previous traumas, suffering and hardship as well as difficulties and social exclusion and rejection in the prolonged process of substance abuse. In second level, related professionals should assist clients to deal with desires for drug. It includes related emotions before, during and after the process of drug taking. It also includes those emotional complexes and intensive emotions in craving for drugs. In the third level, related professionals should help clients with substance abuse to deal with emotions that are induced by drugs. It includes intensive physical senses being stimulated by different groups of drugs. It also contains those emotions being concealed or avoided by drug taking. In the fourth level, related parties should assist persons with substance abuse to deal emotions induced by related social and physical environment in drug taking such as senses of togetherness with drug related peers, trauma, illegal and immoral acts related with substance abuse. In the fifth level, individuals with substance abuse should be helped to resolve emotions after substance abuse such as senses of guilt, helplessness, self-blaming and impotence in controlling oneself. It also includes those unresolved complexes in drug taking.

In interventions within all these levels, related professionals should recognize and ventilate all these emotions, understand related background of these emotions. They should facilitate clients with substance abuse to resolve their needs behind these emotions. They should also facilitate clients to resolve related conflicts among different levels of emotions. Finally, they should help clients to use healthy means to fulfill clients' emotional needs. In doing all these, related professionals should fully beware about consistency, conflicts and various levels of emotions.

Conclusion

As a conclusion, this chapter is a comprehensive discussion about emotionality and drug addiction and substance abuse. According Yip (2012) emotionality consists of four components, mood, feelings, senses and affect. Drug addiction and substance abuse have a substantial negative influence on clients' normal manifestation of mood, affect, sense and feelings. They harbor intense unresolved emotional complexes such love and hate, superiority and inferiority, autonomy and dependence. Furthermore, their normal emotional processing is also blocked by prolonged drug addiction and substance abuse. For a dynamic integrated recovery, related professionals should facilitate clients to deal with their emotions in life frustration, desires for drugs, induced by drugs, from related social and physical environment in drug taking and after drug taking.

REFERENCES

Baker, R., Thomas, S., Thomas, P.W. & Owens, M. (2007) Development of an emotional processing scale, *Journal of Psychosomatic Research*, 62: 167-178.

Liska, K. (1990) *Drug and the Human Body: With Implication for Society*, (4th Edition) New York; Macmillan Publishing Company.

Yip, K.S. (2012) *Emotionality and Mental Illness: A Multi-dimensional Model,* New York: Nova Science Publishers.

Chapter 6

ATTACHMENT IN SUBSTANCE ABUSE AND DRUG ADDICTION: AN INTEGRATED DYNAMIC RECOVERY

INTRODUCTION: ATTACHMENT

Secure and Insecure Attachment

According to Bowlby (1977) attachment is defined as 'a way of conceptualizing the propensity of human being to make strong affective bonds to particular others and of explaining the many forms of emotional distress and personality disturbance, including anxiety, anger, depression and emotional detachment, to which unwilling separation and loss give rise' (Bowlby, 1977:201). With a good and constant attachment, a person feels safe, secure and is emotionally stable. It is crucial for infants, children and adolescents to have secure and constant attachment so to ensure a normal and healthy physical and psychological development process. Secure attachment implies intimate and affectionate relationship that is constant, close, intimate, stable, nurturing, mutual benefiting and autonomous. However, insecure attachment implies insecure and immature relationship that is coming and going, disengaged or enmeshed, unstable, manipulating or exploiting and creating dependency. Holmes (1993) affirmed that 'a person with insecure attachment may have a mixture of feelings towards their attachment figure. These feelings include intensive love and dependency, fear of rejection, irritability and vigilance (Holmes, 1993:67). To ensure attachment, an insecure person tries to cling to his or her unstable attachment figure as hard as possible by means of 'attachment behavior. It refers to 'to any of the various forms of behavior that the person engages in from time to time to obtain or maintain a desired proximity' (Bowlby, 1977: 270). In fact, every child in his/her developmental process needs to develop a close attachment bond with his/her attachment figure. *Attachment bond refers to an enduring attachment which the child confines to very few.*' (Bowlby, 1982: 670). An attachment bond is based on a very secure and enduring attachment. But attachment behavior is simply a reaction to insecure attachment. It represents a fear of losing attachment. A child who does not discriminate clearly between those to whom he has an attachment bond and those toward whom he simply manifests attachment behavior is likely to be severely disturbed. (Bacal, 1990: 216).

For Bowlby, the human dilemma turns on the central importance of an attachment that cannot be entirely reliable, must perforce be shared, and will be lost eventually.

In the process of human development, maturity depends on the capacity to separate from attachment figure and to form new attachments (Holmes, 1993:70).

> People suffering from anxious attachment are chronically fearful that they may lose their attachment figure, and their threshold for manifesting attachment behavior is low. They are often described as overly dependent or immature, and they are likely to develop neurotic symptoms, such as depression or phobia under stress (Bacal, 1990: 214).

In other words, persons are fear of losing their attachment figure. As a result of this kind of fear, they may be immature and depressed or stressful in their emotion (Bowlby, 1969). In fact, anxious attachment happens with persons with borderline personality disorders and those with depression or phobia under stress.

Apart from insecure attachment, compulsive self-reliance is also another type of unhealthy attachment. While insecure attachment result in attachment behaviour in which the child is highly attached to his/her parents with a spontaneous fear that sooner or later, his/her parent/s may leave him/her alone, in compulsive self-reliance, the individual tries all means to detach from any attachment figure. Bacal (1990) described the characteristic of compulsive self-reliance as follows:

> 'Those who are compulsively self-reliant have had similar experience as children to those who manifest anxious attachment. Although this behavior is the opposite of anxious attachment, these people also yearn for love and support. However, their reaction has been to protect themselves from rejection or from having to be someone else's caretaker by withdrawing from close relationships. They take care of themselves under all circumstances. Their resentment is also displaced to weaker people, they tend to react to stress with psychosomatic symptoms or depression. (Bacal, 1990:215)

To escape from the fear of losing their attachment figure, person with compulsive self-reliance tend to withdraw from close and intimate relationship (Bowlby, 1973). They may even display this sort of fear and frustration to other weaker persons. It may be manifested in form of psychosomatic symptoms or depression. That means, individuals with compulsive self-reliance tries avoiding attachment to any persons so as to prevent any abandonment. In doing so, s/he tries very mean to withdraw any close relationship. They appear to be independent, self-caring and self-sufficient. However, deep down in their mind, they are lonely and desperate. They are also full unresolved anger towards their significant others who abandon them. In many ways, they may release their anger towards those weaker people such as their subordinates and supervisees by various forms of oppression, bullying, manipulation and exploitation. For those with slim aggression towards others, they can be persons with schizoid personality disorder whereas they try to avoid contacting and connection to other persons. For those with severe aggression and anger, they can be persons with antisocial personality disorders and narcissistic personality disorders.

As contrary to compulsive self-reliance, persons with problematic attachment in their developmental process can also end up with a compulsive caregiving pattern in their attachment with others.

> 'Compulsive caregiving is a form of attachment behavior in which relationship may be close, but the affectional bond is always one sided. Like the compulsively self-reliant, compulsive caregivers do not seek anything from anyone but, unlike them, constantly extend their attention and concern to others-whether or not they are looking for it. ... . Bowlby equates the compulsive caregivers with False self-personality configuration described by Winnicott. (Bacal, 1990: 216)

Within **compulsive caregiving** attachment, the development of a person's self and personality is manipulated and controlled by his or her caregivers or significant other (Bowlby, 1977). On one hand, the caregivers are actually using their attached objects as a mean to fulfil their urge for anxious attachment. For example, a mother with anxious attachment problem with her previous generation may develop compulsive caregiving for her children as compensation. On the other hand, the person being attached may have difficulties in developing his or her true self and ability to be independent. That means, while the compulsive caregivers actually have anxious attachment on the attached object, the ones being cared are engulfed by their caregivers and have severe difficulties in building a unique self-system with a clear ego boundary. As a consequence, they may be inclined to have a diffused self-boundary and undergo a process of psychotic self-splitting by external oppression (Laing, 1960)

Emotional detachment is another form of problematic attachment in which the individual tries to detach from others emotionally. Bacal (1996) defined it as follows:

> 'The emotionally detached individual, who is incapable of developing a stable affectional bond with anyone, is usually identified as a psychopathic and or hysterical personality. His childhood experience is usually one of early, ongoing maternal deprivation as well as of parental rejection in later childhood.' (Bacal, 1996:216)

According to Bowlby (1982), prolonged detachment from attachment figure may result in an incapability of developing a stable affective bond with others. As a result, the individual may be highly isolated and prompt to have psychotic disorder. That means, that sort of emotional detachment may appear to those individual with oppressive significant others whose attachment may only create harm and hurt rather than warmth and support. Another possibility may that the individual actually grows up in a social environment where attachment or affective bond is not available. That may be the situation that the individual losses parental figures in his/her own developmental process. As s/he does not have any self-confidence on interpersonal relationship, s/he is suspicious about any close or intimate relationship with others. As a consequence, s/he tended to be independent and kept an emotional distance to every one s/he encounters. In doing so, s/he can be safe from any interpersonal harm, oppression and exploitation.

Separation and Loss in Attachment

Within various types of unhealthy and destructive attachment, separation and loss from attachment figures is commonly occurred. Facing the separation and loss from the attachment figures, an individual may have to undergo a process of adjustment and adaptation. Holmes (1993) summarized these four stages which includes:

> **Stage 1: Numbing**
> The very earliest response to a sudden bereavement may be an apparent calmness based on emotional shutdown in which all feeling are suppressed, or reality denied, until the bereaved person is in a safe enough situation to let go a little
>
> **Stage 2: Yearning, Searching and Anger**
> The search of the lost object includes physical restlessness and searching everywhere, hoping that their lost loved one may reappear. The person also goes over in their mind every detail of the events leading up to the loss. Anger also appears towards the outcome by being angry towards anyone who responsible for the loss of the attached figure. Anger also directed towards potential comforter so as to come to terms with the loss figure.
>
> **Stage 3 & 4: Disorganization and Despair and Reorganization**
> Loss throws the inner worlds and life of the suffer into turmoil. All the assumptions and expectation which depended on the presence of the loved one are now thrown into question. The quasi-depressive state which marks the third stage of grief can be understood in facing the loss. The suffer tries to reorganize his or her new life by seeking for a new attachment figure. (Holmes, 1993: 237-8

In other words, the individual in facing separation and loss of constable attachment, at first, they may appear inert and indifferent. Later, as the loss becomes explicit and unavoidable, the individual becomes angry. S/he is angry both with himself/herself and the lost objects. In doing so, s/he searched everywhere for the lost object. In some instable and fragile attachment, s/he earns for compensatory and substituted attachment. In some cases, in which the attachment is permanent and highly enmeshed one, s/he refuses for any compensation and substitution. In both cases, the individual may result in disorganization of self-system that s/he may fixate within the loss of beloved object. For some individuals, they may go through the grief and mourning process so that they can have substantial attachment with other figures and beloved object and retain back to normal ego functioning and self-system. For other individuals, they may regard the loss of beloved object is irreplaceable and they cannot go through the mourning and grief with a result of permanent and chronic despair and hopelessness.

Attachment and Affective Bonding

According to Bowlby's articulation, it is clear attachment is closely related to affective bonding with one's beloved object and attachment figure. There can be different types of bonding and attachment as follows:

- Deprived of parental bonding and attachment
- Secure and insecure bonding and attachment
- Substitution of bonding and attachment

- Frustration, anxiety and insecurity in problematic attachment
- Approach and avoidance complex in problematic attachment.

For those who are deprived of parental love and bonding, they may urge for substitution. Or they may have a total avoidance of possible substituted thinking that people around are apathetic and indifference. Thus, they tend to be compulsive self-reliance or keep an emotional distance from others. Within affective bonding, the attachment can be secured and insecure. In secured bonding and attachment, individuals can grow with normal senses of belonging, self-identity, emotional stability and maturity in dealing with others. For persons with insecure attachment, they are accustomed to be highly sensitive and anxious to incoming attachment bonding and any breakage and separation from attachment figures and affective bonding. They may try every mean including being angry at, craving for the love and self-harm or suicidal threatening to the attachment figures. Despite all these threatening and manipulating mechanisms, the attachment figure still leave or separate from them, it can end up with depressive mood, unless substituted bonding and attachment figures can be thus attained. In the substitution of attachment figures, the new attachment figures may feel highly uncomfortable and unnatural for the sudden but highly attached behaviors from these individuals. Even though they are individuals' newly met friends, individuals with insecure attachment may attach to them as if they are close relatives such as parents, spouses and family members. This can be intolerable and result in breakage and termination of all these substituted attachment. Thus, the individuals may easily trap within an ongoing vicious circle of anxious and insecure attachment to substituted new object, termination of substituted attachment, severe and intolerable sense of loneliness and anxiety in losing attachment object and further anxious and insecure to another new substituted object. Within this vicious circle, individuals with insecure attachment always harbor intensive sense of frustration, anxiety and insecurity in losing trust, love, acceptance and attachment from others. Gradually, they develop an approach and avoidance conflicts in relating to others. On one hand, they have a strong urge to attach to others. On the other hand, they harbor a strong fear that sooner or later, others may leave them alone and abandon them. Thus, they may become highly sensitive to others' comment, criticism or any signs of possible rejection.

For those who are continuously deprived of or being abandoned by attachment objects or they are unable to find substituted attachment objects, they may incline to develop compulsive self-reliance with a continuous emotional detachment from interpersonal relationship. All these have strong implications to persons with substance abuse and addiction.

ATTACHMENT, SUBSTANCE ABUSE AND DRUG ADDICTION

Substance Abuse, Addiction and Attachment: Unhappy Childhood and Abuse

Persons with Addiction always suffer from problems of attachment in their childhood and adolescence. Related studies showed for many male adults with substance abuse usually have with a history of neglect and abuse (36%); basic physical needs were neglected (28%); emotionally abused (18%) by parents; sex abused (18%); in social welfare children institution

(McMahon, et al., 2007). Also, lower level of substance abuse rehabilitation program retention were predicted for women who had been sexually abused and for those had poor parental bonding (Cosden & Cortez-Ison, 1999).

Similar results are also found in local studies. Female adults with drug addiction usually have difficulties in attachment with their parents and other significant others (Yip & Chung, 2008:258). Many local studies (The Hong Kong Federation of Youth Group, 1994; Boys' and Girls' Association, 1994; Central Registry of Drug Abuse, 2000; Chung, 1997; Tang, Lu, & Wong, 1997) showed that major reasons for males in substance abuse were peer influences and curiosity towards drugs. But for females were companionship and assurance with their spouses, boyfriends and family members. These findings were similar to those results in other countries (Stein & Cyr, 1997; Turner & Gil, 2002). Also, Tang, Lu, and Wong's study (1997) showed that 44% of females with substance abuse did have unhappy experience of being sexual abused by their boyfriends, parents, relatives and other persons, which were similar to studies in other countries (Miller, et al., 1987; Rohesnow, Corbett & Devine, 1988).

Substance Abuse, Addiction and Attachment

Addiction and attachment can be related in the following ways:

1. Addiction as a mean to deal with frustration in problematic attachment and bonding
2. Addiction as a substituted bonding and attachment
3. Addiction as a mean to gain bonding and attachment to related peers and social cycles
4. Addiction as a mean to punish related figure in problematic bonding.

Each of this way is also related to different forms of attachment as mentioned above

A. Deprivation from attachment
B. Anxious Attachment
C. Attachment behavior
D. Compulsive Self Reliance
E. Compulsive caregiving
F. Detachment
G. Separation
H. (Childhood, Adolescence, Adulthood)

There are various combinations of addiction and attachment. In type 1, addiction is regarded as a mean to deal with frustration in problematic attachment and bonding. That means, because of various types of attachment problems, the individual feels dreadfully empty, angry, lonely, inferior and fearful. All these feelings are intolerable and unbearable for the individuals. Thus, whenever these feelings appear, individuals have nowhere to escape, or not one to turn to ventilate such feelings. Thus, the only way they can cope with all these are by taking related drugs. During this process, individuals' frustrated senses of mind are being compensated and escaped by a drug stimulated sense of drug. However, once effects of drug eradicated, all these unbearable feelings come back again. They may need to re-take drug to compensate or to escape from all such intolerable feelings. In prolonged deprivation from attachment, individuals harbor intensive senses of emptiness and inferiority; they normally use substance abuse to fill up their sort of emptiness and inferiority. For anxious attachment and attachment behavior feel highly anxious and insecure in facing the predicted leaving of beloved objects and intimate figures such as parents, spouses, good friends and boyfriends or girlfriends. They may express intensive anger and craving to prevent the leaving of these intimate figures. However, if these intimate figures still leave or abandon them, they will end up in a severely depressive mood. To tackle this severely depressive mood, substance abuse especially taking stimulants may be the only or most available alternative for them. For individuals with compulsive self-reliance, individuals may have intensive mistrust of others on one hand and they have sense of insecurity, loneliness and emptiness on the other hand. They try to be independent but detached from others. In doing, drug addiction seems to be a good way to resolve their hidden senses of insecurity, loneliness and emptiness. For individuals with compulsive caregiving, they are actually using caregiving of minors so as to fulfill their need of attachment. They try their best to be overwhelming caregivers so that their minors can be fully attached to them. However, their overwhelming as well as manipulating caregiving in many ways are intolerable to their minors. Sooner or later, their minors may try to rebel or even leave them. Facing the rebellion and leaving of their minors, they feel highly frustrated and worried. They feel lonely, sad and angry as well as severe depressive mood. Thus, substance abuse tends to be the alternative to get away from all these unpleasant feelings and frustration. For persons with different types of attachment problems, it is certain that they have difficulties in facing separation from their attachment figures on one hand and have compulsive or involuntary detachment from others on the other hand. All these imply dreadfully negative emotions that are far beyond their toleration limits. Intensive bodily senses induced by substance abuse are ways for individual to escape from all these negative emotions.

In type 2, addiction is a substituted bonding and attachment. That means, individuals regarded drug as an attachment figures simply to their significant others like parents, spouses, children and friends. Apparently, they have lost or separated from their significant others. Thus, drug and substance tend to the only way in which they can attach to and get rid of their intensive sense of loneliness or being abandoned by significant others. In other words, they loss the love of others or they can never get the love of others. Thus, addicted drugs and abused substances are the only ones they can love or being loved. The process of drug addiction is similar to the process of love and being loved (Peele, S. & Brodsky, 1991 and Hofler and Kooyman, 1996)

Drug Addiction as a Pathological Substituted Bonding

Addicted drugs and abused substance can be a substituted bonding because of the following similarities to an attachment figures:

1. proximity
2. secured based
3. separation protest
4. elicitation by threat

5. specificity of attachment figure
6. Inaccessibility to conscious control
7. Persistence
8. Insensitivity to attachment figure.

Because of unavailability of other social support, drugs become the only available attached object to the individual. In terms of proximity, the easier is the availability, the more the individual is being attached to the drug. Apart from proximity, security basis is also another factor that reinforces the drug attachment and related substituted bonding. Individuals with substance abuse may harbor a strong fear that even they ask for other attention and attachment, sooner or later, they may be rejected and excluded by others. Thus, abused substance tends to the most secure media without any possibility of being rejected and excluded by others. Any time, the individuals like, they can take the drug voluntarily or at their own time and pace. They tend to take the drug within a secure environment without any external disturbance. Substance abuse is also similar to attachment in a form of separation protest. That means, any time, drug cannot be available, or they are forced to quit from drug, there is a serious sense of anxiety or tension. They may try any mean to crave for drug. Anyone who tries to stop them from craving from drug may be severely deterred by them. In some cases, aggressive and violent behaviors as well as illegal and immoral acts will be done by them. Elicitation by threat is also common in drug addiction and substance abuse. Individuals try to release external threat such as external exclusion and oppression by spontaneous drug taking. Furthermore, specificity is also a crucial effect in substance abuse. Different persons attach to different types of drug. Some intend to boost up their emotion and mood by taking physical stimulants. Some intend to release anxiety and worries by taking tranquillizers. Some intend to get away from the stressful world by taking heroine and ketamine. Similar to natures of attachment, individuals embrace problems in self-control (inaccessibility to conscious control). They fully beware the negative and harmful effects of drug on one hand and they intensively depend on and attach to drug on the other hand. In doing so, they deeply regret that they loss their conscious control to addicted drugs. Finally, substance abuse is highly addictive and difficult to quit (persistence). It implies being continuously stuck to related drug regardless of related difficulties, hardships and suffering in taking drug. That means drug is an effective and prolonged substituted attachment simply because of close availability and its power to relieve pain, anger and loneliness in life. If drug removes, there is a strong craving for drug just like separation protest and elicitation by threat.

Different Types Drugs and Attachment Needs

Different persons are dependent in different types of drugs. There is a strong withdrawal and dependent effect of drugs making individuals become highly attached to them. Even if they fully beware of harmful and immoral effects to their addicted drugs, they still fully depend on and attach to their addictive drugs. For those who have long been deprived from secure attachment in which their attachment figures has separated and left for a very long period of time in their developmental process, they tend to loss their trust on their significant others. Compulsive self-reliance with strong sense of emptiness and loneliness are their only coping in life. For them, physical stimulants seem to be a good alternative to cheer up their senses of boredom and emptiness in life. For those who have been suffered from unstable attachment from their significant others, they feel anxious, worry and tense. They harbor strong fear that sooner or later their significant others may left them. Even though they eagerly search for substitutes, they are afraid of establishing intimate contact and connection. They are being trapped with a dilemma that on one hand, they are eager to establish intimate contact with others but they are afraid of actual intimate contact on the other hand. In this process, they become highly sensitive to others' slight rejection, mild criticism or even causal leaving. They would interpret all these as separation as well abandonment and try all means including outburst of anger to avoid being excluded or rejected. If they are exposed to substance abuse, they may finally use it as the most easily available substituted attachment when they feel they are abandoned by others. For female clients with anxious attachment and attachment trauma in childhood and adolescence, they may attach to their boyfriends/spouses with substance abuse as a crucial substituted attachment figures. To gain the togetherness of their boyfriends/spouses, they may take drugs with them together. As a consequence, they may also become substance abusers. For those persons with compulsive caregiving, they need drug as a substituted attachment figures when their minors feel highly frustrated and left them. For all persons who use substance abuse as a substituted attachment, it is hard for them to abstain from drug unless they find another attachment figures from their friends, relatives or even strangers.

Bonding and Attachment with Addictive Peers

Substance abuse and drug addiction is also a mean to gain bonding and attachment to related peers and social cycles. That means, individuals not only attach to related drugs and substances, they attach also to related peers and social cycles. These peers can be school peers, friends, or even strangers in disco, party and social gathering who take drugs together with individuals. Within the similar effects of abused substance, individuals feel that they connect with one another together. Even if they are strangers to one another, under the effects of drug, they feel that they can share their deep seated feelings and emotions in particular those unresolved one. As drug and substance abuse are illegal, they also feel that drug related peers are only those they can trust and rely on. They also protect one another from being discovered by police and their family members in illegal drug trafficking and immoral drug taking. They share information about where and how to get cheaper or better drugs. In many cases, they even advise or warn one another in over-taking drug and substance. In some cases, they help one another in facing the financial and physical difficulties in prolonged drug addiction and substance abuse. For those chronic and prolonged drug users, many of them are isolated or excluded from their family members, friends and relatives. It seems that drug related peers are the only social support and bonding they can get in actual situations. However, different types of attachment pattern may have various responses to drug related peers. For those with compulsive self-reliance, they may prefer to take drug alone rather than together with other drug related peers. For those with compulsive caregiving, they may prefer to take drug together with their minors, subordinates or followers only. For those with anxious attachment, it is certain that they prefer to take drug with any drug related peers so that they can have easily available for their attachment substitutes.

Drug Addiction as a Mean to Punish Related Figure in Problematic Bonding

Drug addiction and substance abuse can be used as a mean to punish related figure in problematic bonding. That means, individuals harbor intensive negative feelings towards their significant others. In their life development, they may be abandoned, abused, manipulated and exploited by their parents, sibling, peers, teachers, boyfriends and/or girlfriends. They feel angry, inferior, loneliness and sad towards these abandonment, abuses and exploitation. Because of various reasons, individuals always fail to express all these negative feelings towards these authority figures. That means all these attachments with authority figures are problematic and difficult. They are trapped within a dilemma that they are very eager to attach all these attachment but authority figures on one hand, but they are angry with these authority figures on the other hand. In addition to that, all these authority figures may be highly oppressive, engulfing or rejecting to the clients' attachment needs. Thus, instead of directly expressing their anger or attachment needs in front of their attachment figures, they prefer attachment to additive drug and abused substance. They transferred their anger towards their authority figures by harming their own bodies through substance abuse and addiction. Underlying their drug addiction, they are expressing a hidden message that '*you hate me and deserve me. That is why I hate myself. I hurt myself so to as to demonstrate that you has been hurting me for years*.' The more they engage in substance abuse, the more their physical and mental health deteriorates because of substance abuse, and the more they feel that they can express their anger fully towards their authority figures.

For persons with compulsive self-reliance, as they are already separated from their attachment figures and they bear no hope to reconnect with them, they are less likely to attach to substance abuse as a mean to punish their attachment figure. However, for those with anxious attachment, as they still harbor hope to connect with their attachment figure or their attachment figure, to certain degree, they are more frequent and likely to engage in substance abuse as a symbolic punishment to their attachment figure. For those individuals with compulsive caregiving, they use their minors and subordinates for substituted attachment. The leaving of their minors may imply difficulties to reconnect with them. Thus, they are less likely to use substance abuse as a symbolic mean to punish their minors.

Vicious Cycle of Addiction and Problematic Attachment

The close connection between addiction and attachment may finally end up with a strong vicious cycle of addiction and attachment. Initially, addiction is used as a way to deal with problematic attachment. It can be a way to deal with frustration in attachment, a substitute, a way to attach to drug related peer, and a mean to induce self-harm so as a symbolic mean to punish one's attachment figures. However, the more it is done, the more severe one's attachment problem become. Apart from drug and drug related peers, individuals with substance abuse are gradually rejected and isolated not only by their own attachment figures but also by members in various social circles. As a consequence, the individual need further drug addiction and substance abuse to deal with their intensified social isolation and social rejection. Finally, drug addiction and substance abuse finally become their own available attachment substitute. They are totally rejected and isolated by others. Drug addiction and

drug related peers become their own 'pseudo but prolonged lovers, relatives and friends'. All these can be illustrated in the following figure.

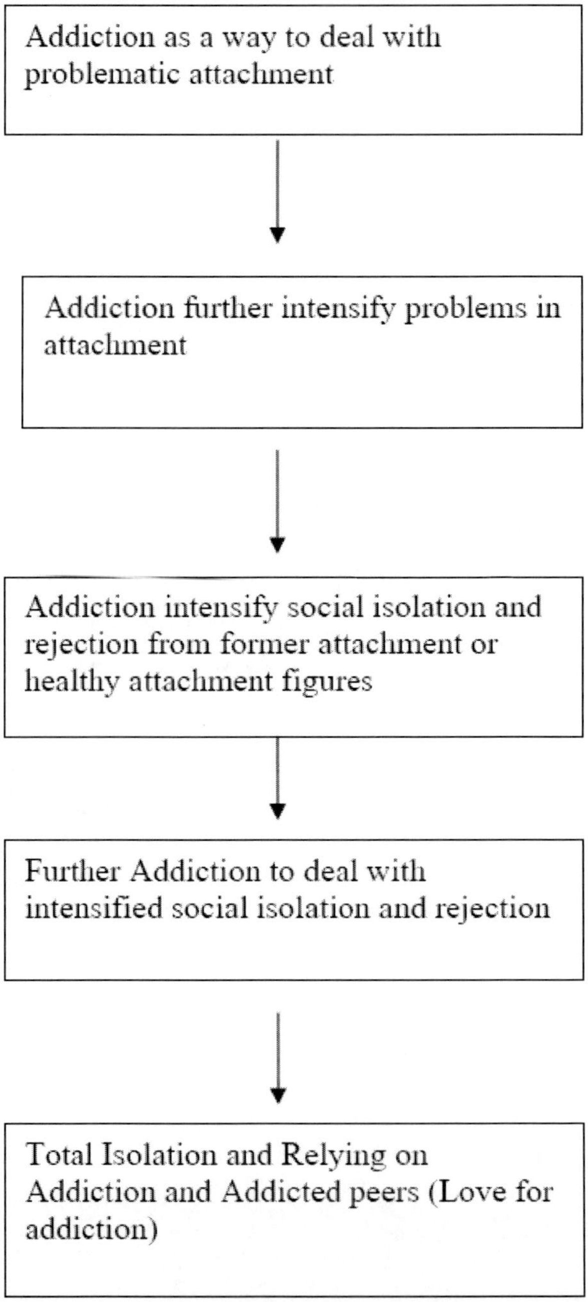

Figure. The Vicious Cycle of Addiction and Problematic Attachment.

Integrated Dynamic Recovery of Attachment in Drug Addiction and Substance Abuse

All these have important implication to integrated recovery for persons with drug addiction. The longer the individual are attached to drug, the more difficult the individual to be abstained from drug. Along this line of thinking, the perquisites of recovery from drug addiction and substance abuse should be facilitating individuals to have good substituted attachment from other constructive, meaningful and healthy attachment object and figures. To attain this, several important intervention strategies are described as follows:

1. Readiness to detach from drug attachment
2. Dealing with trauma and difficulties in attachment in life
3. Establishing meaningful new attachment bonding
4. A note of forgiveness and spirituality
5. Dealing with transference.

Readiness to Detach from Drug Attachment

In integrated recovery from drug addiction, it is important that related professionals should first acknowledge clients' tension among attachment to drug, attachment problems in life and attachment to related professionals. For example, a female client with substance abuse has attachment problem as her father abandons her family when she was only four years old. Later, her mother ran away with another man leaving her with her grandmother. Unfortunately, her grandmother died two years later. From that time onward, she stayed in a children home. When she grew up, whenever she faced frustration in life, she tended to attach to drug to substitute difficulties in attachment. When she sought counseling in a counseling centre for clients with substance abuse, she was also attached to a male counselor who was a middle aged man. He was kind, genuine and caring. In talking with him, she felt that she attached to her father. On one hand, she liked to talk with him as she talked with her father when she was only a small boy. On the other hand, she transferred her unresolved anger from her father towards her male counselor. She was very sensitive to any mild and slight criticism and rejection from the male counselor. It is very important that this male counselor can acknowledge the psychological tension of this client in juggling attachment problems in life, substituted attachment to drug and attachment with him. That means, in the counseling process, he should reflect and facilitate the female client to express and share all this tension. By doing so, he can successfully enable the client to face this tension appropriately, rather than, avoiding this by prolonged drug addiction and substance abuse.

Secondly, related professionals should accept clients' pattern and change of need of attachment according to environmental stress, degree of addiction and life difficulties. That means, the more difficult clients are in their attachment with their significant others, the more intensive they attach to drug addiction and substance abuse. Before, during and after the drug addiction, individuals may also attach to others such as their drug related peers, concerned professionals, and boyfriends or girlfriends. All these may alter individuals' attachment to drug addiction. Related professionals should not simply put the blame on their clients that

they are reluctant to quit drug regardless of their attachment problems. Many clients quit the drug on one time simply because restoration of attachment with their peers or relatives. Similarly, they take up the drug on other time because of the separation and leaving of their attachment figures. That means it is important for clients to have substituted attachment figures before they can detach from drug addiction and substance abuse.

Thirdly, related professional should also recognize clients' fear of detachment from drug that can result in social isolation from drug related peers, and significant others. For females with substance abuse, many of them take drugs simply because as a sign of intimacy and togetherness for their spouses and boyfriends. Some take drug with their close peers. Abstinence from drug may result separation from their drug related spouses, intimate figures and close peers. For individuals with prolonged drug addiction, they have already been excluded from the dominant society. All these drug related peers and intimate figures may mean their final social circles they rely on in dealing with their life frustration and difficulties. Thus, related professionals should fully recognize clients' hidden fear in abstinence from drug. In some cases, clients may enter related intervention and program in abstinence from drug together with their drug related peers and intimate figures.

Fourthly, related professionals should recognize previous trail in establishing new attachment to cope with traumatic former attachment. That means, clients with drug addiction and substance abuse, in fact, have tried their very best to settle or deal with their attachment trauma in life. Nevertheless, without supportive others and a caring social environment, even though they are very eager to establish new attachment and affective bond with people around, they fail. All these substituted attachment figures may finally leave them, betray them or reject them. As a consequence, their attachment traumas increase to an extent that they are no longer harbor trust to people around. However, their urge for being cared and attached with others is still intensive. Thus, the only way they can deal with that is substituted attachment to drug and drug related peers. Related professionals should be deeply empathic with clients' attachment traumas in life and their unresolved dilemmas in attachment needs in life.

Fifthly, related professionals should encourage clients to re-establish new and meaningful attachment with others. With previous experiences in attachment traumas, indeed, it is difficult to do so. Thus, it is important to increase their incentive as well as to re-sparkle their urge to initiate new attachment bonding with their significant others in various social circles. These can be done by the following ways.

1. Construct and restore some meaningful activities for clients with their supportive others. To start with, it can be short but meaningful such as having a good meal or having a game of physical exercises.
2. Encourage clients' significant others to show concern on clients' recent needs, health conditions, financial needs or life difficulties. Sometimes a small gift or a small sum of money or small card with warm and caring word can serve this purpose.
3. Encourage clients to show small concern to their significant others who have been separated from time for a long time because of clients' drug addiction. To start with, it can be a card with warm words or, a small gift to celebrate others' birthday.
4. In doing all these, clients and their significant others may evolve unpleasant memories in previous attachment traumas. It is important that related professionals should avoid going into details of such traumatic memories. Rather they should shift clients and their significant others' attention to current communication and

interactions. Gradually, they can start to establish better understanding and relationship with one another.

Dealing with Traumas and Difficulties in Attachment in Life

With full recognition of clients' attachment traumas in life, as well as their own dilemmas and challenges in facing the detachment from drug, related professionals should begin to deal with clients' traumas and difficulties in attachment in life. Firstly, related professionals should facilitate clients to elaborate feelings and frustrations in difficulties in attachment within a highly supportive, caring and secure social environment with their significant others. This should be done in a natural and cautious way. They should listen to all these triggered former memories and released suppressed and repressed negative emotions. However, they should avoid clients' over-ventilation of feelings. After that, related professionals should engage their clients with meaningful activities and realistic interaction so that they can temporarily recovered from triggered traumatic memories and experiences. Then in the next time, similar process may happen again and again until their clients' suppressed traumatic memories and experiences can be gradually reflected, re-bounced and released.

In the whole process, individuals gradually dissolve all unresolved traumatic memories and experiences in their life.

Following this, related professionals have to accept clients satisfy their needs of attachment in various ways. As the attachment to drug is detached, individuals' difficulties and problems in previous traumatic experiences are dissolved; they certainly express different ways to satisfy their unfulfilled attachment needs. It can be highly attached to related professionals that intervene with them. It can be intensive sense of loneliness that demands togetherness with others. It can be over-whelming urge to attach with different ones in various social circles. It can also be an urge to gain the total acceptance of related others. All these should be fully understood and recognized by related professionals in the process of intervention. In doing so, they should be carefully and patiently acknowledge all these clients' needs without labeling that clients are irrational, difficult to deal with and unable to establish appropriate relationship with others.

Establishing Meaningful New Substituted Attachment Bonding

With that sort of deep understanding of clients' needs of attachment, related professionals should explore clients' other possibilities and experiences to gain good attachment. Very often, related professionals should explore clients' relatives and friends that have been isolated and separated from clients for a long period of time. They should try to help clients to resolve their grudges with their relatives and friends that have been lost in the process of prolonged addiction.

When the client has a good substituted attachment or restore his/her attachment with his/her relatives and friends, it is the time for the social worker to ease up his/her anger and frustration in problematic bonding and attachment with their significant others. The easing out process can be a difficult and comprehensive one in which the individual has to voice out their former traumatic experiences in life. In doing so, related professionals should be highly cautious and careful in avoiding over-ventilation and over-digging into clients' traumatic experiences. All these ventilations and healings should be done within a highly supportive and caring social environment consisting of clients' supportive relatives and friends. Very often a homely and warming environment is much better than a cold and apathetic interviewing room within a social welfare agency. After the ventilation, related clients should be looked after closely by caring others so to avoid that they use drug addiction and substance abuse to compensate their evolved but unresolved negative feelings of sadness, inferiority, emptiness, loneliness and anger. The newly constructed or restored attachment figures can be most suitable ones to care and concern clients after their deep ventilation of negative feelings in their former attachment *traumas*.

A Note of Forgiveness and Spirituality

Within various attachment traumas in clients' developmental process, even though they have ventilated related negative feelings and memories, they still have approach and avoidance conflicts with their former attachment figures. On one hand, they still harbor a strong urge to connect with their attachment figures. On the other hand, former unpleasant and traumatic experiences make them harbor intensive anger, hate, and frustration towards their former attachment figure. Very often, even after the establishment of substituted attachment figures, clients still cannot escape from all these dilemmas and unresolved conflicts. These unresolved conflicts may also deeply affect the stability of all these newly established attachment bonding making clients become highly vulnerable to separation, criticism and comments by others including their newly attachment figures. Thus, to restore stability in attachment with significant others, it is crucial that individuals can develop forgiveness to those attachment figures who hurt them in their previous developmental traumas. The healing power of genuine forgiveness is highly powerful.

Firstly, it is a mean to resolve anger in difficulties in attachment. In many ways, anger is a valid internal means for someone to pull up their own depowered status in being a victim in the attachment trauma. If A is angry with B, that means B has done something wrong to A. In doing so, A has overriding power towards B and B is actually being depowered or victimized by B. Thus, being angry with A is both an internal and external effective way to empower B towards all these victimizations and depowerment. Only if B can take revenge against A, this anger and hate can be resolved. However, in attachment traumas, B may fail to take revenge against A as A mostly be the attachment figures such as parents or other significant others. That means all these anger and hate are sustained without any resolution. The longer this anger is sustained, the deeper the hurt towards the individual is as the anger stir frequent recall of all these traumatic experiences.

Under this condition, the individual with substance abuse and attachment traumas may thus be kept in a dilemma. On one hand, s/he may reject genuine forgiveness to his/her significant others in his/her developmental traumas. Once s/he forgives them, it may mean that s/he becomes powerless, helpless and victimized. On the other hand, prolonged anger and hate may also imply endless recall of all these traumatic experiences together with intolerable feelings of loneliness, anger, inferiority, fear and emptiness. The longer the individual is kept within this dilemma, the more painful and empty s/he becomes and the more s/he needs to adhere to substance abuse as a substituted attachment.

To free the individual from this dilemma, as mentioned in the previous section, the individual first needs to rebuild healthy new attachment to free himself/herself from attachment in substance abuse and drug addiction. Following this should be gradually discharge of anger and frustration in former attachment traumas. Then, the individual, under the help of related professionals, should restore normal and healthy interaction with related significant others in related attachment traumas. When such healthy interaction is sustained and consolidated, the individual gradually able to release his/her dilemma in terms of love and hate, as well as anger and helpless to their significant others.

When related negative feelings can be properly and gradually released, it is the time to develop clients' forgiveness to their significant others who have previously hurt, abandoned, or abused them. However, the development of clients' good genuine forgiveness should have the following pre-requisites:

a. Regain proper and gradual interaction with their significant others who have abused, abandoned or hurt them

The process must be gradual. It can start with a short phone contact or a casual greeting in a social occasion. Then, it can be short social interaction in a social gathering or meal time. Following this can be a sharing of current situation. Anytime if the individual feels reluctant and uneasy, the interaction can be shortened and stopped to avoid further deterioration of relationships.

b. Develop and consolidate a high level meaning of life after the abstinence from substance abuse and drug addiction

This high level meaning can be involvement in religious beliefs such as Christianity, Buddhism and Taoism. Within these religious beliefs, one learns to transcend his meaning of life from secular materialism, attachment to others or taking revenge on enemies to contribution to one's families, society and religions. Being equipped in a high level meaning of life, one begins to recognize that one's life is short and ought to try his/her best to perform meaningful activities rather than confined by previous sufferings and traumas in one's life.

c. Recognize and admit the dilemma and negative effect of anger and hurt in recalling former traumatic experiences done by their significant others

The anger and hurt is deeply complicated and comprehensive. Developmental traumas are also intermingled with hardships, difficulties and rejection in the process of prolonged substance abuse. The recognition of acknowledgement of this complexity and comprehensiveness among traumas and difficulties in various stages of clients' life is crucial in helping clients with prolonged substance abuse. They make clients feel highly ambivalent and are unable to narrate and describe their overwhelming negative emotions or demonstrate strong counter-transference and resistance towards professionals' interventions. Related professionals must accept, tolerate and recognize all these ambivalence and resistance underlying clients' complicated traumas and difficulties in their lives.

d. Develop courage and proper channels to ease out their negative feelings and dilemmas in former traumatic experiences with their significant others

Related professionals should construct a safe and secure environment with supportive others and meaningful activities in helping clients to ease out their negative feelings, dilemmas in former traumatic experiences with their significant others. A safe and secure environment can be a warm setting within a comfortable room, homes of relatives and family members, sunny and beautiful sea beach or meadow within a nice park. All these comfortable settings encourage the client to ease out their negative feelings and memories of former traumatic experiences.

e. Patience to wait for clients' gradual and proper repentance of their significant others who have hurt, abandoned and abused them in attachment traumas

Related professionals must have enough patience to wait for clients' repentance of their significant others. Most clients need several times to release their deep seated negative feelings. Different clients may have various patterns in releasing their deep seated negative feelings. Some may release all their negative emotions within one or two times. Some may need many times. Each time, they can release only a little bit of their negative feeling and traumatic experiences. Many of them may only stop for certain level of traumatic memories and related negative feelings and refuse to go further. Related professionals must work according to clients' own pace without inducing a harmful effect to related clients.

After the above pre-requisites are fulfilled, related clients are able to induce gradual genuine forgiveness towards their significant others who hurt them in previous traumatic experiences. Gradual genuine forgiveness exists in various degrees as the following:

1. Complete Forgiveness

It occurs when both parties are ready to forgive or being forgiven. Clients understand why their significant others hurt them in former traumatic and abusive experiences. Their significant others also deeply repent and regret for what they have done to clients' traumas. In complete forgiveness, communication and mutual understanding is fully attained. Behind traumatic experiences and memories, there are also mutual love, support and care between both parties.

For instance, a client, C, was a female youth with chronic substance abuse. C had been sexually molested by his step father many times. She told this to her mother. She refused to accept this and deterred the client to report to police and even blamed her daughter for her seductiveness to her stepfather. C was deeply frustrated by these traumatic experiences, coupled with endless bullying by her classmates and poor academic performance, she engaged in substance abuse to escape from her prevailing senses of frustration, anger and worthlessness in life. She hated her step father as he sexually molested her. She also hated her mother even deeper than her stepfather. Two years later, her step father died in a car accident. She did not go to her funeral but her hate towards her step father was projected on her mother. As her physical and mental health conditions deteriorated drastically, she sought the help from a social worker in a drug counseling centre. C was facilitated to abstain from her substance abuse. However, she was kept within a dilemma. On one hand, she was keen in abstinence from substance abuse. On the other hand, she was deeply attached to her boyfriend who also engaged in substance abuse. Later, her boyfriend abandoned her. She was deeply hurt by this incident. She committed suicide but was saved by her friend. Her mother visited her during her hospitalized but was rejected by her. It seemed that her mother felt regretted for what she had done to C. She asked the forgiveness from C but C refused to do so. Under the care of the social worker, C was then admitted in a female rehabilitation residential unit in a Christian social welfare organization. In that unit, C was gradually rehabilitated and regained her confidence in daily living. The social worker and the spiritual mentor there also helped C to elaborate her negative emotions in her former traumatic experiences in childhood and in adolescence. Under their arrangement, C's mother also visited C for several times. They did not push C to forgive her mother. Instead, they tried all means to facilitate C's communication with her mother. Gradually, C began to understand her mother's worries, fear and sense of insecurity towards her stepfather. Her step father was a member of a criminal society. She was aware that her mother harbored intensive fear that once C disclosed the sexual molest to others, his step father might kill both of them. Later, her mother was diagnosed as having terminal lung cancer. In that occasion, facing her mother's request and last unfulfilled wish in her life, C finally forgave her mother. The complete forgiveness not only gave C's mother a peaceful ending of her life but also completely dissolved her lifelong deep seated anger in her life.

2. Partial Forgiveness

It means that complete forgiveness is not possible. It may be the victim of the traumatic experiences still harbor anger and hurt that s/he does not want to have any deep recall of related persons, issues, objects, and experiences that relate with traumatic memories. Thus, even with support from others and even with deep ventilation of their unhappy feelings and emotions, they can only have a partial forgiveness of their significant others who have forgiven them. It may also be the fact that related abusive significant others are not ready to repent for their own abusive experience or they still have potentials to abuse or hurt the clients. In doing so, it is better for clients to remain in a state of partial forgiveness so that s/he can be emotionally and mentally stable and enjoy a normal life.

For instance, B is a male adolescent with prolonged and chronic substance abuse. In his childhood, he was spontaneously abused by his alcoholic father who was a member in an underground society. He frequently engaged in drug dealing and trafficking. Whenever he was drunk, he would abuse him and his mother together. B was physically strong and tough. Sometimes, he fought back with his father and tried to protect his father. However, his father was too strong and B's fighting back and even provoked his father further physical abuse on him. Once, B was even terribly beaten by his father and was hospitalized for two months. His school social worker reported to the police and B's father was charged with offence of intentional physical abuse on others. He was sentenced for 3 months prison punishment. B's father was finally released and returned home. Instead of repenting for what he had done to B, he kept on bullying and abusing B and his mother verbally and physically. Finally, under the care of a social worker from Social Welfare Department, B and his mother left him and lived in a public estate unit. Three years later, B's mother suffered from major depressive disorder and committed suicide. B was sad and lonely in losing his mother. He was then under the care of social worker in a boy's home. In the boy's home, B was aggressive and highly irritable. He was then labeled by both his teachers in schools as well as wardens in his boy's home as a juvenile delinquent. He frequently involved in gang fights and became a member of an underground society. He left the boy's home and lived with a gang of delinquents. He also involved in drug trafficking and abused cocaine. B fell in love with a female adolescent who also abused ketamine for many years. Later, they abused ketamine together. Unfortunately, one day, his girlfriend took too much ketamine and died. B was deeply frustrated by the death of his girlfriend. B felt dreadfully lonely as he had lost both his mother and his girlfriend. He was deeply sad, angry and empty with their death. He locked himself in his room for a whole week. Then, he came out of his room, and climbed up a tall building and intended to commit suicide by jumping down. Fortunately, someone in the building discovered that and the police took him to the hospital. He was diagnosed as having major depressive disorder as well as substance abuse. After a week's hospitalization, he was discharged home. In the process of hospitalization, the pastor in the hospital approached him and spread the gospel to him. He began to believe in Jesus Christ and became a committed Christian. He regained his meaning of life to be a peer counselor for those adolescents who had committed in chronic substance abuse. He also aspired to be a Christian minister. He studied theology in a local bible college. Despite changing his meaning of life, his anger with his father was still there. He hated his father as he only abused him and his mother. His father was also the indirect cause of his mother's suicide and his misdeed in his adolescence. His spiritual mentor, the pastor in the hospital advised and facilitated him to forgive his father. He firmly told B that if he did not forgive his father, he could not forgive himself. B tried to find out his father. However, whenever, they talked for a short while, B became furious and tried to curse his father for his irresponsibility and immorality in his life. B's father returned back with cursing and bad words. B became deeply frustrated. The following self-narration could clearly show his conflicts in this issue.

> B: 'As a Christian, I know that I should forgive my father as Jesus Christ had forgiven us. Indeed, it is very hard to do so. My father is a bastard. He abused us when he was drunk. He was very strong and a good fighter in his triad society (the name of a criminal society in Hong Kong). He beat me hardly and even broke my leg and my arm leading to two months' complete hospitalization before I could fully recovered. This was a serious trauma on me. Whenever I saw my father, the memories of this trauma arouse in a way I could never forget about it. Occasionally, I had nightmares that I was beaten to death by my father. In fact, after I became a Christian, I always told myself that I should forgive my father as God had forgiven my sin. I prayed to God hoping He could give me love, patience and faith in doing so. Nevertheless, whenever I saw my father and chatted with him, my anger, my pain and my trauma returned. I would try to challenge him, pick up his fault, allege his past faults and wrong deeds. However, the more I did so, the more reactive he became. He simply responded as a triad member rather than a father. He threatened me by saying that he could kill me if I went on my allegation on him. How could I forgive him? He never repented what he had done to us. He was still a bastard.

From B's self-narration, it was clear B intended to forgive his father. However, every time, he intended to do so, his anger came back. In addition to that, B's father did not repent. Facing B's allegation, B's father fought back. That means, B had motivation to forgive his father. But he needed his father's repentance. Strictly speaking, he only partially forgave his father. It was because that the inner hurt and harm done by his father's former abuse and the death of his mother and his girlfriend had not been healed. As the hurt and harm were still there, it was understandable that once he saw his father, all these traumatic experiences bounced back making him intensively furious and tried to accuse his father. His forgiveness towards his father increased when his father's condition deteriorated. Two years later, his father suffered from lung cancer. His body became weaker and weaker. At first, B did not want to visit his father. Later, under the encouragement of his pastor, he went to the hospital and visited his father. In doing so, his inner conflict came back. He knew that he had to forgive his father. However, he still clung to hurt and harm done by his father. As a Christian, he knew that God forgave him and he should forgive his father. He kept into an intensive dilemma that he did not forgive himself that he could not forgive his father. Fortunately, one day, he was approached by his nephew who had recently visited his father in the hospital. His nephew told him that his father wanted to see him and ask for his forgiveness. At that moment, he knew that God has opened a chance for him. He rushed to the hospital and saw his weak father lying on bed. With tears, his father asked for his forgiveness. He preached the gospel of Jesus Christ to his dying father urging him to believe in Christ. His father nodded his head. From that time onward, his spirit and mind was filled with Jesus' love. He embraced his father and his partial forgiveness finally turned into a complete forgiveness of his father because of Jesus' love and care.

3. Fluctuating Forgiveness

Fluctuating forgiveness means that at one time, the client forgives his significant others who have hurt them, at another time, the client does not. The fluctuating forgiveness may be due to several reasons. First, it can be the problem of the significant other who at one time shows repentance and at another time does not. Second it can be the problem of the client with substance abuse. At one time, s/he repressed the painful memories of being abused by his/her significant other. At another time s/he recalls such painful memories again. Fluctuating forgiveness, in many ways, may be even more frustrating and painful than complete or partial forgiveness. The client with substance abuse may suffer from a fluctuating mood springing from sadness and anger as well as puzzling and confusing. In fact, fluctuating mood is very often is even more painful for partial forgiveness. It always happens for clients with close attachment and relationship with his abusive significant others. What below was the self-narration of a male client with substance abuse who felt highly painful in fluctuating forgiveness with his abusive father.

> D: 'My father abused me whenever he was drunk. Starting when I was just a small boy, he did so. When he was depressive, he went out to drink. When he was drunk, he returned home, whenever anyone in our family including my mother, my sister and me did anything wrong, no matter how small it was, we would be thus be bitten. Once, he used a stick to hit my head and my arm, both my arm and head was broken. I was taken to a nearby hospital. He was then charged by the police for domestic violence and child abuse. However, as he was only bread winner in the family, my mother urged the police to forgive him and from that time onward, even my father abused us, we dared not to report to the police. In fact, apart from abusing us while he was drunk, he was still a responsible father. Also, what puzzled us was that after he abused us, he felt deeply regretted and asked for our forgiveness. Sometimes, he even broke into tears. I understood, he felt dreadfully stressful in his own job that was why he used alcohol to rid off his own stress. The pain for us was that we had forgiven him many times, but he still abused us while he was drunk. The only way to avoid that whenever he was drunk and returned home, we simply closed the door of our room tightly or went outside to avoid him.
>
> As I went outside frequently, I met a group of peers who was frequent substance abuse. They taught me to abuse ketamine and cocaine so as to paralyze my unhappy

> feelings and conflict in facing my abusive father. Finally, they discovered me abused soft drug. My father was very angry. He chased me with a chopper. He wanted to kill me. My mother cried bitterly. From that time onward, I never returned home. Regarding the feeling towards my father, I was very confused and puzzled. On the one hand, I hated him. He abused me and my mother. He made me went outside and committed substance abuse. However, I also loved him. When he was awake from his drunkenness, he deeply regretted for what he had done to us. He wanted me to study university and be an accountant. He urged me to behave well and he also taught me many things while I was a small child. I was deeply trapped within the love and hate dilemma. I wanted to forgive him but I could not. I hated him but I still loved him. It was really painful in doing so. I depended on substance abuse to get rid of all these feelings of confusion and puzzle. In no way, I could escape from all these unpleasant feelings.

It was clear that D suffered a lot from fluctuating forgiveness. His father abused him and his mother when he was drunk. However, his father asked for their forgiveness when he was awake from his drunkenness. The fluctuating forgiveness was painful for D. Whenever he wanted to forgive his father, another new abuse appeared and he diminishes his intended forgiveness towards his father. Thus, the only way he could to use substance abuse to escape from the unresolved love and hate and approach and avoidance dilemmas. The fluctuating forgiveness certainly becomes the fuel and cause of his chronic and prolonged substance abuse. In fact, his father was furious towards his substance abuse and chased him with a chopper. That means, his father still cared about him but expressed his care and concern in a very negative way. It further added to D's love and hate dilemma towards his father.

> 'This dilemma went on in D's chronic substance abuse. D lived an independent but hand to mouth life. He worked as a causal worker in Chinese restaurants. Two years later, D was notified by his relatives that his father suffered from terminal stage of liver cancer. His father regretted for what he had done to his family. He pledged for D's forgiveness and he wanted to see D before he died. D felt painful in hearing this bad news. He rushed to the hospital and witnessed that his father, previously strong and tough, became very weak, thin and pale lying on the bed just like a sack of bones. Facing all these, D's tears poured down. His father, in a very weak voice asked for his ultimate forgiveness. D nodded his hand. His tears had already dissolved his prolonged love and hate dilemma towards his dying father. He forgave his father. His father died with a peaceful mind.

From D's experience, it was clear that D finally forgave his father in his dying process. He forgave his father's past torture towards him. He knew that his father felt deeply regretted for his wrong deeds in the past. He finally recognized his father loved him and urged to be a good father. This was the final unfulfilled wish for his father. All this sparkle his own love towards his father. Once, he felt he was being loved by his father, his love towards his father manifested and he was able to render ultimate forgiveness towards his father.

With genuine forgiveness, individuals gradually develop mental ability (mentalization) to perceive from the stand of the attachment figures within the attachment traumas done the individual. In all three cases, B, C and D, at first, they could not forgive their parents. However, as their parents facing terminal illness, they began to forgive their parents despite their past abuse, ignorance and oppression towards them. Within their forgiveness, their past hurt and harm were spiritually healed. When they knew that their abusive parents asked for their forgiveness or faced terminal illness, they began to forgive them. They knew that their dying parents could no longer hurt them. Their dying parents urged for their care, love and forgiveness. It was also a good chance for them to resolve their lifelong unresolved emotional complex towards their parents. That was why they actively forgave their abusive parents. In doing so, they discharged their lifelong anger, fear, loneliness and inferiority within their past trauma, suffering and hardship. They also felt that they had free from the burden of unresolved love and hate, as well as approach and avoidance towards their abusive parents. Once they were free from all these burdens, they were able to interact, communicate, be empathic and love others smoothly and naturally. Spiritually, profound forgiveness made them feel strongly and deeply loved and cared by almighty God. The togetherness of Holy Spirit enabled them to have profound peace, joy, love, discipline, faith endurance in mind. That means in all these three cases, forgiveness coupled with profound spirituality has the following powerful therapeutic impact.

1. Forgiveness as a mean to resolve anger in difficulties in attachment
2. Forgiveness as a way release one from endless craving of immediate but unhealthy substituted attachment
3. Forgiveness as a way to build up inner space and hope in building new and meaningful attachment bonding.

Within B, C, D cases, it was clear their parents not only abused and maltreat them, they did not provide secure, constant and stable attachment to them making them felt dreadfully lonely, helpless and insecure in their childhood and adolescence. As a consequence, they were trapped within the attachment dilemma, on one hand, they were deeply angry with their abusive parents. On the other hand, they intensively urged for love and care. However, once they began to attach to substituted attachment figures in their lives, their unconscious fear of being abandoned and even abused by their former abusive attachment figure in childhood was activated. Thus, they have prolonged difficulties in attachment and intimate relationship with their significant others in their lives. Only by means of forgiving their abusive parents, they could resolve these difficulties and regain their confidence, security and assertiveness in engaging in intimate relationship with others. That means, with profound forgiveness of their abusive significant others, they are not only free from their love and hate dilemma and attachment hunger, they can also create new inner mental space for new normal attachment with other supportive significant others. In these three cases, profound forgiveness is not merely a mental activities or a sort of mental reflection in terms of mentalization as what attachment theories suggested. In fact, profound forgiveness is found on spirituality. All these three cases, their profound forgiveness is based on a view of life and death, knowing that their abusive figure was facing the terminal days of their lives and recognizing profound forgiveness was the only way to resolve their lifelong unfinished business. In other words, without the connection of spirituality, they do not have the bases in rendering profound forgiveness towards their abusive others. That means, spirituality performs the following pre-requisites for forgiveness

1. Spirituality as an attachment and connection with ultimate meaning of life
2. Spirituality as a reason and justification of forgiveness
3. Spirituality as sources of hope and aspiration in footing new meaningful attachment

4. Spirituality as spontaneous acceptance of changes of attachment bonding.

Different clients may have different interpretation and practice of spirituality. It can be clients' own religious belief, meaning of life, missions in life, fulfillment of their beloved others' final wish and expectation., contribution to one's family, social circle and society. Within profound spirituality, one is connected with hope and love. S/he also develops trust and sense of security towards others. By means of all these, individuals are able nurture a base of forgiveness and transcend from previous life traumas and sufferings.

Dealing with Clients' Transference

All these have strong implications to integrated dynamic recovery for persons with substance abuse. Traumas and hurts in attachment in life are regarded as the cause and source of substance abuse. Thus, intervention should focus on resolving all these hurts and traumas in their previous life experiences. Also, substituted good and supportive attachment should be rendered by related professionals and clients' significant others. By doing all that, individuals can regain a stable, secure and supportive intimate relationship with others in which they are able to love and being loved, to trust and being trusted, to forgive and being forgiven by others.

Transference in Client-Worker Relationship

In the process of intervention, the first challenge faced by related professionals is that they have to work through related transference in work-client relationship. It is regarded as by the client as:

1. As a substituted attachment bonding
2. As a hope for meaningful attachment
3. As a release of past frustration in past attachment
4. As a projection of difficulties in former attachment
5. As a mediator for struggle of attachment to drug versus attachment to abusive others.

That means, related professionals have to face intensive transference, counter-transference and mutual transference within client-worker relationship with their clients with substance abuse.

Within transference, workers are regarded by clients with their substituted good fathers, mothers, sisters, husbands and wives. In their childhood, adolescence and adulthood, their significant others may be bad, abusive, engulfing and/or oppressive. Thus, on one hand, they hate their significant others. On the other hand, they urge for love and concern from substituted attachment figures. Under this condition, related professionals who show empathy, concern and care for their clients may easily be regarded by their clients as substituted attachment figures. Within transference, related clients are highly attached to their professionals. On one hand, they tend to require their professionals to be highly responsive to their demand such as being together with them, fulfilling their needs immediately, or craving for professionals' care and concern. All these are highly demanding for related professionals making them feel suffocated and stressful.

Counter-Transference in Client-Worker Relationship

As an opposite, clients can also have counter-transference with their professionals. That means they regard related professionals as their abusive attachment figures. In that situation, they feel angry with their professionals. They think that related professionals are highly rejecting and critical. On one hand, they may be highly rejecting and resistant to related professionals. On the other hand, they may feel that related professionals hurt their self-dignity and image seriously as their former abusive figures. In extreme cases, even the appearance or words said by related professionals may trigger their former traumatic memories with their abusive attachment figures.

Firstly, facing hunger for attachment in life, related workers are easily regarded by clients as their substituted attachment figure. That means they may be highly sensitive to the response of related professional. On the one hand, they demand related professionals to be highly caring, supportive and even parenting. On the other hand, if related professionals show any slight sign of distancing, reluctance or criticism, they may regarded them as rejecting and abandoning them as their significant others did in their childhood and adolescence. Thus, it is very important for related professionals to be ready to face emotional enmeshment by their clients with substance abuse. By means of proper use of transference, related professionals can enable to their clients to engage in meaningful attachment with a hope to heal their traumas in previous attachment. Related professionals, by means of substituted attachment, facilitate clients to revisit their former traumas and sufferings in their previous harmful attachment in life. They should also facilitate their clients to ventilate their hurt and harm in their attachment with their abusive significant others.

Proper Use of Transference and Counter Transference

Within all these transference and counter transference, related professionals need to be patient and have proper use of these client work relationship. They should recognize and understand clients' intensive needs for attachment underlying their transference and counter transference. On one hand, they should properly disclose and share their own feeling towards clients' transference and counter transference. On the other hand, they should gradually reflect clients' unpleasant experiences in their former attachment. For intensive clients' transference, they should acknowledge clients' trust and attachment on them. Also, they should appropriately diffuse or transfer this transference to a group of supportive others. For instance, a male social worker should transfer or diffuse a female client's transference to a supportive group with male and female mentors so that clients can rebuild a healthy network of substituted family in the process of recovery of their substance abuse.

Regarding counter transference, related professionals should be ready to face clients' resistance, complaint and rejection. Firstly, related professionals should accept clients' anger and frustration without internalizing their comment and criticism as their own inadequacies and helplessness in intervention. Secondly, they should be able to reflect clients' needs of ventilation of their frustration, hardships and anger in their previous life attachment. Thirdly, they should encourage them to share all these frustration and negative emotions within all these traumatic attachment. In actual practice, related professionals should have competence, skills and sensitivity to compare client-worker relationship with their own relationship with their abusive significant others. In doing so, related professionals enable clients to ventilate their deep seated and repressed anger and frustration towards their oppressive significant others. As a summary, related professionals should resolve clients' transference and counter-transference in the following ways:

1. Beware Workers' own attachment needs, difficulties and dilemmas.
2. Accept clients' needs and emotions in transference as well as counter-transference.
3. Resolve worker-client problems in mutual transference.
4. Locate clients' transference to former attachment and relationship with significant others.
5. Transferal and diffusing transference to supportive network, groups & new attachment bonding.

Conclusion

As a conclusion, this chapter is a thorough discussion about attachment and drug addiction. Related studies show that people with substance abuse and drug addiction are usually deprived of sufficient attachment and bonding in early life. Addiction and attachment can be related in the following ways:

1. Addiction as a mean to deal with frustration in problematic attachment and bonding.
2. Addiction as a substituted bonding and attachment.
3. Addiction as a mean to gain bonding and attachment to related peers and social cycles.
4. Addiction as a mean to punish related figure in problematic bonding.

There are several important intervention strategies in dynamic integrated recovery for clients with drug addiction that can be described as follows

1. Readiness to detach from drug attachment.
2. Dealing with trauma and difficulties in attachment in life.
3. Establishing meaningful new attachment bonding.
4. A note of forgiveness and spirituality.
5. Dealing with transference.

References

Bowlby, J., (1969) *Volume I, Attachment*, London: Hogarth.

Bowlby, J., (1973) *Volume 2, Separation: Anxiety and Anger,* London: Hogarth Press.

Bowlby, J., (1977) The making and breaking of affectional bonds: Aetiology and psychopathology in the light of attachment theory, *British Journal of Psychiatry*, 130: 201-210.

Bowlby, J., (1980) *Volume 3, Loss: Sadness and Depression,* London: Tavistock Publication.

Bowlby, J., (1982) Attachment and loss: Retrospect and prospect, *Journal of AmericanOrthopsychiatry*, 52: 666-578.

Bretherton, I., (1992) The origins of attachment theory: John Bowlby and Mary Ainsworth' *Developmental Psychology*, 28(5): 759-775.

Edwards, M.E., (2002) Attachment, mastery and interdependence: a model of parenting processes, *Family Process*, 41(3): 389-404

Holmes, J., (1993) *John Bowlby and Attachment Theory*, London: Routledge.

Holmes, J., (1996) *Bowlby, Fairbairn, and Sutherland: The Scottish Connection in Psychotherapy*, London: Free Association.

Mackie, A.J., (1981) Attachment theory: Its relevance to the therapeutic alliance, *British Journal of Medical Psychology*, 54(3):203-212.

Mitchell S.A (1998) Attachment theory and the psychoanalytic tradition: Reflections on human relationality, *British Journal of Psychotherapy*, 15(2):177-193.

Lewis, J.M. (2000) Repairing the bond in important relationships: A dynamic for personality maturation, *American Journal of Psychiatry*, 157: 1375-1378.

Cosden, M & Cortez-Ison, E. (1999) Sex abuse, parental bonding, social support, and program retention for women in substance abuse treatment, *Journal of Substance Abuse Treatment,* 16(2): 149-155.

McMahon, T. J., Justin, D. W., Suchman, N. E.& Rousavelle, B.J., (2007) Drug abusing fathers: Pattern of pair bonding, reproduction, and parental involvement, *Journal of Substance Abuse Treatment*, 35: 295-362.

Miller, B.A., Downs, W.R., Gondoli, D.M. & Keil, A., (1987) The role of childhood sexual abuse development of alcoholism in women, *Violence and Victims*, 2:157-172.

Peele, S. & Brodsky, A. (1975, 1991). *Love and Addiction.* New York: Taplinger Publishing Co. Inc.

Peele, S. (1985). *The Meaning of Addiction,* Lexington: D.C. Health and Company.

Reading, B. (2002). The application of Bowlby's attachment theory to the psychotherapy of the addiction, in M. Weegmann & R, Cohen, R (ed), *The Psychodynamics of Addiction*, 13 - 30. Whurr Publisher: London.

Rohesnow, D.J., Corbett, R. & Devine, D. (1988) Molested as children: a hidden contribution to substance abuse, *Journal of Substance Abuse Treatment*, 5: 13-18.

Hofler, D.Z. & Kooyman, M. (1996) Attachment transition, addiction and therapeutic bonding – an integrative approach, *Journal of Substance Abuse Treatment,* 17(6): 511 – 519.

Chapter 7

SELF-SYSTEM IN SUBSTANCE ABUSE AND DRUG ADDICTION: AN INTEGRATED DYNAMIC RECOVERY

INTRODUCTION

This chapter is a comprehensive articulation of self-system for persons with substance abuse. The writer will describe how the self-system is affected by the process of substance abuse. Its implications to integrated recovery are also discussed.

TOTALITY OF SELF AND INTEGRATED DYNAMIC RECOVERY

Freud: Ego Consistency between Superego and Id

There are many aspects in describing self-system. Psychoanalysis especially Freud's theory seems to very influential one in describing the conflict within the self-system.

Freud (1933) affirmed that superego and id is in constant conflict as id represents one's instinct bodily desires such sex and aggression whereas superego is one's morality and norm internalized from external society. To ease out this continuous conflict, the ego tries to settle the conflict between id and superego. In fact, the ego is the crux of the whole self-system. It performs the following important function in the daily functioning of the self-system.

1. The ego brings along together, unifies and organize mental process
2. Eliminates contradiction
3. Develop a Coherent and well functioned units
4. Keep an eye of what is going on
5. Check and controls the correctness of perceptions
6. Steers the entire mental system to avoid unnecessary risks. (Freud, 1933: 45)

That means it performs a cohesive and developmental functioning the self-system on one hand. It enable the self-system to interact with others and related environment. In other word, a person with strong ego strength and functioning usually has a cohesive self-system as well as good social functioning. As a contrary, a person with poor ego strength and functioning may have a conflicting self-system as well as poor social functioning.

EGO STRENGTHS AND FUNCTIONING TO PERSONS WITH SUBSTANCE ABUSE

Persons with addiction are weak in ego functioning, their conflicts between id and superego are intolerable and painful. The process of addiction and substance abuse is an addictive suppression of this conflict by a full ventilation of id and desire.

However, after addiction, their suppressed superego may prevail. They may develop related mechanism to suppress their arousal of superego with a high sensitivity to anyone or anything that may arouse their feeling of immorality and guilt in drug addiction (that is the suppression of superego sensitivity to guilt and immorality). Thus, in related interventions, related professionals who arouse clients' senses of guilt in drug addiction may also re-activate clients' mechanism in suppression of their sense of immorality by de-sensitizing their sense of superego. In doing so, clients may develop counter-transference towards related professionals.

They try to label related professionals as hypocritical and apathetic to their needs and emotions. They may also be highly resistant in the process of intervention. In that sense, any intervention that arouse their sense of immorality such as drug education about adverse effects of drug addiction or immorality of taking drug may arouse their super-sensitivity of superego and create intensive resistance on further intervention.

Also, persons with addiction are accustomed to the full ventilation of id, may develop endless drive to id and desires related activities such as sex and intensive pursuit of sensory stimulation.

In terms of counter-transference, they may also challenge the worker by describing their id related activities in details and also confront the worker by requiring the worker to disclose worker's own id related activities. In response to this, the worker my feel shameful, embarrassing or irritated by clients' description of his/her id related activities. The superego of the worker may thus come forward to suppress his or her id arousal. As a result, the worker may condemn the client's immorality.

Then the client with super-sensitivity on superego may criticize the worker as hypocritical and uncaring. All these may become a vicious circle making the worker-client relationship become worse and worse. Thus, suitable intervention should begin with a focus of ego functioning on the clients in dealing with actual difficulties, instead of focusing on client's prevailing id and imposing guilt feeling to face clients' suppression of superego. Coupling with this should be an appreciation of clients' initial id related activities, as well as a toleration of client's testing and challenges on worker's hypocrisy as well id provoking interaction. In fact, only when the clients' ego function is properly improved, the client can thus develop sufficient ego strengths to strive the balance of id and superego. At the same time, his/her ability of superego control can also be improved. Furthermore, it may necessary to facilitate client to elaborate/ventilate his/her id and desires and related activities in a constructive, culturally acceptable way.

Consciousness, Sub-consciousness and Unconsciousness in People with Substance Abuse and Drug Addiction

Freud affirmed that there are three stages of consciousness. They are unconsciousness, sub-consciousness and consciousness. In the stage of consciousness, individual's ego functioning work smoothly with proper articulation of reality and exercise of self-system within an immediate psycho-social context. In the stage of unconsciousness, individual's ego functioning is in a stage of inertia and sleeping. Repressed desires, impulses and unresolved emotional complex and conflicts in ego functioning and self-system prevail and discharge in forms of dreams. In the stage of sub-consciousness, individual's ego functioning and sense of reality is clouded with a transit to the stage of unconsciousness.

In fact, addiction may be interpreted as transit from a stage of painful consciousness to a stage of id-related sub-consciousness. In this stage of sub-consciousness, persons with addiction try to escape from the sense of ontological boredom or insecurity by turning themselves into a stage of full manifestation of id and desires with a full manifestation of drug induced bodily sensory stimulation. However, the frequent occurrence of drug induced sub-consciousness may finally increase the individual tendency in withdrawing from the reality even in stage of consciousness. Ego functioning is also thus retarded and conflict between superego and id is further intensified. The intensified superego and id conflict, as a vicious cycle, further illuminates the needs of drug induced sub-consciousness with a consequence of increasing impairment in ego functioning and absorption to drug induced sub-consciousness. As a consequence, the individual finally turn into a stage of gradual loss and decline of ego functioning and boundary to distinguish consciousness, sub consciousness and unconsciousness. That means, individuals may stay in a prolonged stage of frequent clouded consciousness of reality, prevailing needs and drive to drug-induced or non-drug induced sub-consciousness and frequent and uncontrolled evolvement of unconsciousness. Finally, individuals' repressed conflicts of superego and id is spontaneously evolved but heavily covered up by drug-induced subconscious with a severe withdraw from the actual reality.

Jung's Wholeness between Consciousness and Unconsciousness

Jung (1966. 1967, 1968 & 1970) was one of the distinctive students of Freud. However, he did not agree with Freud's psychosexual orientation. He also had his own view on consciousness, unconsciousness and human development. He advocated the importance of self-individuation and self-realization in human development mental health.

Integration between Consciousness and Unconsciousness

Jung (1968) affirmed that there are five important components in inner psyche system connecting the consciousness and unconsciousness. They are the Persona, Ego, Shadow, Anima/Animus and the Self. Only the Persona and Ego is in conscious level. The other four components are in unconscious level.

The 'Persona' is what one presents to the outside world. It is the presentation of oneself to others in external environment. It is similar to the mask one uses in facing different contexts, roles and demands in external environment. One can have different personas in different social and political contexts. For example, in working or formal organizational settings, the individual needs to use a work related persona in dealing with formal interaction and bureaucracy. S/he may become polite but sophisticated, kind but political, as well as helpful but manipulative in facing the dynamics within office settings. However, in informal interaction with his friends, especially in dealing his/her peers, the individual appears as causal, frank, straight and humorous so as to win the trust and friendship from his/her peers. Thus, there may be consistency or inconsistency among various personas. Personas exist and maintain within individuals' consciousness. In many cases, individuals may be fully bewared that under what conditions, which persona s/he should use or exist in order to maintain a good sense of personal existence within various reality contexts.

The Ego is the centre of consciousness. It is the crux of self-identity in which individual bewares of who s/he was, s/he currently is and s/he will be in the future.

Ego and personas work together in the formulation of one's consciousness. On the one hand, they provide different masks for one to secure and survive within different social, physical and political contexts. Within personas, one tends to hide his/her own inner self, as well as actual emotions and needs. Ego implies one's own consciousness of one's self identity, image, boundary, emotions and needs. There can be various forms of consistency and inconsistency between personas and ego.

1. Inconsistency among different personas as well inconsistency between personas and ego.
2. Consistency among some personas as well as consistency between some personas and ego; Inconsistency among some personas as well as inconsistency between some personas and ego.
3. Consistency among different personas as well as consistency between personas and ego.

Certainly, consistency among different personas as well as consistency between personas and ego is the best condition in which one can freely exercise his/her views in different contexts and situation. For him/her personas in different contexts are no long a mask. Instead, it is a good exercise and actualization of himself/herself in various social and cultural contexts. In actual reality, it is impossible that individuals can attain a full consistency in all aspects of life. Thus, a full consistency among all personas and ego is only theoretic existing. Regarding total inconsistency among different persona as well as inconsistency between personas and ego, it should a stage of extremely high confusion in which the individual is unable to survive existentially. Thus, this stage of total confusion is also theoretically existential.

Individuals, in actual reality, should have consistency among some personas as well as between some personas and ego. In doing so, there is also inconsistency among some personas as well as among some personas and ego. It is common or acceptable that one can perform well or actualize in some social and cultural contexts but cannot perform or actualize in other social and cultural contexts. That means, if an individual have more consistency than inconsistency among personas as well as more time of consistency than time of inconsistency between ego and personas, s/he will be in a comparatively mentally healthy state. As a contrary, s/he will in a comparatively mentally unhealthy state. In fact, inconsistency among some personas and between some personas and ego may be well hidden within unconscious level in terms of the Shadow, the Anima/Animus and the Self.

The Shadow

The 'Shadow' is an unconscious complex in which an individual tries to repress, suppress or disown those experiences, memories and personal qualities that are unacceptable to the conscious self. In facing all these negative sides, individuals use four mechanisms to face their own shadow. They are denial, projection, integration and/or transmutation. The shadow can always be the opposite of the conscious personal qualities (Jung, 1968). A brutal person can be gentle and kind in his/her own shadow. A self-confident person can be inferior and timid in his/her shadow. Different persons may use different ways to cope with their own shadow. A mentally healthy person may discover the positive side of his/her own shadow (gold in the shadow) and incorporates or integrate it into his/her own consciousness. A mentally unhealthy person may try to project or repress his/her negative sides of his/her own shadow. Some may try to represent their shadow in forms of artistic symbols and creation. It is important for individuals to have good awareness of their own shadows and develop constructive ways to integrate them into their own self system.

Anima and Animus

Jung defined 'Anima' as the unconscious feminine components of men and Animus as the unconscious masculine aspects of women. In modern Jungian psychology, practitioners assumed that both 'Anima' and 'Animus' exist together within the individual. Anima and animus exist in our unconsciously. Individuals often project their own anima or animus on others. An aggressive masculine man may tend to love a tender woman at the first sight as he projects his unconscious Anima (his feminine component) onto that woman. Jung also affirmed that rational aspects are of male natures and the irrational aspects are female natures. For immature persons, they may not beware of the anima or animus complexes. They tend to reject, deny or isolate their anima or animus complexes. For mature persons, they tend to accept, integrate and even make good use of anima or animus complexes.

The Self

According to Jung (1966), the self is the totality of our inner experiences. It is highly complicated and serves as the centre of individuals' psychic movement of other archetypes such as shadow, anima or animus as well as ego. It also connected with one's personas in various social contexts.

It is dynamic and paradoxical as there are inconsistencies or even conflicts among different archetypes.

As mentioned above there can be inconsistency among different personas, between ego and various personas, between shadow and personas, between shadow and ego, as well as between ego and animus/anima. All these inconsistencies and conflicts may finally result in paradoxical and dynamic natures of the self. Jung affirmed that individuals, in their whole life struggle for self-realization and self-individualization.

SELF REALIZATION AND SELF INDIVIDUATION

Jung affirmed that individual's self-system is a process of individuation. It is an archetype of wholeness and regulation of inner psyche. It is also a process of awakening of inner psyche into the state of consciousness. That means it should be an integration of unconsciousness of consciousness in which individual is able to realize his/her self through merging personality opposites. Thus, it consists of three important components in the self-system. They are listed as follows:

1. Self-realization as a goal develops out from merging personality opposites related to thinking, feeling, sensing and intuiting.
2. Expose part of the self and personality in different roles and situation.
3. A process of individuation to free the self from false wrapping of persona on one hand and from the suggestive power of the unconscious image of others on the other hand. (Jung, 1966)

That means self-realization and self-individuation work together for the personal development of the individual.

On one hand, self-realization facilitates people to explore and integrate inconsistency among various components in consciousness and unconsciousness.

In other words, various people have their own ways of self-realization so that they can have their own unique characters and personality. Individuation is a manifestation of all these unique features.

Self-realization is a way to nurture and development of all these unique features by means of integration of inconsistency among personas, ego, shadows, anima/animus, and self. Only by means of self-realization, individual is able to develop their maturity and personality.

On the other hand, self-realization is facilitated by the process of individuation. Jung (1966) affirmed that individual's personality is divided into two main stages. The first stage is the development of one's own identity. This stage usually happens within childhood and adolescence. In doing so, individuals try to expel external influence in particular those coming from authority figure.

Thus, adolescents try to appear as destructive as well as rebellious so as to develop their own unique character and self-identity. Also destruction and rebellious emotions and behaviors can also be an effective means to ease out their inner tension in facing inconsistency among different personas, ego, shadow, anima/animus and self. As these conflicts and consistency gradually integrated, adolescents gradually become emotionally stable and more constructive in dealing with others. In middle age, properly around 35-40, individuals are more and more mature. They shift their focus from egocentric and materialistic orientation to collective and spiritual one. They begin to search for spirituality, collective consciousness and meaning in life. They try to connect with the universe (spirituality).

They intend to tune in their tradition, community and society (the collective unconsciousness) and overall attainment direction in life (meaning of life). That means, they urge to develop a true and whole self.

Inconsistency and Mental Problems

According to Jung (1967), mental problems are rooted from inconsistency and disharmony between individual's consciousness, unconsciousness and self. That means inconsistency among personas, ego, shadow, anima and animus as well as self-nurtures various types of mental problems. In facing all these inconsistencies, individuals may develop unhealthy psychological mechanisms such as self-splitting, projection and denials. All these unhealthy psychological mechanisms finally nurture various types of mental problems.

SUBSTANCE ABUSE AND PROBLEMS IN SELF REALIZATION AND INDIVIDUATION

Substance abuse may be regarded as a valid mean for the individual to deal with inconsistency among consciousness and unconsciousness. Individuals with substance abuse may have problems in their own process of self-realization and self-individuation in their childhood and adolescence. On one hand, they may not be able to develop their own unique self-identity. On the other hand, they may not be able to resolve conflicts among personas, ego, shadow, anima/animus and self. Thus, substance abuse tends to serve the following functioning:

1. As an immediate mean for the individual to repress his/her unwanted feelings, cognition, and memories into the unconsciousness in particular the shadow.
2. As a way to deal with unpleasant feelings or negative emotions arouse from inconsistency and conflicts among personas; between some personas and ego, between ego and shadow, between self and ego, between self and shadow, between self and personas, between self and anima/animus, between self and personas, and among personas, shadow, self, ego and anima and animus.
3. As a pathological way to cope with difficulties and problems in self-realization and self-individuation. For example, an adolescent may take soft drug to show that s/he is different and unique among peers. The experience in taking soft drug is the only way to realize oneself in facing highly oppressive and frustrating environment. It is regarded as a way to exercise one's sense of control and mastery in the process of addiction.

Masteron's Characteristics of Real Self

Masterson (1988) affirmed that individual's whole life is striving for the actualization of the real self. Masteron's (1988) characteristics of self can be divided into several groups:

Group A: The Ability to Relate with Others

A1: The capacity for intimacy, which requires the capability of entering into a close and open relationship with another person with a minimal experience of abandonment or engulfment

A2: The ability to be alone, to be alone without feeling abandoned.

Group B: The Ability to Have Constant Self Regulation and Consolidation

B1: The capacity to experience deeply a wide range of feelings, both pleasant and unpleasant.

B2: The ability to soothe painful affects.

B3: The ability to make and follow through with commitment, despite obstacles or setbacks.

Group C: The Ability to Have Self Identity and Uniqueness

C1: The capacity for the acknowledgement of self-esteem, because one cannot always depend on others to shore up one's self esteem.

C2: The capacity for self-activation, and self-assertion, including the ability to identify one's own unique individuality, wishes, dreams, and goals and to be assertive in expressing them autonomously.

C3: The capacity to expect appropriate entitlement, such experience of mastery and pleasure.

Group D: The Ability to Develop and Grow

D1: Continuity of self, the capacity to recognize that the real self persists over time.

D2: The capacity for creativity, the ability to be creative in altering old, familiar pattern of living and replacing them with new and more successful ones.

Substance Abuse and Problem in Actualizing the Real Self

These four groups of abilities relate with one another in helping the individual to develop a healthy and continuous self-system. The ability to relate with other enable to the self-system to outreach and connect with other persons in the actual reality. The ability to regulate and to consolidate facilitates the self-system to be stable, cohesive and harmony. It also helps the self-system to iron out inner conflicts, discrepancies and inconsistencies. The ability to have self-identity and self-uniqueness nurture the self-system to have its own sense of existence and spontaneity without relying or depending on others' approval or comment. The ability to have self-development and growth enables the self-system to develop, to change and to improve according to different events, environment, demands and challenges in life. These four groups of abilities work together making the individual to have a real sense of being, an actual manifestation of self in various situation and real exercise of performance and roles in various social context. It also enables the individual to have a good and spontaneous of self-consciousness and awareness of immediate reality.

For persons with substance abuse, their ability to have self-identity and self-uniqueness are usually hindered by unpleasant past or current experiences of being bullied, abandoned and abused. Their ability to regulate and consolidate inner conflicts and discrepancies is also burdened by all these unpleasant past or current experiences. Thus, within their mind, they are full of unresolved emotional complexes, negative emotions such as loneliness, emptiness, inferiority and fear. They are angry both with themselves and their significant others. All these negative feelings greatly hinder their ability to relate with others. They dare not to express their negative emotions, to assert their rights in front of their oppressive others. As a consequence, their ability to grow and develop is also suffocated. Individuals become highly vulnerable to external frustration and stress. That means, substance abuse becomes a mean for individuals to serve the following functions;

1. To act as a mean to induce a sense of actualizing one's real self.
2. To act a way to paralyze individuals' frustration in actualizing one's real self.

For the first function, various types of drug may serve different functions. Stimulants may help the individual to feel excited and assertive in relating with others. They also induce a feeling of uniqueness, powerful and confident. That means, the ability to have unique self-identity is thus enhanced and boosted up in the process of taking stimulants like amphetamines and cocaine. Hallucinogens tend to serve an important function that they induce intensive delusions and hallucinations with grandiose or imaginative content in gratifying individuals' unfulfilled wishes. For example, an individual who wish to have courtship with a beautiful girl, after taking hallucinogens may delude that he is actually handsome and attractive to beautiful girl. All these drugs serve an important function for the individual to develop an acceptable, good but delusive 'real self' in the process of substance abuse

Regarding the second functions, for persons with substance abuse, most of them have problems in ability in exercising their real self. They may have problems in developing a unique self-identity because of over-enmeshment by their significant others. They may problems in self-regulation and consolidation as they may harbor numerous traumas in their life. They may have problems in outreaching to others as they are spontaneously bullied by others. Any one of these deficiencies may induce unbearable negative feelings of loneliness, anger (in being oppressed by others), ambivalence, love and hate towards others (in being over-enmeshed by others), frustration and inferiority (in being hurt and abused by others). All these negative feelings are intolerable and harmful to the individuals. In many cases, they become unresolved emotional complexes. In other words, they are overwhelmed by their feelings of impaired self. Thus, for persons with substance abuse, the only way to hide or paralyze all these negative feelings is substance abuse and addiction. Usually, tranquilizing drugs such as ketamine, heroine and alcohol seem to serve a function to facilitate individual to ease out internal conflicts and intensive but unresolved emotional complexes such as loneliness and inferiority, fear and anger as well as depression and frustration.

Horney' Achievement of Real Self

Horney (1945), in her famous book: 'Our Inner Conflict' addressed that human beings have ten basic needs that should be fulfilled in life. However these ten basic needs are actually in conflicts. They are needs in moving towards people, moving against people and moving away from people. They are listed as follows:

Moving Toward People

1. The need for affection and approval; pleasing others and being liked by them.
2. The need for a partner; one whom they can love and who will solve all problems.

Moving Against People

3. The need for power; the ability to bend wills and achieve control over others—while most persons seek strength, the neurotic may be desperate for it.
4. The need to exploit others; to get the better of them. To become manipulative, fostering the belief that people are there simply to be used.
5. The need for social recognition; prestige and limelight.
6. The need for personal admiration; for both inner and outer qualities—to be valued.
7. The need for personal achievement; though virtually all persons wish to make achievements, as with No. 3, the neurotic may be desperate for achievement.

Moving Away from People

8. The need for self-sufficiency and independence; while most desire some autonomy, the neurotic may simply wish to discard other individuals entirely.
9. The need for perfection; while many are driven to perfect their lives in the form of wellbeing, the neurotic may display a fear of being slightly flawed.
10. Lastly, the need to restrict life practices to within narrow borders; to live as inconspicuous a life as possible.

Horney believed that these needs have to succeed in human development. However, among these need there are inner conflict. The needs of moving away from people are in fact opposite to the needs of moving towards people. Within a proper harmony and balance of all these needs, individuals become neurotic and may finally get caught into the process of psychosis. Horney (1945) concluded that there are three basic human conditions, compliance, aggression and detachment that are the breeding bed of neurosis or many forms of mental illness.

The first one is compliance in which individuals urge to move towards people. They are the need for affection and approval and the need for a partner. These needs enable individual to comply and to depend on others. If these needs cannot be satisfied, individuals easily have fears of being abandoned. They may involve in a state of helplessness. They harbor a strong urge to attach to others. They become highly sensitive and responsive to others' separation, rejection and criticism. Their emotions are deeply affected by interpersonal relationship. People with compliance are vulnerable to become dependent neurotic (Horney, 1945). All these emotions and needs are highly related to the causes and manifestation of mental problems such as borderline personality disorder, dependent personality disorder, generalized anxiety disorder and phobic disorders.

The second one is aggression in which individuals try to move against people. That means, they tend to be aggressive or protest against people around. It includes the need for power, the need to exploit others, the need for social recognition, the need for persona admiration and the need of personal achievement. All these needs imply individuals outreach and assert themselves in front of others. On one hand, they need to protect themselves from being oppressed, bullied, or exploit by others. On the other hand, they have to get what they want by being powerful, socially recognized and admirable. Finally, they need to develop and actualize themselves so as to affirm their own uniqueness and identity. If people are overwhelmed by these needs and cannot be appropriately gratified in their developmental process, they may tend to be highly aggressive and omnipotent in front of others. They may become hungry for being admirable, outstanding in front of others. In doing so, they may become highly egocentric gratifying their own aggressive needs by hurting, oppressing and/or exploiting others.

They are vulnerable to become aggressive neurotic (Horney, 1945). All these unsatisfied needs may become the roots for people with antisocial personality disorder, narcissistic personality disorder, and manic episodes in bipolar disorder.

For those needs that individuals try to move away from people, it is a kind of detachment. Instead of being aggressive or being dependent on others, individuals choose to move away and detach from others.

They are need for self-sufficiency and independence; need for perfection, need to restrict life practice within narrow border. They are needs for the individual to strive for self-perfection or avoid being criticized and attacked by others. All these needs, if not being properly gratified may make individuals become detachedly neurotic (Horney, 1945). In doing so, individuals consolidate and configure their own uniqueness, identity, assertiveness and power to outreach to others. Without proper satisfaction of these needs, individual may be trapped in their overwhelmed needs to detach themselves from the actual reality and in connection with others.

As a consequence, they may be inclined to become schizophrenic, obsessive and compulsive disorder, obsessive and compulsive personality disorder as well as schizo personality disorder.

Actualization and Realization of Self

Horney defined self as the core of one's own being and potential. Based on a clear concept of oneself, individuals strive to actualize their own potentials in our own live. Horney (1955) affirmed that one have two interactive perceptions on self, the real self and the ideal self.

The real self is what individuals are and the ideal self is what individual aspired to be. A normal person usually embraces a real self with potentials, talents, will power to grow and further development.

It also consists of deficiency and deficits. S/he also harbors goals, aspiration and mission in his/her idealized self for life development and advancement. Horney (1945 further articulated that the achievement of real self is a genuine integration of needs of moving towards, moving away and moving against people. It is also a harmonious combination of the following:

1. the palpating inward life
2. The spontaneity of all feelings
3. The source of interest and psychic energy
4. Growing of self
5. Resuming responsibility. (Horney, 1945:157)

Discrepancies between Ideal Self and Real Self

However, there are always conflicts and discrepancies between one's ideal self and real self. Horney (1955) affirmed that a neurotic person is always overwhelmed by these discrepancies assuming that s/he cannot or should not strive for his/her glory and aspirations. In doing so, s/he gradually develops self-hate and senses inferiority and hopelessness.

Implications to Substance Abuse

For persons with substance abuse, most of them are in the neurotic stage as mentioned by Horney (1945). In other words, their needs for moving towards people, moving against and moving away from people are not properly gratified. They are also unable to seek for the actualization of real self or their real self has severe conflict with their ideal self. In all these cases, individuals feel highly uncomfortable and intolerable. It seems that substance abuse is the best available mean for them to paralyze all these uncomfortable and intolerable negative feelings. Also, substance abuse also tends to be a substitute for unfulfilled needs. For the individuals who are unable to gratify their needs in moving towards people. They harbor an intensive urge to attach and to depend on others. If they do not have any one to depend on, properly substance abuse and drug addiction is their only substitution. They simply regard drug addiction as their significant others/lovers/ or any one they can turn in times of loneliness and emptiness. Regarding those who cannot satisfy their need of moving away from people, they have a strong urge to have self-isolation and separation from other people who spontaneously and continuously abuse and oppress them. In reality, they cannot. In that occasion, drug addiction and substance abuse serves as an immediate way for them to escape from oppressive environment. Among various kinds of drugs, it seems that those drugs that can paralyze related bodily senses making individual feel being out of body, or escaping from reality serve this function well. They are heroin, ketamine and tranquillizers. For those their needs for moving against people cannot be gratified, they may feel their anger and strive for defending from attack and oppression cannot be fully exercised. Thus, substance abuse serves as a way to for them to get substance induced feelings of powerfulness, manipulation and omnipotence. Among various kinds of drugs, it seems that stimulants such as cocaine, amphetamine can serve this function well.

In all these situations, it is clear that substance abuse tends to be a harmful substitute for the individual to actualize his/her suppressed or oppressed real self. That means, in real life, individuals are unable to have examine their inward life. Their minds are occupied by negative feelings. They do not embrace normal source of interest and good inner psychic energy. Instead of feeling of growth and development, their sense of self are deteriorating and withering. They are unable to fulfill their own responsibility. That means, their real self are being repressed and suppressed within a highly oppressed social environment. The more the real self is being oppressed, the more the ideal self is being hindered and suffocated. As the highly oppressive social environment cannot be avoided or escaped in reality, substance abuse tends to be the only way for the individual to actualize a substance induced self. In the process of substance abuse, the addicted mind and body produce delusive senses of spontaneity of good feelings, drug stimulated psychic energy, illusive growth of self, and omnipotent ability to assume responsibility in life. This substance induced self can serve as an immediate substitute for the withering real and ideal self. However, the more individuals indulge in this substance induced self, the more their real self are withered because of deteriorating reality contact and social and ego functioning. As a consequence, their own ideal self is also gradually suppressed. In chronic substance abuse, individuals' real and ideal self are both 'paralyzed' by their substance induced self.

The Phenomenological and Social Self

Individuals' self-system is constantly influenced by social environment. As time goes by, individual's self-consciousness and senses of self-change constantly. In every moment of time, individuals embrace their own sense of existence or being. In phenomenological terms, Hohway (2007) described in terms of 'minimal self'

> 'A minimal self is the pre-reflective feeling that a given moment is performed by me, or that a given perceptual experiences is had by me. This reference to self is distinguished from the autobiographical sense of having a narrative self that persists across experiences. The minimal self is more like an instantaneous feeling of 'mineness' with which experiences are labeled.' (Hohway, 2007: 1)

Hohway further articulate that the sense of self can be further reduced to three continuous cognitive tasks:

1. Self in agency and bodily movement

> 'An individual needs to be able to generate and intimacy track motor commands in accordance with her desires and beliefs about the world. There must be a distinction available between changes in her body and in the environment that are due to her own agency and those changes that are due to other factors in the environment or her sensoimotor system. This agency-based distinction between doings of the mind and the world relates to the sense of self in agency.

2. Self in perception

> 'The individual also needs to be able to represent the real environment causes of noisy, context-dependent sensory signals. This is in part a reality testing competence that grounds a distinction between representation of persistent external objects and the noisy contribution of the sensory system of a perceiving self.

3. Self in planning and attention

> 'The individual needs to be able to distinguish between those environmental causes that she should attend to and act on and those that are not relevant to her current tasks, plan and preferences. This attentional distinction between the world that would affect her plans and the world that wouldn't relates to the sense of a cohesive, extended self. (Hohway, 2007:2)

From Hohway (2007) description, the sense of self should consist of the following components:

A. One's bodily movement due to one's own agency or due to response to external environment
B. One's presentation of self to external object without being disturbed by noises due to external environment
C. One's own plan without being affected by environmental cause.

That means, Hohway (2007) tried to affirm that there are two distinctive but interactive components in the sense of self. One is individual's spontaneous self-awareness and presentation without affected by external factors (S1). That sort of spontaneous self-awareness and presentation present in related bodily activities, perception and related planning. That is a sense of what one actually wants to move, wants to perceive and wants to act in the current moment and to the immediate future. Another one is one's spontaneous responses (related action, perception and planning) to stimuli, events and disturbances from external environment (S2).

Mead described sense of self in terms of two distinguished by inter-related features, the 'I' and 'Me'. The 'Me' is actually the social self in which the individual tries to perform or oblige to certain social roles in interacting with others. It is a sense of self as an object in response to others' demand or related social and physical context. However, 'I' refers to the sense of self as subject in which asserts himself/herself or outreach to others. 'I' and 'Me', in fact, relate to one another. If the sense of self as object is spontaneously negative, it certainly alleviates the positive sense of self, 'I' as subject. As a contrary, if the sense of self as subject 'I' is very positive, it certainly enables the individual to be assertive with a positive sense of 'Me' even in facing negative social contexts. (Mead, 1934)

Hohway (2007) phenomenological orientation is, to certain extent, similar to Mead's (1934) orientation of 'I' and 'Me' in the sense of self. The sense of 'I' is the S1, in which the individual's sense of self is the prime agent without being affected by external environment. The sense of 'Me' is the S2, in which the individual's sense of self is actually the response to external environment.

Jaspers (1946/1923) affirmed that self-awareness has four formal characteristics:

1. The feeling of activity: an awareness of being active
2. An awareness of unity: I am aware at any moment that I am a unity
3. Awareness of identity: I am aware at any given moment that I am a unity
4. Awareness of the self as distinct from an outer world and all that is not the self.

With all these four formal characteristics, self-awareness displays a range of developmental levels from a plain, bare existence to a full life with a conscious wealth of sensitive experience. In the course of such developments, the self grows aware of itself as a personality. (Jaspers, 1946/1923: 121)

For activity of self, Jaspers (1946/1923) described it as follows:

'Self-awareness is present in every psychic event. In the form of 'I think' it accompanies all perceptions, ideas and thought, while feelings are passive, and instinctive drives are impelling states of self. All psychic life involves the experience a unique and fundamental activity. Every psychic manifestation, whether perception, bodily sensation, memory, idea, thought of feeling carries this particular aspect of 'being mine' of having an 'I' quality, of 'personally belonging', or it being one's own being. We have termed this 'personalization'. If these psychic manifestations occur with the awareness of their not being mine, of being alien, automatic, independent, arriving from elsewhere, we term phenomena of depersonalization. (Jaspers, 1946/1923: 121)

In Jaspers' terms, the sense of activity of self is the spontaneous sense of 'I' in every psychic manifestation including bodily sensation, memory, idea, and thought of feeling. All these psychic manifestations are 'being mine'. The individual is independent, autonomous, and being a subject in performing these psychic activities. That mean, the individual also embrace another sense of self as 'me' being controlled or disturbed by external objects, events and persons. In doing so, the individual becomes an 'object'. In extreme situation, the individual feels depersonalized losing his/her own autonomy, independence and even dignity in psychic manifestation.

In terms of 'the unity of the self', Jaspers (1946/1923) affirmed the following:

> 'The experience of the basic unity of the self can undergo some notable changes. Sometimes, for instance, while talking we may notice that we are talking rather like an automation, quite correctly may be, but we can observe ourselves and listen to ourselves. Should this dissociation last an length of times, disturbances will occur in the flow of thought, but for a shorter time we can ourselves experience without disturbance that 'doubling' of personality which patients describes to us in much more elaborated terms. (Jaspers, 1946/1923: 124)

In Jaspers' terms, the unity of self implies the individual can retain his/her self-cohesion despite situations that s/he needs to have double attentions. Even though s/he has to reflect on his/her doing, dissociate because of being distracted by related events, people, objects in the environment, s/he can also retain his/her self-cohesion after that. In other words, the individual is able to maintain a sense of cohesion, consistency and unity in relating with external social and physical environment.

Regarding sense of identity self, Jaspers (1946/1923) described that it is the awareness of one's identity through the passage of time. That means, despite the change of time, individual's identity of self is still consistency. It is a consistency of self-identity in the past, present and future. For example, an individual feels that s/he is a clever person in the childhood and adolescence. In the present, s/he is also a clever person in which s/he can earn a good living within a highly competitive working environment. In the same way, s/he thinks that in the future, s/he will also be smart and able to earn a good living.

For awareness of self-distinct from outer world and not of self, it implies that the individual should beware that in being awareness of activity of self, unit of self and sense of identity, individuals have to involve or relate to object, activities, and persons in the outer world. In doing so, they are spontaneously influenced by concerned stimuli, responses and disturbances from these activities, persons and objects in the outer world. Thus, their own sense of identity, activity of self and unity of self are also affected. In that situation, individuals need to distinct their own senses of self from outer world and not of self. For example, a man perceives himself as a smart person. He is active and always enables to take prompt action in asserting his own right in social interaction and in daily activities. However, in one occasion, he commits a careless mistake because of the fault of his colleague. In that occasion, he is thus blamed by his boss as a stupid and foolish guy. Even though he tries to explain that to his boss, he is also the one to be blamed. All these certainly disturb his activity of self, identity and unity deeply. To maintain his continuous unity, identity and activity of self, he needs to continuously remind himself that the sense of stupidity and foolishness come from outer world. It should be distinctive.

Jaspers (1946/1923) further affirmed that once the individual embraces a complete sense of self awareness in terms of activity of self, unity and identity of self, as well as distinct self of self and outer world and non-self, s/he is actually experiencing an awareness of personality. This, in its totality of content, provides subject matters for the psychology of understandable connection. It is also a full embracement of instinctual drive within the momentum whole. Within the awareness of personality, on the one hand, the individual also embraces his/her sense of instinctual drive in a natural expression within his flow of immediate momentum. On the other hand, the individual also understands and feels that some instinctual drives are also being stimulated and influenced by external environment. The awareness of personality, the totality of awareness of activity of self, unity of self, identity of self, distinct of self and outer world, as well as sense of instinctual drive also changes according with the time. All these show that the phenomenological self within immediate social and physical environment consist of the following interrelated dimensions:

1. The dimension of time and change
2. The dimension of agency and subjectivity
3. The dimension of response and objectivity
4. The dimension of unity and cohesiveness.

In the dimension of time and change, there is the awareness of the presence (current moment), past and the future. It is also the self-awareness of total personality in times of changes. That means, in any given moment, the individual can beware of his/her own current thinking and activities s/he is doing in the immediate moment, as well as his/her thinking and activities in any time in the past, or his/her thinking and activities will happen in the future. In reviewing and comparing thinking and activities in present, past and future, s/he bewares and reflects about changes of himself/herself over times. It is the awareness of the difference/change of himself/herself from one moment to one moment, from one period to another period, as well as from the past to the present, and from the present to the future. It can also be the difference/change of others and related environment in relating to himself/herself over times.

The second dimension is the self-awareness of subjectivity and agency. It is the awareness of 'I', what 'I think, I feel, I act' and 'I want'. It is a self-consciousness of subjective experiences in the immediate moment and social and physical context. The individual bewares of his/her own decision, preference, determination as well as performance and actions. Despite s/he is spontaneously responding to related issues, objects and events in the immediate social and physical environment, s/he still affirms that all related decisions, preferences, performance and actions are exercised within his/her own will and determination. In doing so, his/her sense of self is fully actualized.

The third dimension is self-awareness of response and objectivity. That is self awareness of being 'Me' in every moment and in immediate social and physical environment. It is an awareness of self being an 'object' as a spontaneously passive or even submissive response to related issues, events and persons in the immediate social and physical environment. In doing so, his/her own sense of autonomy, determination, and subjectivity are greatly hindered. However, s/he is flexible, responsive and adaptable to related stimuli, events, persons and object in immediate physical and social environment. Also, as an object to the needs of others and environment, individuals can stay objective to his/her own needs and feelings.

The fourth dimension is unity and cohesiveness. It implies that despite any spontaneous changes in immediate social and physical environment and development of self-awareness, the individual still has to maintain a constant, consistent and cohesive self-identity, self-image, self-perception, self-performance as well as self-actualization. In a full and spontaneous self-awareness, these four dimensions should be present together. They are interacting and relating with one another. In facing different immediate social and physical moments, the individual can shift from one dimension to another dimension. For example, an individual, A, is a member in a formal international conference. While A is a subordinate in hearing his supervisor (B) presenting his own idea. A's self-awareness in terms of response and objectivity should be fully exercised. He must beware that he is an object and his supervisor is a subject in the interaction. He should be highly responsive to his supervisor's idea. He should show good appreciation to his supervisor's presentation. He should appear as humble and even submissive if his supervisor is autocratic and powerful. At the same time, his self-awareness should also focus on time and changes, as there are dynamics within related colleagues' response and reactions. After his supervisor finishes his own presentation, it is the time for A to present his attainment and project. At that moment, A should his self-awareness to the dimension of agency and subjectivity in which A should appear as assertive and affirmative in his own presentation. He should also be highly alert to the responses of related participants. In other words, his self-awareness within the conference should shift from one dimension to another dimension so as to cope with various kinds of demands happening and changing within the immediate and related social and physical environment.

SUBSTANCE ABUSE AND THE PHENOMENOLOGICAL AND SOCIAL SELF

For a normal person, within his/her phenomenological and social self, all these four dimensions can be fully actualized within his social and physical environment in most of his/her life. For persons with substance abuse, these four dimensions are being hindered and even distorted. Before the development of substance abuse and addiction, individuals may be overwhelmed by related traumas and prolonged unhappy experiences. That means, within their constant and continuous immediate social and physical environment, their spontaneous sense of self awareness is greatly disturbed. Very often, being absorbed in their own traumatic experiences of being bullied, belittled, isolated, humiliated and oppressed by others, persons with substance abuse will emotionally absorb in all these experiences or memories. As a consequence, their normal spontaneous sense of time and change are burdened and even fixated. Also, within all these oppressive experiences and memories, they are passively regarded by others as an object for oppression. Their proper responses of ventilation of anger, avoidance of harm, defending themselves as well as taking revenge are all hindered. In other words, their normal sense of self in terms of response and objectivity as well as agency and subjectivity are also deeply hindered. Furthermore, within all these humiliating, isolating or bullying experiences, individual's sense of self cohesion, integrity and dignity are also deeply affected. All these are intolerable for the individual. Thus, substance abuse is a mean to escape from all this intolerable self-awareness. Firstly, within the process of substance abuse, individuals choose their own type of drug, and time, form, place and dosage of addiction. Individuals may think that despite everything is out their control and everything is unpleasant, they can at least control the drug and substance they abuse. In doing so, their senses of agency and being a subject are 'pathologically actualized'. Secondly, being involved in substance abuse, individuals tend to get away from their own unpleasant sense of time and being. For those who take tranquilizers, they may regard their sense of time are slowing down and they engage in a subconscious state of awareness. For those who take psycho-stimulants, they may feel everything change quickly and their sense of self and agency increases accordingly. For those who take hallucinogens, they may evolve their own delusion and hallucinations, with which they evolve or create their own sense of self awareness in terms of agency subjectivity and rapid change of time and space. For those who take heroin and ketamine, they enjoy the senses of being away from reality or the phenomenological sense of being out of their own body.

All these make them feel they are away from the painful reality. All these drugs give individuals a particular sense of self awareness. Thirdly, within clients' unpleasant recent and past experiences, they feel highly split and uncomfortable. However, it seems that the experience in drug addiction is an effective but pathological and temporary way to glue up all this splitting and inconsistency to attain internal consistency and unity.

In the process of drug addiction, the individual is totally absorbed in the drug induced sense of self awareness in which s/he can enjoy a full range of awareness and escape from the painful self-awareness of the oppressive reality and traumatic past memories. However, once the effect of the drug vanished, all these painful self-awareness restore again. As a comparison of the good feelings within the process of addiction, such painful senses of self-awareness increase drastically. Coupled with this is a profound sense of deep frustration, emptiness and boredom.

In addition to that is also a further social exclusion, deterioration of body condition, problems in family, work and social life due to the harmful effects of drug addiction. That means, in the long run, drug addiction does not give the individual a substantial compensation of his/her painful sense of poor self-awareness. Instead, it makes this even worse. However, apart from drug addiction, the individual does not have any way to regain his/her positive sense of self-awareness from constructive, healthy and meaningful social experiences. In other words, the more the individual engages in drug addiction, the more his/her phenomenological sense of self are being blocked and hindered, and the more s/he relies on substance abuse to get a temporary but compensation of a pathological sense of self-awareness within the process of substance abuse. It becomes a powerful vicious circle driving the individual to become more and more hindered in getting a good and spontaneous sense of self awareness in the immediate social and physical environment. As a consequence, the individual's frequency, intensity and dependence on substance abuse increase drastically.

TOTALITY OF SELF AND DRUG ADDICTION

The above mentioned discussion clearly shows that the self-system consists of different aspects. In other words, a totality of self should consist of the following aspects:

1. The Ontological Self: It is a sense of ontological existence in which the individual beware of his/her meaning of life and sense of existence.
2. The Phenomenological Self: It is a sense of ongoing self-awareness towards the immediate social and physical environment (it consists of four dimension, the sense of agency and subjectivity, the sense of objectivity and response, the sense of unity and cohesiveness, and the sense of time and emergence).
3. The Identical Self: It is a sense of self identity and self-image in which the individual develop throughout his/her life development.
4. The Conscious Self: The activities of self-system can be conscious, unconscious and subconscious to the individual.
5. The Conflicting self: The self-system may harbour conflict within various components. There are conflicts among superego and id. There are also conflicts between one's own perception and others perception. Conflicts and discrepancies may also occur between self-expectation and constraints in the reality.
6. The Functional Self: It implies the sense of active self-involvement in various activities in daily life. It is also the sense of outreaching to others and manoeuvring related objects as well as sense of attainment in achieving something in one's life.
7. The Interpretative Self: It is a sense of being rational, cognitively active and evaluative to external and internal condition so that the individual can understand and respond appropriately.
8. The Relational Self: It is the power of the individual to relate with others and performing social roles and functioning.

All these showed that the self is actually a comprehensive system in relating every aspects of life including, mind, body, meaning of life as well as roles and spontaneous

Regarding the impacts of drug addiction to self-system, it is a kind a dilemma. On one hand, the individual's various aspects of self are deeply hindered by past and current unpleasant and even oppressive and traumatic experiences, and substance abuse tends to be only available means to compensate or escape from such painful feeling of poor or even impaired self-system. On the other hand, the consequence of drug addiction and substance abuse further deteriorate the sense of self and whole self-system.

In facing spontaneous unpleasant experiences and even oppression in life, the individual's conflicts between superego and id are deeply intensified. His/her phenomenological sense of continuous self-awareness is blurred. His/her relational and functional self is retarded or regressed. His/her conscious self always focus on painful and unhappy reality or traumatic past. His/her own identity is totally diffused and blurred. His own sense of existence is also greatly threatened. Because of past and current unpleasant and even traumatic experiences, related aspects of self are deeply affected. In the process of substance abuse, the individual may effectively avoid the inner conflicts of self-system, escape unpleasant sense of self-awareness or reduce the consciousness of the painful reality.

S/he uses drug addiction to boast up his/her sense of confidence, reduce the embarrassment in relating to others or develop a grandiose sense that s/he is powerful and energetic.

Nevertheless, enhanced sense and functioning of self in the process of substance abuse are, in fact, temporary and pathological. It just likes sucking one's own blood to stop one's thirsty. The more one involved in substance abuse, the more one's sense, consciousness, liveliness of function of self are impaired and deteriorated. As a consequence, the self-system may finally be collapsed with various manifestation of problems and difficulties in maintain the normal functioning, cohesiveness and sense of self awareness.

Firstly, there may be self-splitting because unsettled inner conflict between superego and id because of the deterioration of ego. Secondly, there may be poor self-awareness and response to immediate social and physical environment. Thirdly, individual functional and relational self-deteriorate accordingly. Individuals with substance abuse not only loss their bodily functions but also loss their self-confidence as well as ability to face difficulties, to assert their own needs, to outreach and to relate to others. The individual becomes socially and self-isolated from others. The withering of the self-system brings along more painful feelings, and deep threatening sense of their own ontological existence that are intolerable to the individual. She has no way except further substance abuse with a final consequence of mental or physical breakdown. His/her own life is totally absorbed by substance abuse and drug addiction. Day by day, week by week and month by moth s/he may closely and only relate to his/her drug related peers, object and events. In some extreme cases, individuals crave for drug on one hand but also cry bitterly on the on the other hand in the process of substance abuse.

As a consequence, the self-system of the individual becomes more and more related and occupied by drug in the process of substance abuse. The whole process consists of several stages. The first stage is a self-exposure to substance abuse. In this stage, the individual is either being seduced by his/her peers, or has curiosity in attempting the first trial of substance abuse, s/he tries to use substance abuse to work through or escape himself/herself from various hindrances and burdens in attaining a good and integrated self-system within an oppressive environment.

The second stage is self-adherence on substance abuse. In this stage, the individual after the first trial of substance abuse with or without his/her peer, begins to abuse drug in a regular and even daily pattern. S/he simply regards abused drug as a daily necessity to deal with frustration in life. Whenever, s/he feels frustrated in the present reality, recall unpleasant past experiences or has uncertainty in facing the unpredictable future, substance abuse seems to his/her only alternative in life to lessen his/her unpleasant feelings and frustration.

The third stage is self-involvement to addiction. Gradually, addiction not only becomes part of the individual's daily life. It also becomes the individual's involvement. It means that the individual begins to attend, concentrate and absorb in addiction. Even though increasing frequency, duration and intensity in substance abuse deteriorates his/her physical and mental health, ruins his/her job, family and peer relationship, s/he still needs to involve in substance abuse. Despite the increasing negative costs of substance abuse, the individual stills regards substance abuse is the most important aspect in life. S/he tends to involve more and more in substance abuse but becomes more and more detached from most aspects of life.

The fourth stage is self-transformation in addiction. That means the individual is no longer a master or subject for the abused substance. Instead, s/he is mastered or controlled by substance abuse and drug addiction. S/he is undergoing a vigorous of transformation by drug addiction. Firstly, s/he daily life pattern is shifted from a regular daily life to a life pattern tailored made for spontaneous substance abuse and drug addiction. S/he may take drug in the morning, afternoon, and/or evening. Secondly, his/her peer groups and social circles before substance abuse is gradually replaced by drug related peers. Thirdly, his/her regular job and family life is severely distorted by his/her frequent, intensive and continuous drug addiction. S/he may even loss his/her job and excluded by family members. Finally, s/he is totally transformed from a normal person to a substance abuser and drug addict. Not only people around label him/her as drug addict or substance abusers, s/he also identity himself/herself as a drug addict or substance abuse.

The final stage is the formation of an addictive self. In this stage, drug addiction becomes his/her own meaning and goal in his/her life. In doing so, his/her self-identity, self-integrity and dignity, ego functioning are gradually deteriorated. S/he sacrifices everything for the sake of drug addiction and substance abuse. Apart from drug addiction, s/he has nothing.

Self Assertion and Drug Addiction: Integrated Dynamic Recovery

Self-Medication & Regulation in Addiction: The Khantizian's Articulation

Khantzian, (1997) asserted that drug addiction is actually a process of self-medication and regulation. He affirmed that individuals, in the process of substance abuse, actually choose their own drug and pattern of drug addiction.

Their own preference, in fact, reflects their own needs and difficulties in various aspects of life. They have primary difficulties in regulating their affects, relationship and self-care. There seems to be a close relationship among specific drug effect on body and emotion. The type of drug and the pattern of substance abuse including intensity, frequency and duration are all influenced by related feeling, self-care, self-esteem, and relationship of the individual. Related feeling implies elated mood or depressive mood. For those with elated mood, they may be more inclined to take tranquillizers.

For those with depressive mood, they may be more prompt to abuse stimulants. In terms of self-care, it seems persons with substance abuse may gradually decrease their ability and concern of self-care. However, taking drug, in particular those anesthetic such as heroin and ketamine, will give the individual a sense of being away, being escaped from unpleasant current situation. Self-esteem is the feeling of self, either sense of inferiority or the sense of superiority.

For those who aspire for the sense of superiority they may be inclined to take stimulants. For those who have indulged in an intensive sense of inferiority, they may be prompt to take tranquillizers. Problems and difficulties in interpersonal relationship also play a crucial role in self-medication. They rely on substance abuse and drug addiction to resolve all these tension, anxiety and psychological distress created. That means, the choice of substance abuse reflects the specific drug effect on body and emotion, inner state of psychological sufferings and disharmony and types of personality.

In real practice, the preference of drug is influenced by the following factors:

- Drug related factors: effects of drug/ stage of usage/Dosage of usage.
- Market/ External factors: availability/ cost/ peer influence/ market.
- Internal/ Personal factors: Relief of psychological suffering/ personality.

These three factors interact with one another in determining what sort of drug and pattern of addiction by the individual.

The Squeezed Ego in Bion's Suggested Emotional Container (William, 2002)

Within the same line of thinking, Bion's emotional container can also be a valid concept in interpreting substance abuse and drug addiction. Based on Freud's articulation of conflict between superego and id, Bion further elaborates ego in smoothing this conflict has its own unique containing capacity. It is a psychic emotional container housing related negative emotions. That means, individuals with a competent ego, are able to accept, absorb and even resolve related negative emotions such as sadness, loneliness, anger, fear and emptiness in normal conflicts between superego and id. However, in the process of development, individuals' ego capacity and strengths may gradually be deteriorated by sufferings, traumas, abuse, oppression and unpleasant experiences. In that sense, the capacity and volume of the emotional container may thus be weakened.

At the same time, the ego is squeezed between a fierce and severe superego and the weakened ego itself, which is left to a powerful id (William, 2002). Under this condition, individuals may emotionally regress to an infantile state in which excess infantile needs and demands which have avoid developmental processes and seek instant relief and satisfaction. Within this line of thinking, substance abuse becomes an immediate way to satisfy all these infantile needs and demands. That means various kinds of drugs do manage to provide an initial containing experience and actually improve poetic products (William, 2002). When one might expect further development and maturity of poetic talents, the drug taking invariably leads to considerable deterioration.

Some drug does more containing than others. Some drugs do more damage than others, but when all drugs tend to do ultimately is to undermine and reduce, and perhaps even destroy, the adapting self of the addict in its capacity to contain and process painful of mind (William, 2002). The whole process can be described in the following stages:

1. Oppressive and frustrating reality weaken the ego boundary and strengths the individual.
2. Emotional containing capacity of the ego decrease accordingly.
3. Weakening ego makes the inherent conflicts between id and superego prevail and uncontrollable.
4. Prevailing conflicts between id and superego further deteriorate the emotional containing capacity.
5. Powerful and regressive id as well as suppressed and guilt oriented superego create intolerable negative emotion. As the emotional containing capacity is limited,

individuals demand immediate relief and satisfaction by substance abuse and drug addiction.

6. Drug addiction and substance abuse further weaken the ego strengths and boundary as well as emotional containing capacity.
7. Further intensified and uncontrollable conflicts between id and superego.
8. Further weakening the ego strengths and emotional containing capacity.
9. Further drug addiction and substance abuse to cater the intensive demand of immediate relief and satisfaction.
10. Drastic increase of impulsivity and irritability in the absence of drug.

The Vulnerable Self and Drug in Kohut's Selfobject

Based on Kohut's selfobject relationship, Weegmann (2002) affirmed that a person with substance abuse has a vulnerable self because of poor self object relationship in the developmental process. S/he is thus highly sensitive to slight rejections or perceived criticism. They have long been deprived from the arousal of narcissistic transference in terms of mirror transference, idealizing transference from self-object until the occurrence of transmuting internalization.

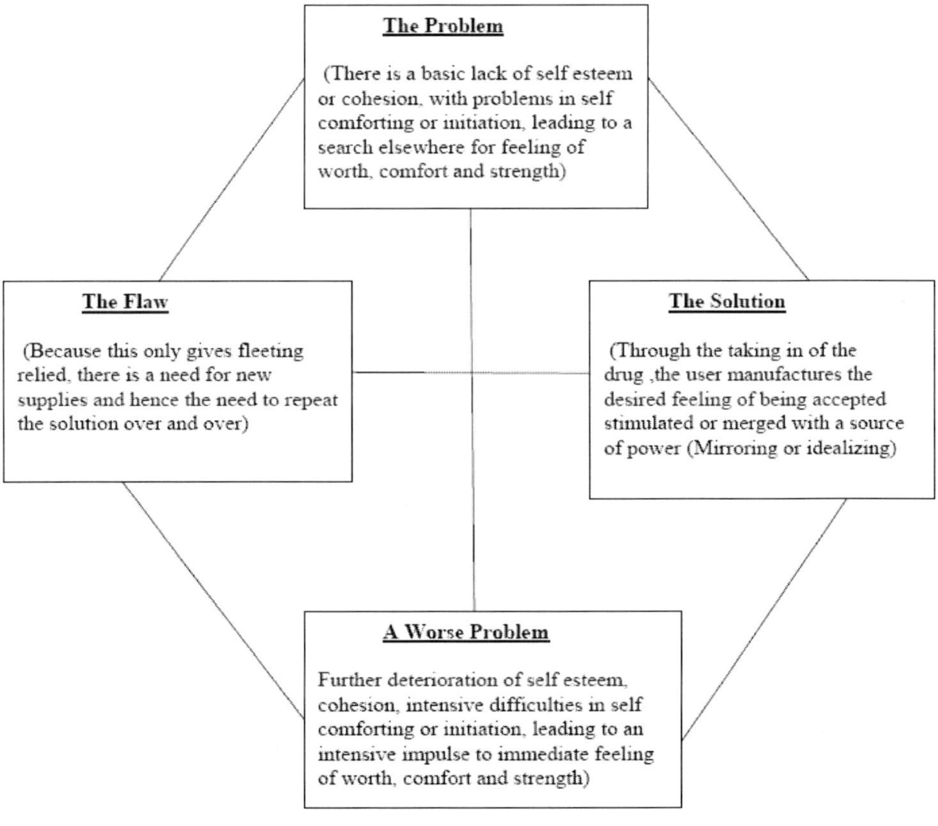

Figure. A Vicious Circle of Self object Relationship in Persons with Substance abuse (Weegman, 2002).

Deprivation of these self-objects may result in further narcissistic vulnerability. In that condition, the drug serves as a compensatory/ replaceable self-object but without actually satisfying the needs of healthy and normal narcissistic transference.

In the process of substance abuse, the immediate effects of the drug may include one or several of the following: an alteration in mood, a rising of self-esteem, an increased vitality or energy, a sense of assertion, an intense affective experience or a nullifying of intensive experiences.

The immediacy of these effects offers a reassuring feeling of control or comfort. As a replaceable self-object, drug addiction makes the individual accustom to an immediate satisfaction of narcissistic transference instead of struggle to search or nurture a substantial self-object (Weegmann, 2002). That means, persons with addiction is enslaved by drug with a progressive weakening of other values or interest. Weegmann (2002) further affirmed for persons with substance abuse, their problem, solution, flaw, and worse problem in pathological self-object relationship are interrelated to one another.

Self Assertion and Drug Addiction

From concepts described by Bion, Kantzian and Kohut, it is clear that substance abuse and drug addiction is spontaneously used by the individual as a valid mean to strengthen his/her weaken ego or self-system including his/her self-identity, image, ego functioning and social functioning. In other words, for persons with substance abuse, drug is a mean for immediate self-assertion. Under an oppressive environment in which the individual is deeply depowered, drug is a powerful but destructive way of self-empowerment. The individual can use any place, any time and any intensity to have a substance induced sense of power and ability.

In other words, substance abuse is also a way to exercise will power and sense of mastery and control over oneself and related drug. It can be a heightened sense of elation or a way to escape from depowered memories, current frustration and future hopelessness. It is also a glue to link up the fragile self-system.

That means substance abuse serves as a harmful mean to glue up individual's internal conflicts and discrepancies between expectation and reality. For persons with substance abuse, they may use substance abuse and drug addiction as a defense mechanism to external threat and a shelter from the frustrating reality. They adhere to drug when their beloved object abandons them, when they are oppressed or bullied by other, and/or when they face unavoidable trauma and hardship.

As mentioned above, addictive self in persons with substance abuse have an important and vital impact and functioning of the self-system. They are closely related to the development of various types of mental illnesses. Its process and stages and development can be described in the following diagram.

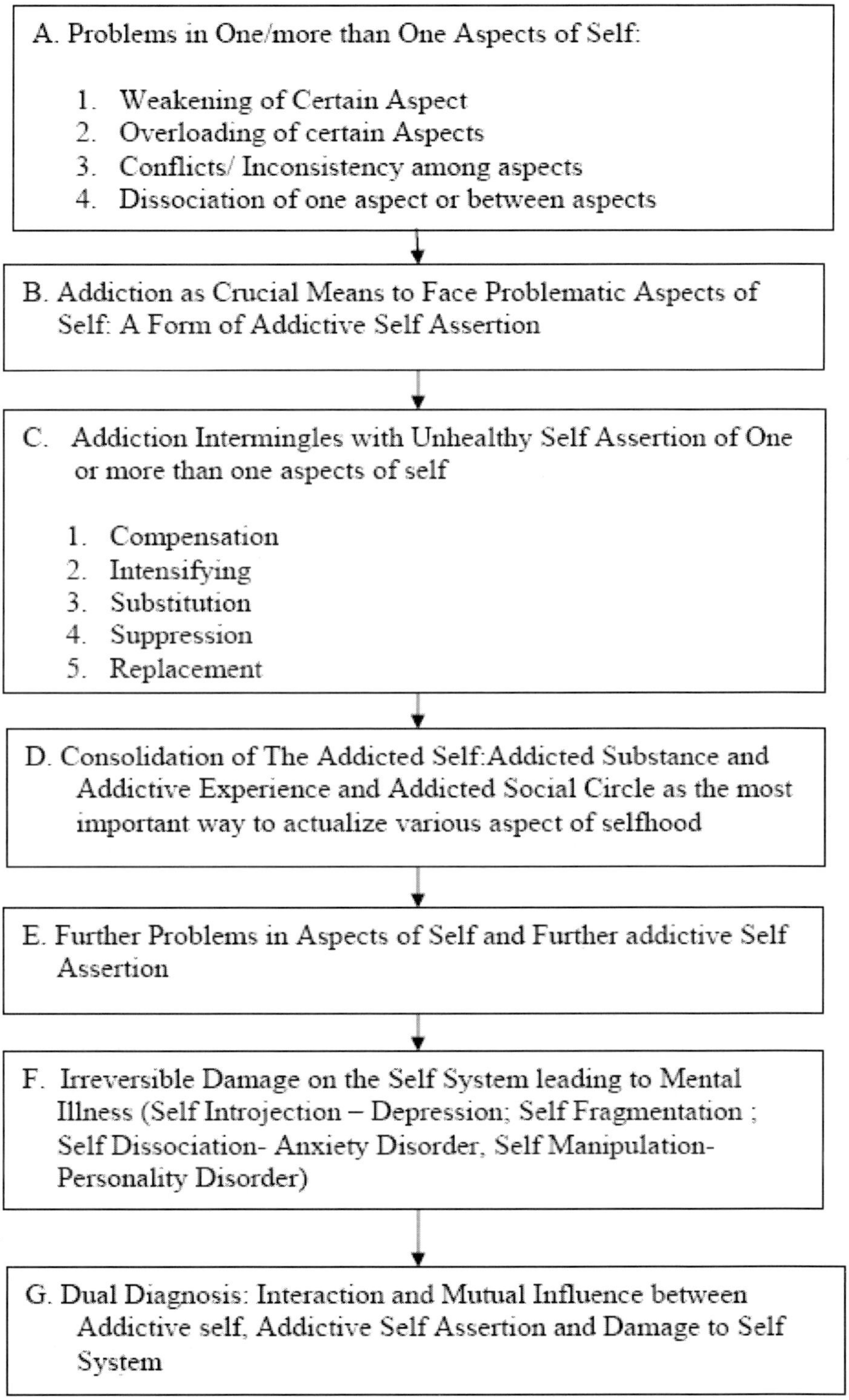

Figure. Process of Self Assertion in Addictive Self in Persons with Substance Abuse.

Implications of Integrated recovery: Understanding Clients' Aspects of Self

Within different concepts of self, there should be a strong implication in rendering related intervention strategies for the integrated recovery for persons with substance abuse. Related stages of intervention can be briefly listed in the following:

1. Understanding Client's Different Aspects of Self and the Formation of Client's Addictive Self.
2. Communication of Clients' Unhealthy Self Assertion.
3. Rebuilding Client's Healthy Self Assertion by Re-affirmation Clients' Life Aspiration and Will to Recovery.
4. Reconstruction of Clients' Normal Aspects of Self.

Understanding Client's Different Aspects of Self and the Formation of Client's Addictive Self

In helping clients with substance abuse, it is very important that related professionals can understand client's different aspects of self-including the ontological self, the phenomenological self, the identical self, the conscious self, the conflicting self, the functional self, the relational self and the interpretive self. In understanding clients' different aspects of self, related workers should beware of the following:

1. Their current stage of existence, whether each aspect of the self is in good or inadequate conditions, and is there a vicious circle in the process of substance abuse.
2. In what way the client's recognizes or interprets strengths, problems and difficulties in every aspects of self.
3. Compare and contrast every aspect of client's self before, during and after the substance abuse and addiction.
4. Are there any conflicts and inconsistencies among different aspects of client's self?
5. What are client's inherent urges and past efforts for striving for the consistency, continual emergence, wholeness, realization and presentation of self in their life?
6. Any external frustration, burdens and difficulties that hinds the aspects of self.

In understanding all these, related professionals should beware that all aspects of self are indeed closely related to different domains and levels of the individual including the meaning of life, mind (morality, cognition and emotion), body (figure, health and clothing), role (social functioning in family, work and environment) and behaviors (performance and deeds in various social circles in everyday life).

To attain a thorough understanding on clients' self-system and other layers of life, related professionals have to know client's life history and background in refined details. For persons with substance abuse, especially those with chronic addiction, they may try to repress their memories on their unpleasant history by substance abuse.

So it is bit hard for related professionals to know their life history and emotions in details. Thus, related professionals may need a long period of time in building rapport with clients with substance abuse so that clients can gradually ease out their deep seated emotions and unpleasant past experiences and life history in details. Only by doing that, related professionals can have a thorough understanding on related aspects of self before, during and after substance abuse.

Indeed, it is a great challenge for related professional in facing the addictive self of clients with substance abuse and drug addiction. First of all, clients may have a strong dependence and even attachment to drug addiction so as to replace, compensate and substitute various attachment and traumas in life.

In that sense, it is really hard for related professionals to convince their clients to abstain from substance abuse unless there are immediate or powerful substitutes and attachment in facing their deep frustration in life and in addiction. Very often, the genuineness, empathy, warmth and understanding of related professionals can be regarded as a temporary substitute and attachment for clients to face ongoing and prolonged frustration and challenge in life. All these are also important motivational factors for clients to abstain from drug and substance abuse.

In doing so, it also means a great challenge for related professionals in which some of them may not have sufficient psychological space to render all these to their clients. In addition to that, clients' narration of their traumatic psychological experiences may also trigger professionals' their own unpleasant and unresolved past experiences. Related professionals may be reluctant to listen, to accept and to contain clients' dilemmas and frustration in the process of formation of addictive self. In that situation, it is very important that related professionals should be well supported by other members in the professional teams. Their supervisors or seniors should share their wisdom in understanding and accepting clients' addictive self. Their colleagues should share their own frustrations in recognizing and accepting clients' addictive self. Coupled with their seniors and clinical supervisors, they should support one another to work through and resolve their own difficulties, traumas and suffering in their lives so that they can ease out their own frustration and create sufficient psychological space and ego strengths to contains clients' frustration, difficulties and problems.

After that, related professionals should move on to look into clients' plight and pains in isolating themselves from normal aspects of self in reality because of spontaneous substance abuse and chronic drug addiction. They should also able to discover clients' occasional effort in breaking their addictive self by trying to quit their drug addiction and substance abuse. It can appear in forms of reducing the dosage of their drug intake, joining harm reduction programs, harboring a sense of guilt towards their significant others in craving for drug, and finding a job and seeking professionals' help. Related professionals should also provide home visit or counseling to clients' significant others who have long been frustrated by clients' chronic drug addiction. Many of them may be physically or mentally exploited by their relatives and friends with substance abuse. Related professionals should recognize their frustration and sparkle their hope again in supporting their relatives and friends in recovery from substance abuse.

After years of chronic drug addiction, clients usually harbor intensive confusion in their normal self-urge (urge for love, care, support and actualization), addictive self-urge (urge to taking different kind of drug to cover up their frustration in unfulfilled self-urge) and fragmented self-urge (inability to describe their own needs, frustration and urge). They may regard as the addictive self-urge is the only way to gratify their normal self-urge. As a consequence, their normal self would gradually turn into fragmented self-urge in which they can hardly describe their own feeling, needs, frustration and urge. For inexperienced professionals, they may wrongly regarded fragmented self-urge as their clients have no insight in their own difficulties. Coupled with clients' prevailing addictive self-urge, related professional may wrongly conclude that their clients have no motive to abstain from drugs or have no will to recovery.

Thus, related professionals should recognize and accept clients' confusion of normal self-urge, addictive self-urge and fragmented self-urge in the process of chronic addiction. Even though clients appear to be inert and highly adherent to their chronic addiction, under their fragmented self-urge and addictive self-urge there are still unfulfilled normal self-urge of being loved, cared and supported. In that sense, related professionals should never confine their intervention in terms of harmful reduction and relapse prevention simply by warning clients about the harmful effects of drugs or institutionalization of clients into detoxification programs within highly alienated residential institutions. Instead, they should encourage clients to develop or restore their normal self-system with sufficient ego strengths to express their normal self-urge, to formulate a good self-image, and to establish capacity in relating and interacting with others in the immediate social and physical environment. Only by doing so, related interventions rendered by professional workers can at least inhibit their further aggravation of their addictive self and give them another opportunity to rebuild a new and normal self-system.

Communicating with Clients' Unhealthy Self Assertion

It is always a challenge for related professionals to communicate with their clients' unhealthy self-assertion in the process of substance abuse. Within their chronic drug addiction, individuals' unfulfilled self-urge is achieved by their unhealthy self-assertion through the drug addiction. For them, drug is used as a mean for a manifestation of their self-defence and aggression towards others. Drug is also a way for self-elation and getting a sense of omnipotence to cover up their senses of inferiority and helplessness in facing frustration in life. It is also a kind of self-isolation and regression in facing the highly oppressive environment and difficulties in everyday life. Persons with substance abuse are lonely and being excluded by their significant others as members in the communities. In that situation, substance abuse seems to be a valid mean for substitution and compensation of all these sense of loneliness and isolation. Finally, prolonged substance abuse makes the individual develop mental symptoms such as self-dialogue in hallucination in schizophrenia. This unhealthy self-assertion greatly complicates related interventions performed by professionals. Firstly, related professionals may come to a conclusion that their clients are heavily dependent on drug in everyday life with a slim hope of recovery. Secondly, as clients assert and relate to drug rather than relating to others, related professionals may get a feeling that their clients are distant and unmotivated to interventions and programs in recovery. Thirdly, facing all these pathological ways of unhealthy self-assertion, related professionals may likely label these as mental problems and personality problems that demand immediate medical treatment rather than fulfilling clients' self-urge. Thus, for the recovery of persons with substance abuse, it is important that related professionals can accept and recognize clients' unhealthy self-assertion is normal in the process of substance abuse and drug addiction. They should try the best to communicate with clients' unfulfilled needs, repressed emotions, and suppressed normal self-urge behind unhealthy self-assertion. By means, proper meaningful activities and group interaction, they should facilitate clients to understand their need of unhealthy self-assertion. For example, for an adolescent with prolonged abuse of ketamine, s/he may be highly reluctant to express their suppressed negative emotion and normal self-urge. Thus, they tend to compensate this by abusing ketamine with their peers. To ease out their repressed emotions, suppressed normal self-urge, related professionals may organize some healthy group activities such adventure training, physical exercise, dancing or internet games, within which adolescents with substance abuse can involve and interact smoothly and normally. Gradually, they begin to trust and establish good sharing with one another. Finally, within a normal and supportive group environment, they able to ease up their negative feelings of being neglected, excluded and rejected by others. They are also able express their normal self-urges of being respected, loved, cared and included by others in interpersonal interaction.

They should facilitate clients to revisit their healthy self-assertion before their formation of addictive self. When clients with substance abuse is able communicate their normal self-urge, regain a sense of ontological and phenomenological self in normal daily activities, they feel more at ease to tell their own stories in their childhood, adolescence and adulthood. Within all these personal self-narrations, there are difficulties, traumas and hardships in attaining normal self-urge, as well as some repressed emotions and history of abandonment with their significant others. All these unfulfilled normal self urges in unpleasant experiences are repressed and transformed into unhealthy self-assertion through the process of substance abuse and drug accidents. Only when these unfulfilled normal self urges are fully elaborated and acknowledged by related professionals and their significant others, persons with substance abuse will begin to abandon their unhealthy self-assertion through substance abuse and drug addiction.

With the restoration of clients' healthy self-assertion behind previous and current traumas, hardship and suffering in life, related professionals should acknowledge clients' suppressed urge for self-integration, self-cohesiveness and self-actualization. They should have some positive experiences in being cared, loved and supported by others, actualizing their strengths and talents, proving that they are unique and special and showing that they can also care, love and support others. All these positive experiences are crucial in attaining their self-integration, self-cohesiveness and self-actualization.

Finally, they should maximize clients' significant others' aspiration for clients in healthy self-assertion and rebuild of healthy aspects of self. Related professionals should recognize clients' significant others' frustration and hardship in clients' substance abuse including the craving for drug, deterioration of physical and mental health, failure in fulfilling their own responsibility, as well as self-isolation and exclusion from normal daily life. In extreme cases, they even reject to meet their relatives with substance abuse. Unless, clients with substance abuse can have substantial actions in their own recovery, their relatives may not believe in them or assist them in the process of recovery. Thus, related professionals need to facilitate communication among clients and their significant other in acknowledging their motives, actions in recovery. This can be motives and actions in finding a suitable employment, entry into a detoxification program, sense of regret in taking drug.

Reconstruction of Clients' Normal Aspects of Self

To have a full recovery, persons with substance abuse should be helped to have a good reconstruction of their normal aspects of self.

1. Reconstruction of clients' healthy phenomenological self

It can start with the reconstruction of the phenomenological self by develop a normal life pattern and by engaging in meaningful activities and constructive social interaction with others within clients' own community and social circle. This can be normal social activities with friends or family members, healthy recreational activities and physical exercise, normal sleep and meal times, work and employment By doing so, clients begin to have healthy involvement of sense of reality and engagement with their significant others so that they can feel substantial and integrated in every moment. Once their phenomenological self is developed, their sense of emptiness, boredom and detachment from reality can be substantially increase. It greatly reduces their needs to depend on substance abuse to alleviate their senses of emptiness, boredom and frustration in life.

2. Reconstruction of clients' healthy ontological self

In developing their healthy ontological self, it is important that related professional should facilitate persons with substance abuse to engage in meaningful activities and search for their own meaningfulness of life. Instead of losing their meaning of life because of physical, mental and social deterioration in chronic drug addiction and substance abuse, clients should be facilitated to develop a new meaningful life. This can be attained by engaging them into volunteer work in serving deprived and vulnerable groups such as the fragile and lonely elderly, the children with mental and physical disability and delinquent adolescents. All these volunteer work makes clients feel that their life is still meaningful and worthwhile. Despite their chronic substance abuse, they can still serve as important helpers for others. After that, they should encourage to refocus their own life in riding off their chronic substance abuse. They should also be facilitated to be a peer mentor in helping others to alleviate their own substance abuse. In doing so, they spontaneously remind themselves that substance abuse should not be their purpose in life. They still have other meaningful purposes to attain. They should re-affirm clients' life aspiration and will to recovery that should include the following intervention strategies.

1. Explore clients' unfinished life aspiration in childhood, adolescence, youth or adulthood.
2. Facilitate clients' significant others to acknowledge clients' aspirations.
3. Help clients to take an initial step in actualizing their life aspiration gradually.
4. Enhance clients' significant others to appreciate clients' initial effort in actualizing their life aspiration.

Very often, clients' aspirations in life are closely connection with their meaning of life in their life development. They can be unfulfilled wishes or dreams in clients' own life such as being good parents for their new born babies, actualizing the wishes of their deceased or dying parents, and being good husbands/ wives for their spouses who always remind/help their to quit substance abuse. All these unfulfilled aspirations should be shared and acknowledged by clients' significant others. This can be done by professional counselling with related family members.

3. Reconstruction of clients' healthy and normal self-identity

In developing clients' self-identity, there are two important intervention strategies. One is the development of client's own healthy self-identity. Another one is the development of acceptance and appreciation of others towards clients' healthy self-identity as well their unique talents and attainment. The enhancement of clients' own healthy self-identity is based on development of clients' unique talents and strengths. This can be talents in art, sports, computing, design, body make up and dressing, language, and social interaction. Once these talents can be properly recognized, developed and appreciated by others, clients' self-image and identity are thus properly enhanced and rebuilt. At that moment, all these well developed talents should be further formally developed and trained. For example, a client with good dancing talents should be trained by a professional dancer and engaged in dancing competition. Then s/he should be encouraged to become a professional dancer or go back to college to receive formal dancing degree training in creative art and professional dancing. By doing all these, clients' self-image and identity can be gradually enhanced from being a chronic substance abuser to a person with special talents and skills.

4. The Construction of Ego Strengths and Meaning of Life

In fact, the development of a healthy identical self and an ontological self can always work closely together. After the restoration of a healthy and good identity, the client with substance abuse is able to establish a meaningful life goal in fulfilling his/her roles to be a good and responsible husband/wife, son/daughter, citizen and friend with remarkable contribution to his/her family, community and society. In the same way, within the process of establishing a meaningful life, clients' self-image and self-identity are also greatly enhanced and developed. They begin to beware that they have special calling and mission in his/her unique contribution to their own families, communities and societies. In doing so, they link up their own self-image and self-identity with all these unique contribution and position within their own social circles. They are not only a person with special talents and ability but also a highly responsible member within their own families, communities and societies. In fulfilling and actualizing all these, they are no longer egocentric persons focusing on their own substance abuse. Instead, people around begin to recognize their drastic changes, appreciate their unique contribution, struggle and effort in fulfilling their social responsibilities.

5. Development of Other Aspects of Self

After the development of a good identical self and a meaningful ontological self, clients with substance abuse become a person with dignity, integrity and responsibility. Moment by moment, day by day and month by month, they are fully engaged in meaningful activities and healthy social interaction. With a proper development of a normal and healthy ontological, identical and phenomenological self, other aspects of the self-system can also be properly enhanced. Firstly, it is the time for the individual to tackle related inner conflicts. In the process of prolonged drug addiction and substance abuse, individual's ego strengths gradually deteriorate with a prevailing conflict between superego and id. However, after the cessation of drug addiction and substance abuse and with proper development of ego strengths, the conflict between superego and id can thus be harmonized and regularized. Repressed memories of traumas, sufferings and hardships in life in prolonged substance abuse and drug addiction begin to re-bounce as individuals' ego strengths and consciousness increase. Under the help of related professionals, it is the right time for the individual to ventilate negative emotions and resolve related conflicts, dilemmas underlying these repressed traumas, hardships and sufferings. With the proper resolution of all these negative emotions, conflicts and dilemmas, individuals begin to embrace enough emotional and mental space to forgive themselves and their significant other who has done harm to them in their life development. In doing so, clients begin to recovery their normal and healthy sense of self consciousness. Their oversensitivity towards others' comments and criticism decreases as they embrace good mental space and acceptance of people around. As a consequence, their interpersonal relationship with their significant others and other members in their social circles increase accordingly. All these can help them to have better good social functioning in their work, family and social circles.

HEALTHY SELF ASSERTION IN FACING PERSONAL DIFFICULTIES AND HARDSHIPS

Once, the healthy aspects of self are developed, individuals not long dependent on substance abuse and drug addiction to face their personal difficulties and hardship. Individuals are able to have health self-assertion in resolving and coping with their personal difficulties and hardships. The healthy assertion can include the following:

1. From Self Defense to Self Advocacy

Within a normal and healthy self-system, individuals are able to lessen their inappropriate self-defense to appropriate self-advocacy in facing personal difficulties and hardships. Self-advocacy implies that individuals are able to advocate and assert their own strengths and rights in facing personal difficulties and hardships. For example, in past, if an individual faces an oppressive boss who imposes unfair treatment and even abuse him/her. As his/her aspects of self are inadequate and unhealthy, s/he dares not to assert his/her rights and advocate his/her own strengths to bargain with his/her oppressive boss. Instead, s/he tends to suppress all these unfair treatment and abuse. As a consequence, s/he feels deeply frustrated and intolerable. S/he tends to commit substance abuse so as to ease out these sorts of frustration and intolerable feeling. However, once his/her aspects of self are enhanced and healthy, s/he will be courageous and confident enough to assert his/her personal rights to bargain with his/her oppressive boss. Or s/he has enough confidence to find another job so as to free himself/herself from these oppressive environments.

2. From Self Isolation to Self Integration

For a healthy and normal self-system, individuals are able to integrate with others. Sullivan (1956) interpreted this as an integrating tendency in which persons are able to establish close connection and intimate relationship among one another. It is also a kind of inherent urge in which the individual tries his/her best to relate to other, to tune in a group, to build up normal and spontaneous interaction with one another. These inherent urge may or may not be fulfilled or developed in one's developmental process. However, within one's development process, his/her significant others may be not be able to satisfy all his/her need of integrating tendency. Under that sort of conditions, the individual may always harbor an unfulfilled need of intensive attachment and dependence on others. S/he may thus be trapped within a vicious cycle. On one hand, s/he earnestly and eagerly looks for someone to depend on or attach to. On the other hand, s/he is easily hurt by others' separation, criticism and leaving. To avoid this intolerable, individual is deeply trapped within an avoidance and approach conflict towards others. As a consequence, substance abuse may become the only available object for the individual to temporarily gratify his/her unfulfilled but burning integrating tendency towards others. When related aspects of self, the individual is able to maintain his/her own self integration. With proper appreciation from significant others and exercising and developing their own ego strengths, individuals gradually develop appropriate relationship with newly established peers, friends with healthy and normal hobbies, engaging in interaction with colleagues in normal work environment and establishing new intimate relationship with their significant others. Gradually, his/her integrating tendencies are fully and continuously gratified. S/he no longer needs to depend on substance abuse as a substituted attachment object to fulfill his/her needs for integrating tendency.

3. From Self Suppression and Dialogue to Self Expression

Persons engaged in chronic substance abuse are always engage in self-dialogue of their painful and intolerable situation of mind and body. They told themselves that they are painful and intolerable to related traumas and suffering from life and from chronic substance abuse. They also told themselves that they want to quit from all these drug related traumas and exclusion by others. The more they feel painful, the more they rely on substance abuse to ease out their pain and sufferings. Thus, they also told themselves that they feel guilty and hopeless about themselves and their future.

All these self-dialogues are conflicting and highly dynamic and paradoxical to one another. As a consequence, individuals with substance abuse are very hard to express their conflicts and complicated feelings. Intensive and chronic substance abuse becomes the only way to conceal all these painful feelings and intolerable reality. However, once related aspects of self are reconstructed in normal ways, individuals with substance abuse record begin to regain their sense of integrity, cohesiveness and power to relate to the reality. With normal and healthy supportive others, they are able to express their negative feelings and painful traumas in life.

By doing so, they are able to clear their unresolved emotional complexes towards former traumas and difficulties in life. Once these are cleared, their ego strengths, normal social functioning and self-capacity are greatly improved.

4. From Self Elation and Self-Regulation

Individuals with substance abuse usually suffer from intensive sense of inferiority and inadequacies. The more they engaged in substance abuse, the more inferior and inadequate they feel. They are heavily dependent on substance abuse to pull up their mood and sense of self in life. However, after substance abuse, their sense of inferiority and inadequacy return again. Gradually, they may lose their ability in regulating their sense of self and emotions. However, once their substance abuse are reduced and their normal aspects of self are restored by related intervention of professionals, thy may be able to regain their sense of self-regulation. Instead of relying of substance abuse to conceal and regulate their negative emotions, individuals are able to use healthy activities and normal means such as physical activities, sharing negative emotions with others, doing healthy positive events to evolve positive feelings, resolving conflicts and frustration with others. Healthy positive events can be visiting good old friend, finding out solution for current and past personal problems, helping others, and having interesting recreational activities. All these mean that individuals' self-system is strong and integrated with proper functioning to face and regulate one's difficulties and negative emotions.

5. From Self Delusion and Self Realization and Acutalization

Individuals with substance abuse are usually depowered by oppressive others in their social environment and developmental process. Very often, this oppressive social environment are getting worse and worse as the individual is more and more involved in substance abuse. S/he is thus spontaneously excluded by labeled by others as a hopeless and useless substance abuser. To get rid of all these intensive senses of hopelessness and worthlessness, the only available means is only further substance abuse and drug addiction. As a consequence, individuals are heavily involved and absorbed in drug induced senses of delusive images, feelings, and bodily responses. However, with proper restoration of various aspects of self, related individuals are able to realize their ego strengths, talents and social functioning even in times of difficulties and hardship. The more they can realize all these, the less they are dependent on substance abuse. Finally, their senses of hopelessness and worthlessness are gradually replaced by senses of hopefulness and self-confidence. They are thus totally free from substance abuse and drug addiction.

6. From Self Compensation and Substitution to Independence and Autonomy

As mentioned above, individuals with substance abuse have a poor sense of self and encounter numerous oppression, labeling, traumas and hardships in life. They need substance abuse as a mean of compensation to all these frustration. Gradually, they are totally dependent and addicted to drug. Only with proper restoration of various aspects of self, the individuals are able restored their own ability to regain their ego strengths, self-confidence, self-image, interpersonal relationship and proper social functioning, they are able to cope and facing various difficulties in life. They also to restore their own self autonomy in determining their own life, own work, own future and own life pattern without being addictive and independent to substance abuse and drug. The sense of autonomy is crucial in the process of recovery. It gives individuals a sense of being. It makes individuals assert their own rights, make their own decision, go their own way, live their own life. It also gives individuals a sense of uniqueness and integrity. Only when all these normal senses of self are fully implemented and actualized, individuals can restore their self-autonomy without reliance on drug and substance abuse especially in times of frustration, hardship and suffering.

It is clear that self-advocacy, self-integration, self-regulation, self-realization, self-actualization, and independence and autonomy are crucial in the recovery of individual with substance abuse. All these imply that individuals' normal aspects of self, such as spontaneous healthy phenomenological self, normal and assertive relational self, meaningful ontological self, good and competent self-image and self-identity, continuous and healthy self-consciousness, normal and good social functioning and integrated self-interpretation are gradually restored. With a normal and competent self-system, individuals are able to face hardship, frustration and suffering constructively. There is always a challenge for professionals in helping individuals with substance abuse to restore their normal aspects of self. They may always focus their attention on helping clients to have immediate drug detoxification or harm reduction of substance abuse. Once, these are attained, they claim success on their interventions and programs. No sooner, as clients' aspects of self are still inadequate and even deteriorating, their substance abuse relapses again. Thus, it is crucial that related professionals can develop clients' different aspects of self so that s/he can have good ego strengths, positive self-image, self-confidence, and adequate social functioning and assertiveness to face challenges, difficulties and hardships in life. Only by doing so, individuals with substance abuse can be fully recovered with proper integration into a normal social life.

CONCLUSION

As a conclusion, this chapter is a comprehensive discussion about self-system and drug addiction. It is clear that drug addiction and substance abuse is in fact a way to glue up the gap of the self-system on one hand, On the other hand, it creates further problems and in extreme cases, it fractures the already vulnerable self-system.. In integrated and dynamic recovery, it is important that related professionals can help clients with substance abuse and drug addiction to develop healthy means to strengthen their self-system including their self-identity, self-image, self-regulation and self-recognition.

REFERENCES

Freud, S. (1933) *New Introductory Lectures on Psychoanalysis,* Penguin Freud Library 2: 105–6.

Hohway, J. (2007) The sense of self in the phenomenology of agency and perception, *Psyche*, 13(1): 1-20.

Horney, K. (1945) Our inner conflict: A construction Theory of Neurosis, New York: W. W. Norton.

Jaspers, K. (1946/1923) General Psychopathology (Trans. Hoening, J & Hamilton, M. W.), Manchester: Manchester University Press.

Jung, C. G. (1966) Two Essay on Analytical Psychology, 2nd edition, translated by R.F.C. Hull, Princeton, New Jersey, Princeton University Press.

Jung, C. G. (1967). *The Development of Personality*. 1991 ed. London: Routledge. Collected Works Vol. 17.

Jung, C. G. (1968). *Analytical Psychology: Its Theory and Practise* (a.k.a. "The Tavistock Lectures").

Khantzian, E. J. (1997) The self medication hypothesis of substance use disorders: A reconstruction and recent applications, *Harvard Review of Psychiatry*, 4(5): 232-244.

Kohut, H. (1977) *The Restoration of Self,* New York: International University Press.

Mead, G. H. (1934) *Mind, Self and Society,* Chicago: University of Chicago Press.

Sullivan, H. J. (1956) *Clinical Studies in Psychiatry*, New York: W.W. Norton.

Weegmann, M. (2002) The vulnerable self: Heinz Kohut and the addiction, in M. Weegmann, M. & Cohen, R. (Edited) *The Psychodynamic of Addiction,* pp. 31-51, London: Whurr Publication.

Chapter 8

Meaning of Life in Substance Abuse and Drug Addiction: A Dynamic Integrated Recovery

Introduction

The Need of Existential Perspective in Substance Abuse

While the cognitive behavioral perspective assume that substance abuse is merely a problematic cognitive schema in facing stress and frustration in life, the behavioral perspective tend to assume physical senses induced by related drug is a valid and powerful reinforcement in avoiding frustration and difficulties in actual life situations. However, including the disease and biochemical models fail to address the complexity of human life. They merely assume human thinking and action can be articulated in a highly reductionistic t simplified measurement and controlled physical and mental mechanism. They fail to acknowledge human being is continuously strives for profound meaning and sense of existence in life. Most clients with severe substance abuse or chronic drug addiction are empty and meaningless in their life endeavor.

There seems to be a strong need of employing an existential perspective in understanding and perceiving addiction.

> There is a clear demand from existentialists to examine the concept of addiction. They point out that much addiction research already highlights existential issues even though the author may use other terms to describe them. However, these 'givens' are unlikely to be assessed during evaluation of treatment if the treatment modalities are based on narrow, reductionistic models of alcohol use and human behavior.' (Wright, 2013: 1)

In existentialism, people in drug addiction are regarded as having choice. They are not 'dependence' and 'addiction'. The choice of drug addiction is a way to ease out their pain, anxiety, meaninglessness and frustration in life (Wurm, 2003). It is a humanistic perspective in regarding people as not drug addicts or abusers. Instead, they are people with value and responsibility. Frankl (1997) affirmed that everyone harbors a strong will to meaning. Everyone urges for meaning of suffering and love. For clients with drug addiction and substance abuse, they are actually deprived for meaning in life. They deprive of love and their sufferings are lack of meaning. Thus, drug addiction becomes their immediate and preferable choice in escaping from the sense of meaninglessness and existential frustration. Related studies show that people with a better meaning of life decreased their frequency and amount of drug addiction and substance abuse at (Waisburg & Porter, 1994; Wright, 2013)

Meaning of Life in the Process of Addiction

For persons with substance abuse, most of them have a poor meaning of life in their prolonged process of addiction. Firstly, before of their substance abuse, many of them have already encountered numerous frustration and difficulties in time to an extent that they think they cannot live a life with meaning and purpose. To free from that sort of ontological and existence frustration, they turn to drug for temporary release and immediate substitute. However, the more they engage in drug addiction and substance abuse, the more meaningless and hopeless they become. Finally, their own sense of existence is also deeply threatened. They sacrifice and loss their bodily health, they loss or quit their normal job, they betray or loss the trust of their family members and friends, and they loss their normal and healthy self-identity in the prolonged process of substance abuse. They fully acknowledge that apart from substance abuse, they are in fact, entirely meaningless and worthless. Thus, in the process of recovery, their meaning of life must be restored. Otherwise, even though their drug addiction is detoxified, sooner or later, their deep sense of ontological emptiness and meaninglessness will certainly push them to re-engage in chronic drug addiction and substance abuse. In this chapter, the writer tries to describe the importance of change of meaning of life in persons with substance abuse. Its implications to integrated motivational interviewing are also described.

The Importance of Meaning of Life to Human Being

A Multi-dimensional Articulation of Meaning of Life

Meaning of life has long been the concern of scholars and professionals. There are many interpretations of the meaning of life. I can be a philosophical interpretation of the values of human being in the society. It can be an ultimate search for meaning in religions. It can be a connection with supernatural beings. It can be a presentation of values of life in fiction, movies, and artwork. Finally, it also can be an articulation of human values in defending one's country, maintaining morality, securing righteousness and presenting of love to our beloved one. Yip (2012) has a multi-dimensional summary of meaning of life as follows:

1. As a Scientific Articulation (as a materialistic existence, different interpretation, driving forces, final cause of everyone.)(Cottingham, 2003; Artistole, Physics, 325 BC)
2. As a Religious Christian Articulation (positive axiologyical meaning – intrinsic values, teleological meaning – achievable and non-trivial, both meaning in Christ)

(Following Christ as deprived living, as being despised and being offensive to dominant society) (Quinn, 2005; Kieikegaard, 1991)

3. As a question for self-reflection (meaning of life in encounter certain condition, values and worthlessness of one's existence, meaning of life of mankind, ontological meaning of life in universe) (Wohlgment, 1988)
4. From Repetitive Meaninglessness to Meaningful Living and Existence (life is highly meaningless, find ways to deal with meaninglessness, meaning of existence in doing things rather than consequences, once purpose is attained, sense of meaninglessness may come back and another purpose needs to strive for) (Taylor, 1970)
5. Being moral and intellectual (activity of the soul, contemplative activity, the search of wisdom, should not related to goals and attainment, leisure related activities and true self manifested in these activities) (Aristotle, 1962)
6. Being happy and playful (seeking for real can be creative playfulness and play rather than goals and purposes or repetitive and boring work) (Schlick, 1974)
7. Meaning of life ascribed in Suffering (Frankl, 1984)
    a. The will of meaning (unique and specific, must fulfill by individual)
    b. Existential frustration (question about values. meaning of existence)
    c. Noogenic neuroism (frustrated by unpleasant encounter in life)
    d. Noodynamics (inner tension rather equilibrium in search of meaning)
    e. Existential Vacuum (Loss of instinct and tradition, a state of ontological boredom)
    f. Essence of Existence (meaning of existence if one can live a second time) (served ones beloved persons, actualizing oneself, creating work or doing a deed, unavoidable suffering
    g. Meaning of love (one essence of existence interact with others)
    h. Meaning of suffering
    i. Life transitories. (Yip, 2012: 406)

Based on above mentioned multi-dimensional articulation, the writer tries to articulate various related elements in articulation of meaning of life. They are:

1. Meaning of Life as a Struggle for Survival
2. A Connection of the Infinite
3. An Ultimate Insight and Wisdom
4. Sense of Ultimate and Ontological Existence
5. Sense of Continuous Existence
6. Constant Search for Meaning of Life.

Meaning of Life as a Sense of Existence

Meaning of life is crucial for every human being. It encompasses our sense of immediate existence. Every moment, we need to engage or involve in any related activities or interaction so as to ensure our own sense of existence. Very often, when we are disengaged from such activities, our sense of existence is immediately being questioned and challenged. We feel empty, puzzled and even boring. We are doubtful about where, when, what and how to do next. We need to engage in the next activity so to ensure our sense of existence is being anchored and actualized. In normal daily life, in particular within busy and competitive city life, every moment we have a certain thing, event and person to be involved with in terms of work, education, family life, social life and recreational life. Even if we do not have a tight schedule, within a city life, there are plenty of enjoyment, recreation and issues to be involved. We think, we act, we feel and we acknowledge our own existence within all these engagement. However, once we are free from a busy city life and we are being excluded from work, from education, from family or/and from friend, we immediately loss our own meaning and sense of existence. We need our type of involvement to confirm our existence. It can be spontaneous entertainment such as watching movie, playing internet or electronic games, and social interacting. Strictly speaking, it is a kind of phenomenological and ontological existence. In which individual find meaning out spontaneous and continuous involvement.

Meaning of Life as a Struggle for Survival

Meaning of life can also exist in a form of struggle for collective or individual survival. It can be a clerk who works very hard under an oppressive and bullying work setting to struggle for a minimal wage so that s/he can support the daily living of his/her family. It can also be an industrial worker who works 14 hours a day and seven days a week to earn enough money for his/her children. It can be a soldier who fights bravely with his enemies so to save his life. It is common that when one struggles for survival or when one's life and existence is under severely threat, s/he greatly treasures the values of life is to survive under adverse environment. Within traumas, suffering, hardship, terminal illness and warfare, every moment of existence, life or death, kill or being killed, existence or vanishing is of crucial importance to the individual. Under that sort of conditions, the individual uses or exhausts his/her physical, mental and psychic energy to save his/her life or maintain his/her sense of existence. All these are traumatic experiences for the individual. The more the individual goes through traumatic experiences, the more s/he becomes detached from external reality as it is predictably painful and traumatic and the more s/he becomes egocentric and apathetic to others' needs. S/he may be fixated to the belief that life for sake of minimal survival and self-interest, anyone who hinder his/her minimal survival should be suppressed, removed or even diminished. S/he becomes highly and even over alert to others' ignorance, criticism, rejection, exclusion and attack. S/he may appear as relaxed and polite, but deep down in his/her mind; s/he may manipulate every chance to ensure s/he is safe, secure and able to get his/her own benefit.

Interaction between Minimal Survival and Sense of Existence

This sort of surviving meaning of life is different from phenomenological meaning of life. The former is an intensive struggle for minimal survival. The latter is a continuous sense of existence within related activities. Within an intensive struggle of minimal survival, the individual is fully engaged in any person, event, activity and relationship that focus on survival. The individual is highly selective, extremely focusing and responsive to anything that increase his/her chance of survival. In many case, his/her normal sense of phenomenological existence is hindered or suppressed, so that the individual can focus all his/her mental and physical energy to struggle for survival. As an opposite, if the individual normal phenomenological sense of existence is fully exercised, the individual is in a stage of security and regularity, his/her sense of struggle for minimal survival is lessened, his/her awareness to related risks and hindrance for his life and survival is decreased. Facing traumas, hardships, and sufferings in life, individuals may be involved in a tough stage of struggling from survival. Their sense of immediate existence is thus suppressed and hindered. Gradually, they may become more and more detached from external reality and in relating to others. Unless, their traumatic experiences, memories and fear are properly ventilated and comforted by supportive significant others, they may not able to retain and restore their spontaneous sense of immediate existence.

Meaning of Life as a Sense of Ultimate and Ontological Existence

Meaning of life can also interpreted as a sense of ultimate and ontological existence. It is not a sense of immediate sense of existence and a sense of minimal survival. Instead, it is totality of meaning in one's whole life. A rumination of what one has done and experienced in his/her childhood, adolescence and adulthood. Behind the rumination is a full articulation of meaning and worth all these life long effort and experiences. It is a deep evaluation of one's past and present with a projection towards the future. Within this sort of evaluation, one is searching for his/her ontological sense of existence. For example, a poor single mother has worked very hard to bring up her two sons. If her two sons are very smart, have good academic performance, good career and show good respect and care to her, she certainly feels what she has struggled in the past has a definite return in the present and in future. Her meaning of life and ontological security and existence is worthwhile and meaningful. However, if her two sons are rebellious, have bad academic performance, poor career and do not show any respect and care to her, she certainly feels what she has struggled in the past is in vain. She feels empty, meaningless and worthless for her whole life. The sense of ultimate sense of ontological existence is deep and profoundly linked with one's sense of hope, spirituality and urge for eternity. It sparkles our urge for connection with god, religion, infinite and universe. It enables us to search for purpose in our life. There may be several levels for meaning of life. The lowest level (Level 1) is the endeavor for materialistic attainment, accumulation of wealth and fortune. It is full engagement in investment, trying all means including those illegal and immoral ones to get money, and riding others' wealth and fortune. The next level (Level 2) is self-actualization of one's sense of self-worth, identity and image. It can be using one whole life to achieve high attainment in sport, physical exercises, academic performance, promotion in career and being respected by others. The high level (Level 3) is living for the sake of taking care, bringing up and showing concern to others. It can be one's children, aging parents, students, spouses and other persons with special needs. The highest level (Level 4) is sacrificing oneself for the benefit of others. It can be a solider sacrificing his life to protect his country from the invasion of enemies. It can be a mother sacrificing her life to save her children. It can be a committed missionary sacrificing his/her life to spread gospel to other deprived areas. Thus, meaning of life in terms of ultimate ontological existence is the manifestation of spirituality in life. It determines ones' sense of ontological security, meaningfulness and inner psychic and mental energy in facing various types of suffering, hardship and traumas in life.

Meaning of Life as a Constant Search for Meaning

Meaning of life as constant search for meaning is a combination of a sense of ultimate ontological existence and a continuous sense of existence. That means in every moment in life, one has to be engaged in activities such as social interaction, work, learning, house chores and observation and response to immediate social and physical environment. In doing so, one also reflects whether or not these engagement and involvement are really meaningful in connection with his/her ultimate sense of ontological existence.

For example, after a long day's work, one may feel dreadful tired and fatigue both physically and mentally. However, if the work is very positive and constructive such as helping others to work through difficulties and hardships, achieving a breakthrough in one's work and academic performance, educating one's children to do a good job, or winning an important games, one certainly find it is meaningful and worthwhile. However, if the work is boring or stressful such as being blamed or oppressed by one's boss unreasonably, reading or attaining a boring lecture, watching an aimless movie or failing to do something important, one will find it is meaningless and worthless. It is a waste of time and effort in doing all this. The sense of meaninglessness or meaningfulness not only a spontaneous reflection of what one has done recently or within a period of time, it is also a reconnection of this with one's meaning and purpose in life. So that one can have a deep sense of worth in every moment of life or things one has attained recently or within a period of time. It is a connection of the present with one' past with a hope into the future.

It is a sense of completeness and hope in one's life with what one have done in the current moment. The connection of past, current and future would finally make individuals get a feeling that his/her life is meaningful and worthwhile. As an opposite, if there are discrepancies among individual current endeavor, past experience and effort, the individual may feel painful and intolerable.

Meaning of Life as a Connection with the Infinite

In the search for ultimate sense of ontological existence and a constant search of meaning, individuals always feel that things are unpredictable and uncontrollable. Human beings are weak and complicated. Even the most powerful one may one day become powerless, the most strong one may be weak, the rich may become poor, as well as the healthy can be sick. In dealing with all that, individuals feel that s/he is weak, helpless and even impotent. Facing all that, human beings embrace an inherent urge to worship god, connect with the infinite, and actualize his/her spirituality. In doing so, an individual exists in the world not solely by himself/herself but also with others, in particular with the connection of a powerful omnipotent god.

Also, his/her existence in this world is not within a short period of time but with possibility to be eternal and everlasting. With the connection of an infinite and powerful god, and with possibility of an eternal spiritual life, the individual, no longer feels lonely, helpless, powerless and hopeless even in times of hardship, suffering and traumas. The more s/he is connected with the powerful and omnipotent god and believes in eternal life, the more s/he feels hopeful, powerful, capable and substantial in facing his/her hardship, trauma and suffering in life.

As a consequence, with the connection of the infinite, the individual assumes that after current hardship, suffering and traumas in life, there will be happy eternal life in the future. Also, what s/he has done in his/her life will be counted in his/her eternal life. Life is not a full stop after death. Life is not an unfair endeavor in which the wicked is rich and the sincere is poor. Life is not empty in which no matter how hard one struggles, his/her effort will be in vain after his/her death. Within the connection and belief of a powerful god and the infinite, life is still fair and worthwhile. If one does good work, s/he will be rewarded in the eternal life. If one does bad work, s/he will be punished endlessly in the hell.

Meaning of Life as an Ultimate Insight and Wisdom

As mentioned above, meaning of life can be described as a constant search for meaning in life, sense of ultimate ontological existence, minimal survival and continuous sense of existence and connection of the infinite. The more one experience all these, the more one embrace an ultimate insight and wisdom in life. It is a sense of totality and a sense of know how and what to do in the future. It is also a sense of transcendence in life. This kind of ultimate ontological wisdom can be illustrated in religious and spiritual literature. For example in the Holy Bible, the book of

> 1:2 Vanity of vanities, said the Preacher, vanity of vanities; all is vanity.
> 1:3 What profit hath a man of all his labour which he taketh under the sun?
> 1:4 One generation passeth away, and another generation cometh: but the earth abideth forever. 1:5 The sun also ariseth, and the sun goeth down, and hasteth to his place where he arose. (The Holy Bible, King James Version: Ecclesiastes, Chapter 1)

The Book of Ecclesiastes is written by King Solomon. He was a king full of wealth and wisdom. He had experienced the most luxurious life and enjoyment. He had been a king working very hard to serve almighty God and his people. He had built the temple of God but also build temples for idols. His riches were countless and his wisdom was profound and powerful.

However, after experiencing of all these, by the end of his life, he began to realize that all these were meaningless. All things vanished no matter how much fortunes, wisdoms we accumulated and how hard we worked to maintain them. He recognized that apart from God, nothing is long last. Things come and things go. Human beings die and are born. Events happen and vanish.

Similar to King Solomon, anyone who had plenty of life experiences, especially those experiences of fluctuation of ups and downs, begins to formulate his/her profound meaning in life. A man who gains a lot of money but finally losses it realizes that money is not long lasting and accumulative. When he sees someone who struggles very hard in accumulating wealth and fortune, he embraces a transcendent view that this struggle and hard work is meaningless and unnecessary.

Totality of Meaning of Life

These several forms of meaning of life are closely related to one another and equip the individual to face various conditions in life. In times of extreme adversity and life and death situation, the individual struggles hard for survival. In times of hardship and suffering, the individual needs to connect with the infinite so that s/he can gain extra spiritual power and support to face hardship and sufferings.

In normal daily life, every moment the individual needs to have a sense of continuous sense of existence so that s/he can feel his/her own being. Otherwise, s/he may feel deeply bored and being excluded from the outside world. Coupled with the spontaneous sense of existence is the continuous search for meaning in life in every daily activity we engage. We try to compare the meaning, values and sense of ultimate and ontological existence. It is a kind of purpose and values in our whole life in which we struggle and strive hard for. Within our life long endeavor, we are living for materialistic attainment, actualizing ourselves, serving and nurturing our significant others, or contributing and sacrificing ourselves to our, religion, mission, society and/or wellbeing of mankind.

The constant search for meaning, the sense of continuous existence, the sense of ultimate and ontological existence work closely together to shape our direction of life, to give us a sense of being of every moment in life and to construct our phenomenological consciousness of ourselves.

We survive and give meaning to ourselves and things surrounding us. Within this spontaneous endeavor, we develop our insight and wisdom. We know why we survive. We conclude what purposes is our lives for. We formulate our own view towards ourselves, others and our society.

Gradually, we beware that in our lives sufferings, hardships, traumas and accidents are unpredictable and uncontrollable. We also beware that life is far more than secular desires and attainment. We have doubt in where we go and what happen after death. We harbor strong spiritual needs and have a strong urge to connect with gods and the infinite. Only by doing so, we can have hope and meaning in facing uncontrolled hardship and suffering in our lives.

It is clear that all sorts of meaning of life are closely related to one another. The sense of ultimate and ontological existence, the search for meaning and the sense of continuous existence work together to give the individual a sense of existence, an anchor in life and a direction what to do in the present and in the future. Within various situations, these three mechanisms manifest in different ways.

In times of extreme crises, risks and emergency, the individual struggles for minimal survival. In times of hardship, trauma and suffering, the individual tries his/her best to connect with the infinite. In evaluating one's whole life and past experiences, one develops one's ultimate wisdom and insight in life. All these can be represented in the following figure.

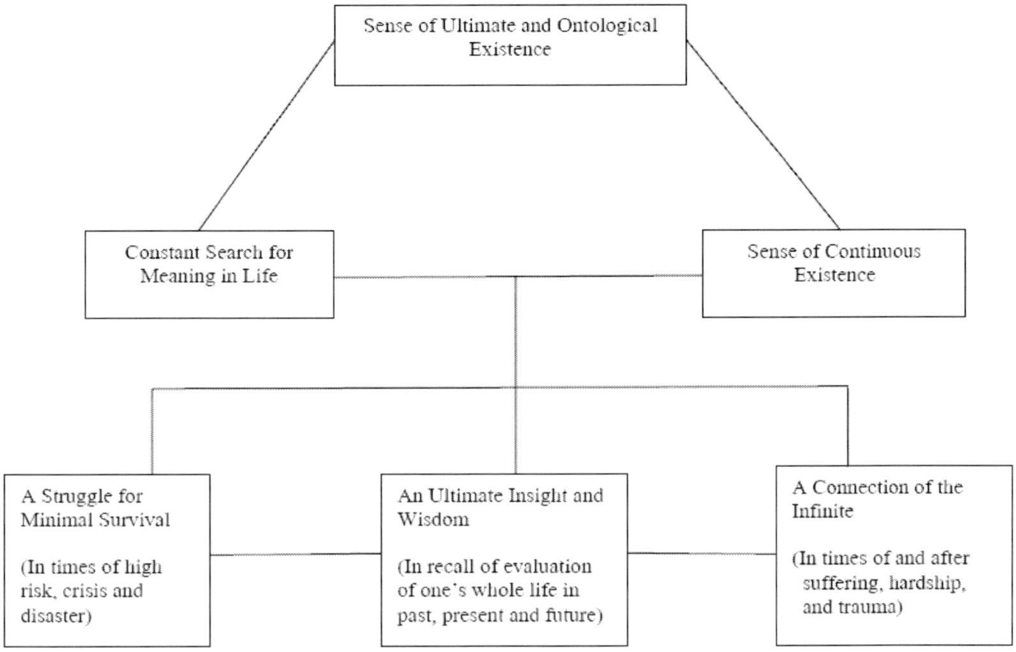

FRANKL' SEARCH FOR MEANING OF LIFE

From Will to Meaning in Life to Existential Vacuum

From the above figure and description, it is clear that meaning of life is so important that every human being has an inherent will to meaning in life. Frankl (1984) affirmed that it is a will to meaning. The will to meaning is very powerful and embraces the following natures:

1. The will to meaning (the primary motivation in life and not a secondary rationalization of instinctual drives.
2. The meaning is unique and specific, must be achieved by one only).
3. Men search for meaning to achieve significance which will satisfy their own will to meaning.
4. Men are prepared to sacrifice and even to die for their own meaning.
5. Men may camouflage their meaning of life by superficial and secular attainment; the deep concern of full meaning of life is covered by inner conflict. Once these inner conflicts are removed, they still aspire for a full meaning of life. (Frankl, 1984:122)

The will to meaning of life is so powerful as meaning of life is a full combination of constant search for meaning, ontological and phenomenological sense of existence, connection with the infinite, an intensive struggle for minimal survival and attainment of prolonged insight in life. However, in times of being camouflaged by secular pursuit, conflicts and hardship in life, individual's will to meaning is hindered. It makes him/her feel highly uncomfortable. According to Frankl (1962), it is a kind of 'Noogenic Neurosis' in which the existential frustration is intensified and diffused to every aspects of life. It consists of the following characteristics:

Noogenic Neurosis (Frankl, 1962: 123-126)

a. existential frustration end up with noogenic neurosis
b. it does not emerge from conflicts of drives and instinct, it emerge from existential problems
c. the will of meaning may be frustrated by some unpleasant encounter in life
d. individuals are unable to fulfill his meaning of life
e. individuals are continuously stay in a state of frustration in an aimless but continuous search for meaning of life (Yip, 2009)
f. Individuals are neurotic in search for real and deep meaning but replace and compensate their need by more immediate and secular attainment (Yip, 2009)
g. The secular and immediate attainment cannot satisfy one's inner search for meaning so the search and eagerness still goes on and on non-stopping. (Yip, 2009) (E. g., the replace of love and dignity by the endless search of corrupted power.)

That means, in times of existential frustration in which the individual is fully disguised and burdened by life difficulties and frustration and inner conflicts, his/her constant search for meaning, ontological and phenomenological sense of existence, connection with the infinite, an intensive struggle for minimal survival and attainment of prolonged insight in life were greatly hindered. They become an intensive but concealed urge and endeavor. The stronger is this concealed urge and endeavor, the more frustrated the individual become existentially. On one hand, the individual questions about his/her own values, meaning and state of existence. On the other hand, their direct search for meaning and values are hindered and suffocated. The existential frustration turns into a state of 'noogenic neurosis. The individual engages in a state of approach and avoidance complex in his/her will to meaning. The individual tries to engage in superficial engagement in secular attainment, addiction as well as other pathological behavior so as to conceal his/her will to meaning. However, more the individual engages in these superficial engagement and pathological behaviors, the more s/he feels empty and meaningless. Finally, the individual may turn into a state of 'Noo-dynamics'. Frankl (1984) refused to put a pathological label on all these superficial engagement and substitutes. He affirmed that it is a state of inner tension pushing the individual to search for ultimate meaning in life. This tension should be regarded as the pre-requisites for one's mental health. That is a tension between what one has already achieved and what one still ought to accomplish, or what one is and what one should become. Frankly (1984) affirmed this as noo-dynamics. That is the source of inner psychic energy for one to strive for attainment of his/her unique meaning of life. It motivates the individual to re-orientate his/her own current situation to a better meaning of life that suits his/her own needs and aspiration. The inner psychic energy transforms the will of meaning to manifest different types of meaning in action. In times of accident, trauma and disaster, the inner psychic energy is greatly intensified and facilitates the individual to struggle for minimal survival. In times of normal daily life, the inner psychic energy is diffused into every daily activity and involvement helping the individual to formulate his sense of continuous existence. It is also a constant search for meaning in which the individual consumes his/her psychic energy to reflect what s/he has already in recent moment is meaningful or not to his life. The inner psychic energy is limited and the will of meaning can be exhausted in times of prolonged hardship, suffering and frustration. At that moment, the individual needs to re-charge his/her inner psychic energy and will to meaning to connection of the infinite. With that sort of connection, the individual's will to meaning, inner psychic energy and state of noo-dynamic becomes highly intensified and durable in facing prolonged difficulties, extreme hardship and severe trauma in life. It makes the individual harbor hope to face the painful presence and unforeseeable future. In times of reviewing what one has done in life, particularly when one has a long struggle or endeavor in working through difficulties and hardship or when is growing older and older, the psychic energy is the state of noo-dynamic will enable the individual to look for ultimate insight and wisdom as well as to formulate his/her sense of ultimate and ontological existence. In doing so, the individual is actually re-directing and re-focusing his/her psychic energy towards a clear goal and purpose in which the individual can be fully engage in evaluating his/her past, living with the presence and looking for the future.

In the state of existential frustration, individual enters into a state of noogenic neurosis in which his/her search for meaning cannot be actualized. Then, his/her will to meaning becomes intensified to a state of noo-dynamics in which s/he earnestly engages in various forms of endeavor for meaning of life. Very often, the endeavor can be successfully attained in terms of manifestation of continuous existence, connection with the infinite, search of meaning in related experiences, and sense of substantial ontological existence and good security even in times of adversity, hardship and risks. However, there can be times when the struggle and endeavor are finally in vain making the individual engages into *a state of existential vacuum.* Frankl (1984) described this in the following details:

> 'Existential Vacuum
>
> In the search for meaning and the will for meaning, individuals may capture within an inherent an existential vacuum. That is a loss of basic animal instincts as well as a loss of one's tradition. The loss of these important inherent instincts and traditions, individuals becomes an ontological vacuum. In this vacuum, the individual does not have his/her own ways to search for his/her own meaning of life. It exists in a form of boredom. Or individual compensate this sort of ontological boredom by involvement in meaningless activities. It can be a will to power, a will to money or an involvement in secular stimulation such as sex, addiction and substance abuse. It is a vicious cycle, the more one involves in noogenic neurosis and compensatory activities, the more serious the boredom becomes. For persons with addiction, substance abuse, depression and other mental problems, such boredom and existential vacuum is common. Only with this vacuum being filled, can their mental problems be resolved. (Frankl, 1984: 132)

Essence of Existence and Meaning of Love and Suffering

In no way, the state of noogenic neurosis, noodynamics and existential vacuum is tolerable for the individual, the will to meaning influences the individual to have a vigorous search and actualize the essence of existence. Frankl (1984) described the essence of existence is to live fully in one own life. It resembles to what described mentioned in terms of the ultimate and ontological sense of existence. It transcends one's past, present and future.

> 'Facing all these existential vacuum, noogenic neurosis and noodynamics, the essence of existence is deeply needed by any individual. It is an attitude towards one's life regarding one can live a second time. It assumes that the present can pass and the past can be changed so that one can live fully in his/her own life. The essence of existence can be actualized in various ways such as:
> 1. serving one's beloved persons;
> 2. actualizing oneself;
> 3. creating a work or doing a deed (achievement and accomplishment);
> 4. experiencing something or encountering someone who is good, genuine, loving or being loved;
> 5. facing unavoidable suffering.' (Frankl, 1984:136)

Meaning of Love

Frankly (1984) asserted that the meaning of love and meaning of suffering are vital for individual to construct his/her essence of existence. Without the meaning of love and suffering, individuals become a vacuum of existence with prolonged and chronic existential frustration. The meaning of life in Frankl (1984) asserted that love is a connection of one's essence of existence to another one's essence in life. With love connection to beloved persons, the individual is able to anchor his/her essential traits and features. The loving person can actualize his/her potentials and ability fully in life.

In other words, the individual needs to formulate his/her essence of existence with love connection with others beloved persons. If the love connection is being lost or terminated, one's own essence of existence is being threatened. It is common and understandable that the loss of one's beloved persons and the loss of beloved persons' love are painful and unbearable for the individual. S/he feels sad, frustrated and empty. In some cases, the individual may even harbour suicidal ideation and attempts. His/her essence of existence is thus deeply threatened.

In fact, the will of meaning being transformed into constant search for meaning, ontological and phenomenological sense of existence, connection with the infinite, intensive struggle for minimal survival and attainment of prolonged insight in life are closely connected with the meaning of love. That means, with the meaning of love, being loved or showing love to our beloved one, one can struggle through hardship. Without the meaning of love, one may loss the courage to face hardship and suffering. When our beloved one faces life difficulties and illness, we pray to God and affirm our connection with the infinite. With the togetherness of beloved persons, one feels every moment of life is meaningful and enjoyable. Without the presence of them, one feels every moment is boring or even empty. For many persons their ultimate sense of ontological existence enable them to bring up their beloved children, to serve his aged mother, and to devote to their beloved God, religion, profession and country. With love, one can have profound meaning, insight and wisdom towards life. The insight and wisdom is that love, hope and faith are far more important than secular attainment and materialistic ownership. Without love, one's insight and wisdom in life is restrained to actualization of one's secular desires, attainment of secular objects and achievement. In fact, throughout the whole life, everyone is searching for genuine love, empathy, care and hope among supportive ones. If all these are reached and connected, one certainly feels that his/her whole life is entirely meaningful. If all these are not reachable or lost one certainly feels that his/her whole life is empty and meaningless, s/he will keep on searching until the end of his/her life.

Meaning of Suffering

Frankl (1984) affirmed that meaning of suffering and hardship is crucial in the meaning of one's life. Frankl (1984) was one of survivor in the death camp of the German Army in the Second World War. Within this prolonged and severe torture in the death camp, he tried his best to make meaning of every moment by recalling the past memory of his beloved family members.

By doing so, he was able to survive within numerous horrible experiences of torture and trauma. Frankl (1984) illustrated that with concrete meaning of suffering, the individual is able to manifest the deepest and most unique human potentials. Those with profound meaning of sufferings are able to transform personal tragedy into a triumph, to turn a predicament into human achievement. With meaning in one's suffering, his/her sense of suffering will thus be reduced (Frankl, 1984: 138). For example, a mother worked very hard to live a hand to mouth life so that she could bring up his three children. Her husband died only when their children was very small. In the whole process, she suffered a lot. She worked day and night and she had to take care of their three children. She felt dreadfully tied and fatigue. Even when she was sick, she had to work. When she was bullied by others, she still has to tolerate. Sometimes, when she could not earn enough money to support his family, she even had to starve so that she could let her children eat. She suffered a lot. However, she found profound meaning in his suffering. She suffered for the sake of bringing up her children. Whenever she was tortured and bullied by others, she thought about her children. When she was tired and fatigue, her love towards her children enlightened her giving her extra mental and physical energy to endure and sustain her. It was clear the meaning of suffering is sparkled by the meaning of love. In suffering, one not only feels unhappy but is also being happy because of one's own unhappiness. That means, in suffering there is dual hardships. One is the suffering itself. Another one is suffer because of one's suffering. That means a sad person is not only sad about unhappy events in life. S/he is also sad about his/her own sadness. Similarly, a depressive person is depressive because of the loss of beloved person. S/he is also depressed about his/her own depression. It is a double loop of suffering enabling one to interpret the meaning of suffering. Within the process of suffering, the individual asks why s/he suffers so much, what makes him/her suffers, and whether s/he deserves the suffering. If the individual cannot find sufficient meaning for his/her sufferings, s/he is angry and rejects his/her experiences in sufferings. As suffering is unavoidable and inescapable, one must learn how to search meaning in suffering. In search for meaning of suffering, One is actually questioning and articulating how his/her own meaning of suffering. That is the meaning of meaning of sufferings (The super meaning of suffering). Only if the super meaning of sufferings is actualised, can one feel suffering is bearable and meaningful. It can be

1. for the sake of sacrifice of ones we love
2. for our religious beliefs in fulfilling the ultimate truth
3. for ensuring ourselves that we have really tried our very best to pursue our very best in doing 1 & 2. (Frankl, 1984:162)

The crucial point is this search must be done by the individual himself/herself. The meaning of suffering is firmly articulated so that the suffering becomes a meaningful and happy experience.

Meaning of Life and Life Transitoriness

Frankl (1984) described that the meaning of life in terms of meaning of suffering, essence of existence, meaning of love as well as nooneurosis and noodynamics, changes with individuals' life transitory. It merges with one's own perception, memories and articulation of the past, present and future. In the past, one's memories are stored including suffering and pleasant experiences. For unpleasant memories, one feels sad and regrettable. For pleasant memories, one feels happy and enlightened. In the present, individuals may be frustrated by current difficulties or enlightened by happiness. Within current happiness, one enjoys life and time flies. Within existing suffering and torture, time freezes and it seems that torture and suffering are endless. Facing the predictable future, one may feel insecure or be contented with forth coming blessings and fortune. If the future is unpredictable and sad, one may lose hope in his/her whole life. In other words, the struggle for minimal survival, a constant search of meaning, a continuous sense of existence, an ultimate insight and wisdom, a connection of the infinite and a sense of ultimate and ontological existence should all concern with the perception, memories and articulation of the past, present and the future.

The meaning of life depends on whether one can have a positive and consistent meaning in articulating and interpreting the past, the present and the future. It also depends on an individual in making a sensible choice in actualizing his/her present potentials, in recalling and accepting the realities happened in the past, and determining to live the fullest in the future. The meaning of life anchor in the urges for wholeness, whereness and meaningfulness of the past, the present and the future (Frankl, 1984).

Meaning of Life and the Urge for Wholeness, Whereness and Meaningfulness

Frankl (1984) asserted the search for meaning consists of three crucial elements. This is the urge for wholeness, whereness and meaningfulness. The urge of wholeness is gestalt with three sorts of integrations. Firstly, it is the integration between past, present and future. Secondly, it is the integration between thinking, feeling and behaviours. Thirdly, it is the integration between the expectation and attainment.

In the first type of integration, as mentioned above, individual has a consistent sense of meaning within different period of time. For example, a person who was a good son with a good father in the past, a good father with a good son in the present and will be a good grandfather with a good grandson in the coming future certainly feels highly meaningful and consistent in his whole life.

In the second type of integration, the individual acts, thinks and feels coherently. That is integration within and outside a person. S/he does not have conflicts between his/her words and deeds, s/he is not a hypocrite, nor s/he dissociates his action from his/her feeling. That means, if s/he is angry with someone. Emotionally, s/he can express such angry feeling. Cognitively and morally, s/he can justify his/her anger. Behaviourally, s/he can act out such anger or s/he can punish or take revenge on the person s/he dislikes (Frankl, 1984; Yip, 2012).

In the third type of integration, individual feel gratified as s/he has reached what s/he expected in his/her life. A student feels happy as s/he has successfully completed the course. A worker feels deeply enlightened as s/he has finally promoted to be the supervisor of the team of which s/he has expected for years. A mother feels extremely impressed as her daughter has married a good husband. What one expects is what one attains is, no doubt, the happiest experiences in the world. At that moment, individual asserts life is meaningful and enjoyable. The longer and harder one struggle one can attain his/her expectation, the more meaningful and enjoyable s/he feel at the final moment.

Based on Frankl's insight on life transitoriness, Yip (2012) further develops it into the following poem:

The Past, the Present and the Future (YIP, 2012: 412)

The immediate existence is full of endless responsibilities and spontaneous action but also with substantiality and actuality as we act, we feel, we speak, we see, and we smell.

Time passes away and anchors our work, our deed and our suffering in which we triumphed, we failed, we enjoyed and we feared, we loved and we hated.

Future is full of uncertainties and doubts to be unveiled. It can be full of hardships and difficulties, but it can also be plenty of opportunities and challenges.

When the predictable future is uncertain and stressful, enjoy our current livelihood and our past triumphs towards sufferings.

The past can hurt us previously but cannot confine our actions in the present and our extension in the future.

When the immediate realities are painful we can dip ourselves in our triumph in our past sufferings.

When the past was traumatic, we can rely on the livelihood of the present.

The present can make us busy and breathless but cannot ignore our experiences in the past and limit our hope in the future.

The future can be insecure and even stressful but cannot suppress our substantiality and actuality in the present and our triumphs and joys in the past.

So live the fullest in the present, ruminate your experiences in the past, enjoy the challenges in the future.

In fact, various component of meanings of life and the will to meaning, meaning of love and meaning of suffering, as well as noo-genic neurosis, noodynamics and life transitory as well as the urge for wholeness are all inter-related with one another. All these can be represented in the following figure.

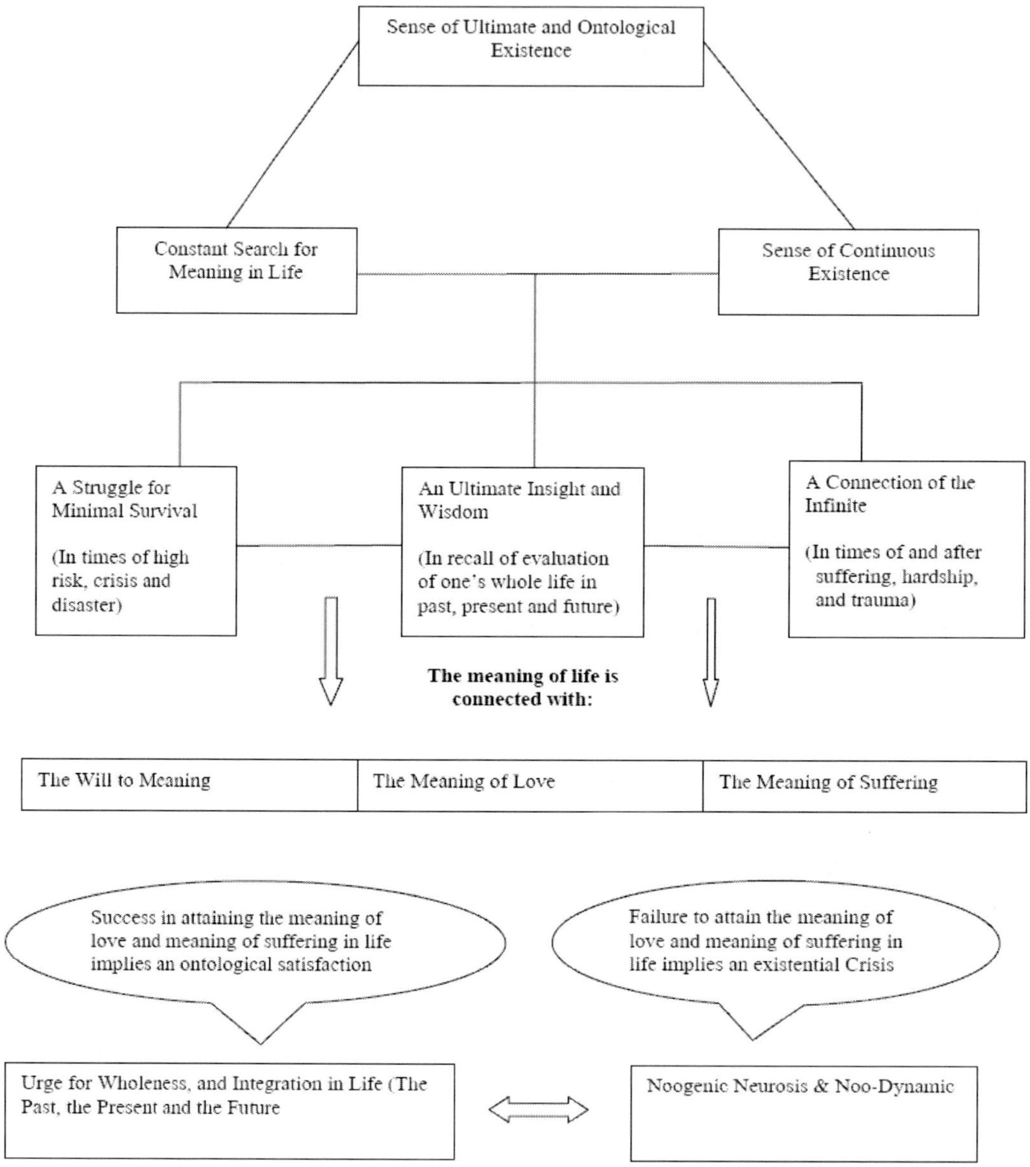

A Comprehensive Articulation of Meaning of Life.

MEANING OF LIFE, DRUG ADDICTION AND SUBSTANCE ABUSE

Drug Addiction and the Sense of Existence in the Meaning of Life

For persons with addiction, they usually have problems in their sense of existence. They may have frustration and even traumas in life. In facing that sort of traumas and frustration, they feel empty, puzzled, and even dreadfully bored. In some cases, the constant re-bounce and triggering of unpleasant past traumatic experiences make the individual feels highly intolerable and uncomfortable. They usually have no one to turn to or they do not believe that others can ease out their inner pain and emptiness. In doing so, their sense of continuous existence is being threatened. Instead, they continuously feel that their lives are entirely empty, painful and meaningless. To ease out all these, they may regard addiction and/or substance abuse as the way to escape from their painful sense of reality. Within the process substance abuse, they absorb in the sensory stimulation by the drug. It can be an intensive sense of euphoria from taking stimulants such as amphetamines and cocaine. It can also be an intensive sense of dysphoria from abusing barbiturates, alcohol and minor tranquilizers such as GHB. It can be a sense of out of body experiences by inhaling ketamine. In doing so, the individual's continuous sense of ontologically meaninglessness, emptiness and painfulness can be shifted to an intensive sense of drug induced senses of excitement, relaxation or transcendence from the painful reality. However, all these senses of excitement, relaxation and transcendence vanish as the effects of the drug diminish. Following this is a return to the meaningless, empty and painful reality in which the individual's continuous sense of existence is deeply threatened. As far as the individual has tasted the sense of relaxation, excitement and/or transcendence from the painful reality, s/he may also become less and less tolerable to the meaningless, empty and painful reality. As a consequence, his/her search for continuous existence may gradually transform into a continuous search for absorption and addiction in drug induced experiences. That means his/her search for continuous existence becomes a continuous search of addictive existence. Only within addictive and substance induced experiences, s/he feels substantial and real. In doing so, s/he gradually increases the dosage of substance abuse or s/he tried different types of drugs or mixed drugs. The increase of intensity and involvement in drug addiction implies that the individual becomes more and more detached from the reality. As a consequence, as the drug addiction prevails, the individual's feeling, thinking and acting are related to substance abuse. S/he may even sacrifice his/her health, her family relationship, her self-esteem and dignity in craving for drug. Continuous sense of existence with drug addiction tends to be his/her only way of existence.

Drug Addiction and the Struggle for Survival in the Meaning of Life

Meaning of life can exist as a struggle for survival. Everyone needs to struggle for survival in times of his/her life is under severe threat. For the individual, the experiences in struggling for survival, is in fact, highly traumatic and painful. To escape from all these traumatic recalls and re-bounces, it seems drug addiction and substance abuse is a good mean to numb all these traumatic senses and memories. Only by numbing all these painful memories and traumatic recall, the individual can keep himself/herself survive in his/her daily functioning.

Drug Addiction and Sense of Ultimate and Ontological Existence in the Meaning of Life

For persons with substance abuse and drug addiction, their life experiences can be listed and described as follows:

1. Experiences in childhood, adolescence and/or adulthood before onset of drug addiction and substance abuse.
2. Experiences in childhood, adolescence and/or adulthood after onset of drug addiction and substance abuse.

For the second type of experiences (after the onset of drug addiction and substance abuse), it can be divided into two types:

2a: Experiences in life without any relationship with drug addiction and substance abuse, including:
   i. Normal daily experiences (such as working, accommodation and social interaction) without being affected by substance abuse.
   ii. Normal development in life span such as childhood, adolescence and adulthood.
   iii. Normal manifestation of one's own meaning of life, self-identity, interest, potentials and strengths.
   iv. Normal evaluation and articulation of life experiences.

2b. Experiences in life with direct relationship with drug addiction and substance abuse, including:
   i. Experiences in the process of drug addiction and substance abuse (immediately before, during, and immediately after the drug addiction).
   ii. Experiences in getting and craving for related drugs and substance.
   iii. Experiences in relating with drug related peers and persons.
   iv. Experiences in suffering from the impacts and effects of drugs (physical, social and mental deterioration).
   v. Experiences in the struggle to abstain from drug.

Meaning of Life according to Pattern of Substance Abuse

Within all these experiences, the individual with substance abuse tries to have a deep evaluation of his/her past and present with a projection into the future. S/he is searching for his/her ontological sense of existence. In doing so, s/he is actually comparing and contrast and his experiences in the following ways.

1. Before the onset of substance abuse or before the individual becomes a regular substance abuser, the individual may feel his/her life is full of frustration, meaninglessness and unpredictability in a way that s/he feels that only the experiences in substance abuse can give them a sense of meaning in life.
2. However, the more the individual engages in substance abuse, the more the individual feels that his/her meaning of life is empty, meaningless and worthless and the more s/he needs to engage in substance abuse to get rid of the sense of meaninglessness, emptiness and worthlessness.
3. Gradually, the individual engages in a state of chronic substance abuse and addiction. The individual engages in a state of entire meaninglessness, emptiness and worthlessness. His/her life is full of drug induced traumas, hardship and suffering.

Levels of Meaninglessness in Substance Abuse

In all these reflection and deep rumination, the individual is actually actively comparing experiences before the onset of substance abuse and experiences after the onset of substance abuse. As mentioned before, individual meaning of life in terms of ontological existence can be described into four levels:

Level 1 is the endeavor for materialistic attainment, accumulation of wealth and fortune.
Level 2 is self-actualization of one's sense of self-worth, identity and image.
Level 3 is living for the sake of taking care, bringing up and showing concern to others.
Level 4 is sacrificing oneself for the benefit of others.

For persons with substance abuse, their level of meaning of life is should be far low than those in level 1. That means the level of meaning of life should be divided into two main groups. The first group is level of meaningfulness. The second group is level of meaninglessness. The above mentioned four levels in meaning of life are levels of meaningfulness. The level of meaninglessness in life means that individuals' meaning of life is deteriorating and they live with an empty and meaningless life. With reference to four levels of meaning of life (meaningfulness), related levels in meaninglessness can also divided into 4 levels. They are listed as follows:

Level -1: Despite spontaneous struggle by the individual, his/her endeavor of materialistic attainment is in vain, s/he lives in poor and deprived situation. S/he feels empty and meaningless in life.

Level -2: Despite spontaneous struggle by the individual, s/he loses his/her self-identity and image, s/he feels dreadfully inferior and empty.

Level -3: Despite spontaneous struggle by the individual, s/he is rejected, isolated, neglected and oppressed by others.

Level -4: Despite spontaneous struggle by the individual, s/he needs to maintain minimal survival by committing illegal, immoral and risky deeds and actions.

Within these four levels, for persons with substance abuse, their sense of meaninglessness can be modified as follows:

AD Level -1: Because of spontaneous substance abuse, the individual cannot maintain a normal life in work, family and in social life. S/he lives in poor and deprived situation. S/he feels empty and meaningless in life.

AD Level -2: Because of continuous substance abuse and the craving for drug, the individual loses his/her self-identity and image, s/he feels dreadfully inferior and empty.

AD Level -3: Because of continuous chronic abuse of drug, the individual is rejected, isolated, neglected and oppressed by others.

AD Level -4: Because continuous and chronic drug addiction, the individual has to maintain minimal survival by committing illegal, immoral and risky deeds and actions.

For persons with substance abuse, before the onset of drug addiction, their meaning of life may already be meaningless. The sense of meaninglessness and emptiness is prevailing. It is really intolerable and unbearable. To rid off this sense of meaninglessness, the individual involves in drug addiction. Within the stimulated effects of drug, s/he is temporarily withdrawn from the intensive sense of meaninglessness. Nevertheless, the process of substance abuse does not enable to pull his/her sense of meaningfulness. Instead, it makes him/her even worse. Finally, the individual may gradually pull down from the levels of meaninglessness. S/he may start from level -1, then, gradually decreases to level -2 and onwards. The change of levels of meaning of life for persons with substance abuse can be demonstrated in the following case illustration. Related parties' consensus in using this story for academic purpose was sought. For the sake of confidentiality, related personal information and identity was properly disguised.

> D was an adolescent with substance abuse. He was in a low class family whereas his parents had to struggle very hard to earn a hand to mouth living. At first, D still had good care from their parents as their parents tried to make D and his younger sister to have a decent living. Unfortunately, his father died in a car accident. From that time onward, D's mother had to shoulder the whole family. Despite she worked very hard, they could not have sufficient income to sustain their basic living. She had to work day and night with one full time job as a cleaner and several part time jobs to make the end meet. D was responsible to take care of his younger sister and finished all the household chores. Whenever D's younger sister did something wrong, D was the one to blame for his mother. D felt very unfair and angry with his younger sister. He became rebellious to his mother's command and started to wander around the neighborhood. He joined a delinquent gang and began to engage in drug addiction as well as drug trafficking. His mother was furious about D's delinquent behaviors. She tried to curse and hit him and D fought back. From that time onwards, D did not return home. D fully engaged with his gang. He became an active drug dealer and earned a good sum of money from selling and trafficking drug. With the money earned from drug, he lived a luxurious life. He drove good car, dine in good restaurants and date with beautiful girlfriend. While he enjoyed fully in his luxurious life, he was caught by the police and they charged him for illegal drug dealing and drug trafficking. He was then sentenced for two year imprisonment. In the prison, he felt deep regretted for what he had done in the past. A Christian missionary visited the prison and persuaded D to repent before God. Then, D became a committed Christian. Three years later, after he was discharged from the prison. He dedicated his life to help delinquents.

From this case, it is clear that D experienced various levels of meaning of life. Before the process of substance abuse, D's level meaning of life does not dependent on drug addiction. At first, he had to take care of his younger sister, doing the household chores so that his mother could earn a hand to mouth living for the whole family. That means, when D was a child, his meaning of life reached level 2 (living for the sake of taking care, bringing and showing concern to others). However, he did not receive any appreciation from his mother. Instead, her mother put the blame of her young sister's wrong doing on him making him very angry and frustration. At that moment, his meaning of life dreadfully dropped from level 2 to level -3 (Despite spontaneous struggle, he is rejected, isolated, neglected and oppressed by his mother). That means D felt highly intolerable and unbearable. As a consequence, D needed to depend on drug addiction to rid off his sense of meaninglessness and emptiness as well as his anger towards his mother and sister. Being engaging drug addiction and drug trafficking, D ran away from home. Drug trafficking and dealing made D become rich and live a luxurious life. At that moment, D's meaning of life rose to level 1 (endeavor for materialistic attainment, accumulation of wealth and fortune.). However, spontaneous dependence on drug addiction made D's life depend on drug. Despite he had money to spend, he actually lived a socially deprived life. He was afraid of police. He dared not meet his family members and his previous peers. His social circle was restricted to drug related peers. Thus, at that moment his meaning of life in addiction was confined to AD Level -1 to AD Level -3. Within that sort of levels of meaninglessness of life, D felt empty, meaningless and even frustrating. The only way he could cope with that was by heavily involvement in materialistic attainment, accumulation of wealth and fortune and further heavy drug addiction. It became a vicious circle. The more he engaged in drug addiction, drug trafficking and drug dealing, the more he needed to engage in materialistic attainment and fulfillment of secular desires as well as the more he involved in drug addiction. Finally, he was caught by the police and sentenced to imprisonment. D's meaning of life became entirely meaningless. Despite spontaneous struggle, he was rejected, isolated, neglected and oppressed by others. His minimal survival by committing illegal and immoral drug dealing was also in vain. He was deprived, poor, and being labeled and punished as criminals by the society. At that moment his level of meaninglessness of life should a sum of level -1 (poor and deprived), level -2 (poor self-identity), level -3 (neglected and oppressed). That mean, he was entirely meaningless and empty.

As he becomes poor, deprived and empty with free from drug addiction, he can undergo a vigorous process of self-reflection of his own meaning of life. In doing so, he knows that the endeavor of materialistic attainment, accumulation of wealth and fortune should be finally in vain. He began to recall his previous meaning of life in living for the sake of taking care, bringing up and showing concern to his family life. He might also reflect how meaningless he was in being addictive to drug. Because of drug addiction, he lost his self-image, his materialistic attainment, his peer and his family members. He lived in a deprived environment. He craved for drug and he was controlled by drug. He began to beware that life under the control of drug was aimless. His mother's unfair treatment to him is negligible in comparing with the destructive effects of drug addiction. He started to research his meaning of life in the prison. Fortunately, at that moment, a Christian pastor visited the prison and preached the gospel of Jesus Christ to him. He admitted his sins and asked for the forgiveness of Jesus Christ. He accepted Jesus' salvation and began to be a committed Christian. He devoted his meaning of life to serve others and save those who were restricted by drug addiction by preaching the gospel to him. His level of meaning of life began to change from AD-3 (Despite spontaneous struggle, he needed to have a minimal survival by committing illegal, immoral and risky deeds and crime) to Level 3 (living for the sake of taking care, showing concern to others.)

Drug Addiction and Constant Reflective Search for Meaning

As mentioned above, meaning of life as constant search for meaning is a combination of a sense of ultimate ontological existence and a continuous sense of existence. That means in every moment in life, one has to be engaged in activities such as social interaction, work, learning, house chores and observation and response to immediate social and physical environment. In doing so, one also reflects whether or not these engagement and involvement are really meaningful in connection with his/her ultimate sense of ontological existence. The sense of meaninglessness or meaningfulness is not only a spontaneous reflection of what one has done recently or within a period of time, it is also a reconnection of this with one's meaning and purpose in life. It is a sense of completeness and hope in one's life with what one have done in the current moment. The connection of past, current and future would finally make individuals get a feeling that his/her life is meaningful and worthwhile. As an opposite, if there are discrepancies among individual current endeavor, past experience and effort, the individual may feel painful and intolerable.

For persons with substance abuse, individuals may embrace a constant search for meaning in life. Before drug addiction, individual may feel highly inconsistent and discrepancies in the following:

1. His/her own expectation and others' expectation.
2. His/her current endeavor and the extensive and introversive reward.
3. His/her current and his/her past experience.
4. His/her past and current situation and his/her future.

In first discrepancy, individuals may have their own expectation in work, education, family and other aspects of life in which is vastly different from others' expectation in these social context. For example, an individual may expect s/he is the lovely child of his parents, however, his/her parents only regard him/her only as a trouble maker in the family. In the second discrepancy, the individual may feel that despite s/he works extremely hard, his/her effort is not being appreciated by others. For instance, a young man has tried all her means to please his girlfriend. He spends all his saving on her. He even owes a huge for the expanse of his girlfriend. However, his girlfriend finally leaves him. In the third discrepancy, the individual has intensive discrepancy between his/her current and past experiences. For example, an adolescent who is born in a very rich family and spend his/her childhood in living a very luxurious life is very hard to face the current deprived and poor life because of his father's bankruptcy In the final discrepancy, individuals may not harbor hope and embrace a lot of uncertainty in facing their future. Even though they have a good past and stable current situation, their future is unpredictable and fearful. A good example of this discrepancy is a well-educated professional with a good social status and stable family life suddenly discovers that s/he suffers from terminal stage cancer. His/her days are numbered.

Within these four types of discrepancies, individuals tend to feel puzzled and frustrated. Thus, they undergo a stage of self-reflection and rumination in which they try to question about their aim and values of life. For those persons with substance abuse, within these four types of discrepancies, they seem to have no way out. They feel painful, powerless and empty. The more reflective in this process, they more they feel empty and meaningless and they more frustrated they become and the more they are absorbed in reflective search of life meaning.

Finally, they reach an unbearable break point that they have to engage in constant drug addiction so to paralyze the continuously reflective but painful search for life meaning in resolving all these discrepancies.

It seems that drug addiction works effectively for a short while in which they individual, under the effect of related drug, is able to absorb in stimulated or tranquilizing mood or out of body experiences to escape from the reflective search for life meaning. However, once the effect of drug comes to an end, the painful trip to search for life meaning and intolerable reflection of discrepancies in life returns. In addition, the harmful effects of social life, mentality and physical conditions prevail. That means individuals have to increase their dependency on drug addiction to avoid deep reflection of their life experiences. Gradually, the individual engages more and more in drug addiction to escape from painful search for meaning in life. Apart from the above mentioned discrepancies, the individual engages in further discrepancies in life after drug addiction. They are:

1. His/her own expectation before and after drug addiction.
2. Others' expectation before and after drug addiction.
3. His/her life endeavor before and after drug addiction.
4. His/her unsatisfied past (before drug addiction), regrettable present (drug addiction) and poor future (with severe physical, mental and social harm induced by chronic drug addiction).

With so many discrepancies in mind, it is clear that the reflective search for meaning of life for persons with drug addiction is painful and may ends up with a deep sense of meaninglessness and emptiness in which the individual has to cover up and conceal by increasing dosage of drug. In addition, the deep sense of pain and frustration also paralyze the individual's sense of reality and normal ego functioning. They become highly inert and self-absorbed in unresolved discrepancies in life before and after drug addiction. In other words, apart from drug addiction, the individual becomes more and more alienated, withdrawn and passive in family, work and social life.

Drug Addiction and Connection with the Infinite

As mentioned above, all human beings harbor an inherent urge to worship god, connect with the infinite, and actualize his/her spirituality. In doing so, an individual exists in the world not solely by himself/herself but also with others, in particular with the connection of a powerful omnipotent god. Also, his/her existence in this world is not within a short period of time but with possibility to be eternal and everlasting. With the connection of an infinite and powerful god, and with possibility of an eternal spiritual life, the individual, no longer feels lonely, helpless, powerless and hopeless even in times of hardship, suffering and traumas. The more s/he is connected with the powerful and omnipotent god and believes in eternal life, the more s/he feels hopeful, powerful, capable and substantial in facing his/her hardship, trauma and suffering in life. For persons with drug addiction, the connection of the infinite is usually blocked. They may be the following issues in hindering their connection with the infinite:

1. They may encounter hardship and even suffering in their life making them feel that life is full of misfortunes and God is unfair too.
2. They may not have chance to connect with related religious belief and religion.
3. They may have encountered people in religious group such as monks in temples or pastors in church but their impression is that all these people are highly hypocritical and unfaithful.
4. Their life is full of anger, sufferings and unfair treatment. They do not feel that god is there.
5. They feel too painful in life and the connection of the infinite is far too distant or delayed for him to get rid of the pain and suffering in life.

Under all these conditions, individuals urge for immediate and powerful release of all these negative feelings in facing the discrepancies in life. Thus, instead of connecting with the infinite, they connect with drug. Many persons with drug abuse admit that the effect of taking drug is so powerful that they feel not only release from pain in life but intensively elated mood, out of body experiences, grandiose delusion as well as tranquillizing peace and quiet induced by drug is so happy that they feel they are in heaven. In other words, they regard the drug taking is a connection of self-induced infinite. Some even declare that the intake of heroin is far better than sex orgasm.

Nevertheless, drug induced heaven and sense of infinite is highly harmful and destructive. It destroys one's aspiration and endeavor in life. As a consequence, the individual relies more and more on the self-constructed of the drug induced 'pseudo heaven' as the replacement of connection of the infinite. Finally, they regard drug addiction as the only aspiration and endeavor. They may even sacrifice their family, their career, their own life for the sake of drug taking. In some case, persons with drug addiction may even have compulsive gambling, they may become highly superstitious. In doing so, they think that once they connect with the local superstitious god or have fortune telling power, they can have good luck again and their life will change entirely.

Drug Addiction and Ultimate Insight and Wisdom

For a person with drug addiction, s/he may embrace three types of ultimate insight and wisdom in perceiving his/her life. The first type usually occurs before the drug addiction in concluding his/her whole life. S/he may conclude that despite s/he struggle a lot, his/her life is still empty, frustrated, unfair, painful and/or meaningless. That is why s/he becomes a regular or chronic user of drug. At that moment, the induced effect of drug tends to act as an induced 'heaven' to escape from painful reality. It is the second type of his/her ultimate wisdom that s/he drug addiction is the only available 'happiness' and 'aspiration' for him/her in his/her After the effect of drug, s/he fully bewares his/her life becomes even more meaningless, empty, frustrated and confusing than before the taking of drug. In that moment, s/he harbors strong feelings of inferiority (being a drug abuser is shameful and a complete loser in life), lonely (everybody reject him/her because of prolonged drug addiction), anger (being angry with himself/herself why taking drug to spoil his/her life and being angry with others who make his/her life so confused and frustrated that s/he has to depend on drug) and fear (fearing that one day s/he will die because of taking drug). All that mixed feelings make his/her drug taking becomes highly conflicting and confused. His/her search for the ultimate wisdom of almighty God, religious help and ultimate meaning in life becomes highly confused and conflicting. On one hand, s/he concludes that his/her life is entirely empty, hopeless, meaningless and in vain. S/he simply waits for the day that drug addiction take over his/her life. On the other hand, s/he earnestly hopes for ultimate forgiveness, salvation and rescue from a powerful and almighty God to save him/her from chronic drug addiction. S/he hopes that there really exist some ultimate wisdom in life that can explain his/her plight and suffering and gives him/her insight, courage, support, and determination to get away from the muddle of chronic drug addiction. This is why many chronic users of drug are trapped within an existential dilemma. On one hand, they are highly materialistic, urging for money to crave for drug. On the other hand, they have deep, philosophical and sophisticated search for meaning of life. They hope that they can find the real ultimate wisdom in life. Putting these two contradictory positions together, persons with drug addiction tend to be quite confused in their search for ultimate wisdom in life. At that moment, if they can have a deep spiritual encounter with almighty God, many of them can regain sufficient psychic power to abstain from drug addiction and turn a new page in life. That is why spiritual recovery and religious intervention is still one of the major intervention approaches for detoxification of drug addiction.

The Will of Meaning in Addiction

Similar to other normal persons without drug addiction, persons with drug addiction also have a strong will for meaning in life. However, their will to meaning is entirely blocked by frustration, hardship, unpleasant events and even traumas and abuses in life and developmental process. They camouflage their will of meaning by addiction and/ or use addiction to resolve their inner conflict. The more addictive they become, the more restricted for they to search for their full meaning, the more they limit their search for meaning by addiction only, and the more they aspire for a real and full meaning of life. Once their inner conflict remove, his camouflage their meaning by addiction will lessen, His aspiration for full meaning will manifested and his urge for an ontological meaning in life is restored. This is why spiritual intervention and recovery is important model in serving clients with drug addiction, in particular those chronic and serve cases.

Existential Frustration and Drug Addiction

For people with drug addiction, taking drug is a form of existence in which they can find their own meaning and escape from empty, meaningless and highly frustrated life. Absorption in drug, involvement in the physical stimulation by the effects of drug, and the senses of heightened mood, tranquillized feeling, or out of body experiences are the only way to sustain the individual to continue their daily life. Drug addiction should be a manifestation of ontological despair towards one's own life.

Noogenic Neurosis and Drug Addiction

People with drug addiction have many unpleasant events or even traumas in life in which their normal search for meaning are totally blocked. Instead, they depend on drug addiction to ease out the intolerable tension in noogenic neurosis. Drug involvement seems to be the most crucial mean to stay away from frustration in the aimless and continuous search for meaning of life. Whenever the individual feels empty, frustrated, anxious and helpless, addiction is the most immediate and accessible way to cover up all these unpleasant feelings. It also serves an immediate gratification for existential frustration and ontological empty.

Existential Vacuum and Drug Addiction

As mentioned above, in the state of existential vacuum in which the individual urge to fill up the vacuum by the will to power, to money or involvement in sex and secular attainment. Drug addiction becomes the quickest and most easily available way to fill up the existential vacuum with a result of endless dependence on drug addiction.

Essence of Existence and Drug Addiction

For people with drug addiction, the essence of existence shifts from a life with meaning to serve one and another to become a life in craving for and totally dependent on drug. At first, one tries to use drug to gratify his/her urge for escape from frustrating past and present condition. Gradually, s/he depends on drug in everyday life. As the deteriorating effects of drug increase, it is not the drug being abused by the individual. Instead, it is the individual that is ‘abused’ by drug. The essence of life of one’s life is totally focused on drug. Because of chronic drug addiction, s/he is excluded by friends and relatives before drug addiction. S/he can only relate to those relate to drug.

Drug Addiction and Meaning of Love

For people with drug addiction, they are the ones who deprive of true and genuine love in their life. They may be abandoned by their significant others. They may be socially excluded, rejected, bullied and oppressed by others in their life. Drug becomes the only object they can engage and connect with (Peele, 1985). That means drug addiction serves as the love objects. Many regular and chronic drug users are in fact deprived of love and concern from their significant others.

To cope with all these frustration in life, they regard drug addiction as the substituted object of love or being loved. At first, the relationship between individual and addicted drug is merely erotic in which the individual only attached to the stimulating effect of the drug just like s/he is being attracted by the physical beauty of others. Later, as the drug addiction prevails, the drug becomes the object of egocentric and dependent love in which s/he tries to use drug to fulfill his/her egocentric interest, to escape from reality and to comfort their frustration. For chronic users of drug, their love for drug may be so profound and transcendent that they are willing to sacrifice their physical health and mental health for taking drug. In extreme situations, when they crave for drug, they can even commit immoral and illegal acts for drug taking. They may stole or borrow money from their friends and relatives. They may also commit drug trafficking. For them, their love towards their drug is far more intensive than their love towards their parents, spouses, children and their best friend. In other words, the meaning of love in addiction has the following components:

1. Love is the only for persons with addiction to reconnect their essence with others.
2. By love, they are able to see the genuineness with others.
3. Through love they can actualize their potentiality despite addiction.
4. Help them to recognize and re-actualize love rather than sex, concern rather than stimulation, support instead of addictive isolation.
5. Transcend them from one levels of love to another.

Drug Addiction and Meaning of Suffering

For persons with addiction, suffering is complicated. On the one hand, drug addiction is used to escape or lessen the pain in suffering in life (SL). On the other hand, drug addiction creates various kinds of suffering (SD) such as deterioration of physical and mental health, loss of employment, being excluded and labeled by significant others. These two types of suffering interact with one another. People with addiction may have difficulties in transcending suffering or turning predicament into a human achievement. In other words, their resilience and coping for hardship and suffering are usually weak and inadequate (Weak R= WR). The process of drug addiction, in fact, further weakens their resilience and coping mechanism in facing hardship and suffering. That means they become more fragile and vulnerable in facing hardship and suffering. However, after a prolonged period of drug addiction, in addition to suffering in life (SL), individuals have to face suffering due to drug addiction. In other word, individuals have to rely more on drug addiction to face both suffering in life and suffering from addiction that is far beyond individuals' already weaken resilience (SL + SD >> WR). In other words, they need to rely more and more on drug addiction with an increasing suffering both from life and drug addiction.

The individual is thus kept in a complicated dilemma. In the search of meaning of suffering, s/he full addresses that suffering from drug addiction is entirely meaningless and masochistic. S/he also acknowledges that drug addiction can only seal up his/her meaninglessness in life but it can never resolve it or make it even worse. On the other hand, s/he has no way out. S/he needs spontaneous drug addiction to cover up all unpleasant feeling and increasing suffering and tortures in life and in drug addiction. S/he fully acknowledges that sooner or later, s/he will end in a vacuum of life meaning. S/he witnesses himself/herself being totally swallowed by meaningless suffering and torture. At that moment, s/he becomes the inescapable slave of suffering of life and suffering from drug addiction. S/he may embrace intensive senses of loneliness, emptiness, helplessness and meaninglessness. In extreme cases, individuals may harbor intensive urge to end up their life.

Drug Addiction and Meaning of Meaning of Suffering

For people with drug addiction, the super meaning should be the meaning of meaning of suffering in life and the meaning of meaning of suffering in drug addiction. In the process of addiction, the meaning of meaning of suffering of life is gradually declining from having frustration in life, to being empty as being suffocated by drug addiction, and finally to having regret and guilt feeling for one's whole life. For the meaning of meaning of suffering in addiction, it gradually changes to having mild suffering in drug addiction to replace or substitute severe suffering in life to severe suffering in drug addiction together with very severe suffering in life. In other words, the meaning of meaning of suffering in drug addiction becomes more and more meaningless and empty. There are three types of meaning of meaning (super-meaning) of suffering for people with drug addiction:

a. suffering from meaninglessness in life;
b. suffering from meaninglessness in suffering;
c. suffering from meaninglessness caused by sufferings from addiction.

These three types of super-meaning of suffering interact with one another making the individual with drug addiction feel dreadfully empty, meaningless, and aimless in his/her life.

Drug Addiction and Meaning of Suffering and Meaning of Love

For people with drug addiction, the love of drug addiction and the suffering from drug addiction combine together and penetrate into every aspect of meaning of life. Within drug addiction, the meaning of love in drug addiction and the meaning of suffering in drug addiction also intensifies quickly. The sense of ultimate and ontological existence, constant search for meaning in life, sense of continuous existence, a struggle for minimal survival, ultimate insight and wisdom and connection of the infinite are also minimized and deteriorated by the deprivation of love, and increased sufferings in drug addiction.

- **Life Transitoriness in Persons with Addiction**

For people with drug addiction, they usually harbor many discrepancies among their past, present and future. For their past, they are full of regret and frustration. For the future, drug addiction with deteriorating physical and mental health make them conclude that they do not have any future. All they can do is to choose those transitoriness according to their current situation. They share those painful but neglect those joyful and meaningful endeavor and experiences both in the past and in the present. In fact, their transitoriness before and after addiction cannot be done away. They become pessimistic when they observe with fear and sadness that their future withers with addiction.

Urges for Wholeness and Persons with Drug Addiction

For people with drug addiction, their urge of wholeness is broken by the discrepancies between having no addiction in the past and having addiction in present and the further addiction in the future. Their urge for whereness is lost in addiction as their life is targeted only for further withering and deterioration.

The Past, the Present and the future of Persons with Addiction

For people with drug addiction, the immediate existence is full of pain, failure and spontaneous suffering as well as escape. As time passes away aimlessly, addiction engages them in a temporary shelter from the flow of reality but they can still feel the pain and endless sufferings in it. For them, future is hopeless and deteriorating. The presence is painful and intolerable suffering. The past is traumatic. As the present is busy and breathless with endless addiction related activities, they ignore and escape from the painful past and cast no hope on their future. All these can be summed by the following figure.

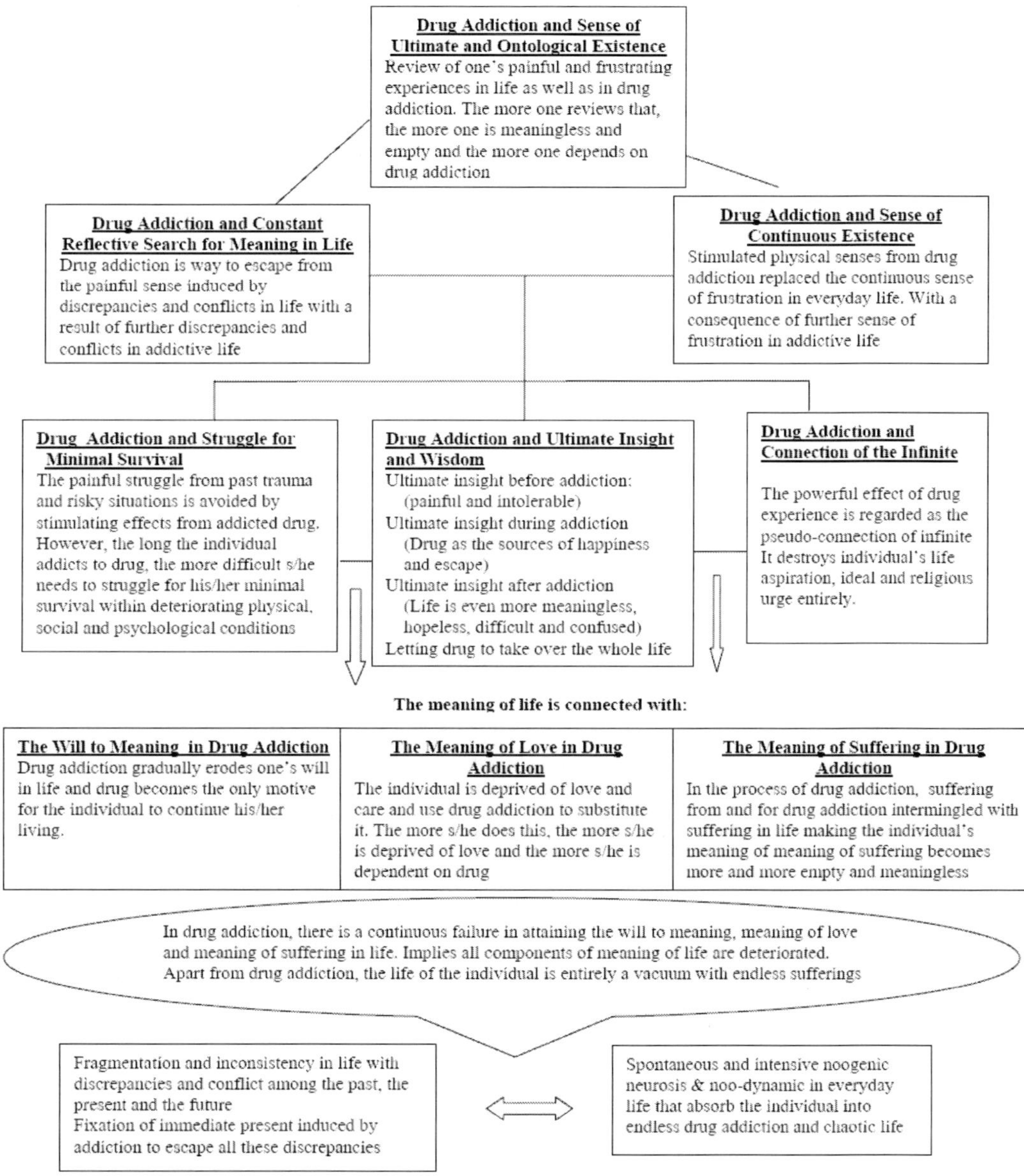

A Comprehensive Articulation of Drug Addiction and Meaning of Life.

Integrated Dynamic Recovery of Meaning of Life in Drug Addiction

People with drug addiction need to reconstruct a meaningful life in recovery. It consists of several dimensions:

1. The breaking and time out of the vicious circle of meaninglessness of life and pseudo-meaningfulness in drug addiction.
2. The substitution of pseudo-meaningfulness in drug addiction by others less harmful or even healthy life involvement.
3. Good exposure and support for the individual to search new meaning in life in normal relationship, interaction, work, education, social and recreational activities.
4. Re-establishment of new aspiration in one's whole life or re-connection of unfulfilled needs and life aspiration.
5. Actualization of all these life aspiration and unfulfilled gradually, realistically and substantially.

Integrated Recovery of the Sense of Ultimate and Ontological Existence

In the process of drug addiction, people with drug addiction constantly review their painful and frustration experiences in life as well as in drug addiction. Before drug addiction, they may properly be frustrated by developmental traumas in which they sense of ultimate and ontological existence is threatened. They need drug addiction to ease all these senses of emptiness and meaninglessness. However, the more they engage in drug addiction, the more they feel empty and meaningless after drug addiction, and the more they depend on drug addiction.

To break this viscous circle, in terms of ontological sense of existence, the breaking of vicious circle must be accompanied by a glimpse of hope in the meaning of life, a flash of meaningfulness and aspiration in one's life. It can be shown by the following case illustration. Related parties' consensus to use their stories for academic purpose was sought. To ensure confidentiality, their personal identity and information was properly disguised.

> 'Mr. T had involved in the abuse of ketamine for seven years. He was born in a low class family. His parents had to work very hard so as to earn a hand to mouth life. T had a younger sister. When he was young, he was responsible to do all house hold chores and take care of younger sister. His younger sister was very naughty and always got into trouble. However, he was the one to be blamed by his parents. T felt very unfair and was angry with his parents. He always engaged in a gang of juvenile delinquents. They began to engage in drug addiction. Gradually, T became a drug addict in abusing ketamine. T also engaged in drug trafficking so that he could earn enough money to support his substance abuse and addiction. Finally, his parents discovered that and cursed T seriously.
>
> At first, T was determined to quite the drug addiction and joined some detoxification programs for youngsters. When he was discharged from the detoxification program, he felt emptiness, bored and inferior. He was unemployed and his previous peers tried to isolate him. No sooner, he committed in drug trafficking and drug addiction again. His

parents and his younger sister were deeply frustrated by him. Finally T moved out to live with other drug related peers. He became an active member in drug business. He earned a good sum of money from drug trafficking and sales. He had his girlfriend and his own car as well as his own drug business. At that moment, his meaning of life in terms of ontological existence was highly secular. He concluded that if he got the money, he could do and get whatever he wanted. Then, life was meaningful and interesting. No sooner, he was caught by the police and sentenced to three months' imprisonment. Three months later he was released. He immediately took ketamine again to ease out of his frustration. He was poor, helpless and no one helped him. Under this condition, he felt dreadfully empty and meaninglessness. He took a heavy dosage of ketamine to ease out his uneasy feeling. He fainted and in a close risk of committing suicide. Fortunately, his friend called an ambulance to take him to a nearby hospital and stay there for three days. Within these three days of hospitalization, the hospital pastor visited him.

1. Taking a break from the vicious circle of ontological meaninglessness and endless addiction by proper insight in rough bottom period

Within the rough bottom of life, T began to reflect about what he had done in his whole life. He began to beware that his entire life was meaningless. The pastor preached the gospel to T. He began to realize that Jesus died for his sin and his whole life could restart again with the total forgiveness and salvation from Jesus.

2. The substitution of pseudo-meaningfulness in drug addiction by healthy life involvement

Within the help of visiting pastor, T began to accept Jesus' salvation and urge to start a new meaningful Christian life to be free from drug addiction. He joined a residential detoxification program organized by a Christian Organization. He stayed there as an inmate to abstain from drug addiction. He tried hard to follow a highly disciplined life pattern in the residential care unit. Every morning, he got up at 6 a.m. and had prayer and exercises with other residents. After that, they involved in various forms of vocational training. T learnt how to operate computer design and graphics in which drawing cartoon was his interest in childhood. After lunch, T was assigned to cleaning and repair duties of the residential units. He learnt how to repair electrical fans, lighting and many other utensils. At evening times, he needed to join the bible study group in members support one another in knowing God's love and Jesus salvation. They also help one another to continue their endeavor in being free from drug addiction. They regarded group members as brothers in Christ. After six months' residential program, T's life had a total new meaning.

It was clear that within the residential detoxification program, T began to start a new life pattern. He engaged in normal and healthy life pattern such as doing morning exercise, learning new thing and skills, getting along with supportive brothers and sisters in Christ and engaging in meaningful bible study and fellowship.

3. Good exposure and support for the individual to search new meaning in life in normal relationship, interaction, work, education, social and recreational activities

'Instead of spending his whole life on destructive drug addiction to cover up his frustration in life, T determined to begin a new meaningful life within the love of Christ. He went home and asked for the forgiveness of his mother and father. They were very happy in seeing the return of T from his drug addiction. T witnessed that it was the power of the Holy Spirit and God that made him change. They began to understand and admire the healing power of God. They also followed T to go his church. Gradually, they also became Christians. With good support from the church members and pastor, T began to develop a mission that he should help those adolescents who were tortured by drug addiction. He felt highly enlightened by this new ontological meaning of his life. The pastor encouraged him to enroll in a certificate course in training indigenized missionaries in a theological seminary.

With good exposure and support for T's parents, church members, and his pastors, T was able to start a new meaning of life. This meaning of life should a new ontological sense of existence. He anchored his life in saving adolescents from prolonged drug addiction.

4. Re-establishment of new aspiration in one' s whole life or re-connection of unfulfilled needs and life aspiration

'Within the new aspiration of saving other adolescents from drug addiction, T was very excited. Under the proper guidance of his pastor and members in his church, T vigorously started his new life. He enrolled in an evening secondary school and continued his secondary school education. In the daytime, he worked as a peer counselor in a social welfare agency for rehabilitation of persons with drug addiction. T worked diligently for his new life. He no longer felt empty, boring and frustrated. On Sunday and Saturday, he preached God's gospel by doing personal testimonials how Jesus changed his whole life. He also enrolled in a part time distance learning certificate course in theology'.

5. Actualization of all these life aspiration and unfulfilled gradually, realistically and substantially

'T worked very hard in actualizing his life aspiration. Apart from his meaningful day time job as a peer counseling, at night, he had to go the evening school to finish his secondary school education. On Saturday and Sunday, he went out to give his personal testimony in church and in social welfare agency. He also had to study distance learning certificate course in theology. He stretched himself too hard that was far from his body could tolerate. Two years later, he was sick and suffered from a severe health problem. He got the initial stage liver cancer. He felt dreadfully tired and fatigue. He felt hopeless and caught in a thinking that God did not appreciate his work and he was worthless in front of God and in front of others. His sense of contribution his life to fight for adolescent drug addiction was deeply challenged. He was depressive and tired assuming that his final day was come. He lied on bed without doing anything or even refused to eat anything saying that sooner or later Jesus would take him away. His pastors approached him and prayed with him. He sadly aired out his anger in life. He did not understand why God put so much suffering in his life. He was unfairly treated by his parent. He committed in drug addiction and He was betrayed by his friends......He worked hard to repent and to serve Jesus but he was thus caught by liver cancer... . His days were numbered. The pastor understood that he put too much on himself. T had very good ontological meaning to serve God and to help those adolescents with drug addiction but he worked too hard far beyond the tolerance of his own body. His pastors comforted him and prayed to God to heal his liver cancer.

Fortunately, one of his church members, G was a very famous specialist in healing liver cancer. He gave T the most effective treatment. Within the care and concern of T's good pastor and G, T was finally recovered from his initial stage of liver cancer. He began to recognize that he need to attain his life goal in serving God and adolescents with drug addiction in a gradually way. From that time onward, he changed in his full time job to half time job and finished his secondary school education within two years. Then, he finished his certificate course in the next year. T then became a junior ministry in a drug addiction rehabilitation agency who was run by a Christian organization.

Integrated Recovery of Constant Reflective Search for Meaning

Before drug addiction, individuals may feel highly inconsistent and discrepancies in the following:

1. His/her own expectation and others' expectation.
2. His/her current endeavor and the extensive and introversive reward.
3. His/her current and his/her past experience.
4. His/her past and current situation and his/her future.

Within these four types of discrepancies, individuals tend to feel puzzled and frustrated and they try to be reflective in resolving these discrepancies. They reach an unbearable break point that they have to engage in constant drug addiction so to paralyze the continuously reflective but painful search for life meaning in resolving all these discrepancies. Then, individuals engage in further discrepancies in life after drug addiction. They are:

1. His/her own expectation before and after drug addiction.
2. Others' expectation before and after drug addiction.
3. His/her life endeavor before and after drug addiction.
4. His/her unsatisfied past (before drug addiction), regrettable present (drug addiction) and poor future (with severe physical, mental and social harm induced by chronic drug addiction).

With so many discrepancies in mind, the individual becomes more and more alienated, withdrawn and passive in family, work and social life. Facing all these conflicts and discrepancies in mind, integrated recovery of reflective search for meaning should involve the following dimensions:

The breaking and timing out of vicious circle of increasing reflective discrepancies in life and increasing drug addiction by discovery of the consistency of her mother's love.

To take a break from increasing discrepancies in life and increasing drug addiction, related professionals should help the client to recall and reconstruct some good consistency in their lives. This can be shown in the following case illustration. The consensus in using their stories for academic purpose was obtained. Their personal identities and information were properly disguised to ensure confidentiality.

> 'Betty was a female youth who had engaged in abuse of ketamine for seven years. She was born in low class family where her parents had to struggle for basic survival. She also had a brother who was only one years younger than her. When Betty was 4 years old, her father died of liver cancer. Her mother felt very sad and worked very hard to support the whole family, but they still lived a very deprived life in which Betty and his younger brother were mal-nutritious.
>
> Two years later, her mother married another man whose wife died several years ago. He was a small business man. At first, Betty felt happy about her step-father and her step-sisters. At least, Betty and her younger brother could have enough food to eat. Unfortunately, her step father's business ran down two years later. He was bankrupt. He worked as manual labor in a nearby factor.
>
> From that time onwards, he became depressive and involved in alcohol addiction. Whenever he was drunk, he physically and psychologically abused Betty, her mother and her step sisters. One night, when he was severely drunk, he climbed on Betty's bed and sexually abused her. Betty told her traumatic experiences to her mother. Her cursed his step-mother but refused to notify the police and threaten Betty to keep her mouth shut in front of others. Betty was seriously hurt by her mother's ignorance of traumatic harm. She became highly rebellious and emotionally fluctuated. At the same time, her academic performance declined drastically.
>
> When she was 15, one day after a severe quarrel with her mother she ran way and lived with her boyfriend who was a delinquent. He engaged frequently in gang fight, drug trafficking and other antisocial and criminal behaviors. Under his influence, Betty engaged in addiction of ketamine as well as amphetamine. At first, they went well and loved each other. No sooner, her boyfriend fell in love with another beautiful girl. Betty was very angry and sad. She attempted suicide and was fortunately saved by her friend. She was hospitalized and diagnosed as suffering from depressive disorder. Two weeks later, she was discharged and her mother urged her to return home and took care of her.

From the above case description, it is clear that Betty suffered a lot from discrepancies in her life. Initially, she thought that drug addiction could help her to face the painful reflective search for meaning in life. However, the more she engaged in drug addiction, the more meaninglessness she felt in self-reflection.

> Betty: Indeed, my life was painful and meaningless. When I was young, I loved my father and my parents. Despite they were very busy working. They still brought me to the

park and arcade. At that time, I did think that my life would be happy forever. My father died when I was only four. I cried bitterly. My mother even said he was only sleeping.

Sooner or later, he would wake up. I trusted my mother's words but my father never woke up. My mother worked very hard to support the family. Apart from paying the rent, the food and my school fee, my mother had to pay back the debt in paying the medical treatment of my father. We were in a desperate position. We did not have enough to eat and enough money to spend. We became highly mal-nutritious. One day, my mother told me that we would have a new father. He would give us enough money to spend and enough food to eat. I and younger brother were so happy. We thought our good days finally came. In our stepfather family, we had enough food to eat and we could go to school. Also we had two step elder sisters to play with. Everything seemed fine and in right direction.

At first, my stepfather treated us well. I harbored a hope that we would have good days thereafter. Hi, my life seemed to be circled around bad fate and misfortune. Two years later, my step father was bankrupt. The whole thing changed. He simply became a drunken monster. He abused us whenever he was drunk. One night he even sexually abused me. Indeed, it hurt me most. I expected my mother to comfort me and to put this bastard in jail. She did nothing to save me. Instead, she even complained to me and insisted that I was seductive to my step-father and I should keep my mouth shut. I hated my mother. She did not protect me at all. She simply put my whole life in a mass. I hated her. I did not expect her to act like this. This was completely out of my expectation.

I hated my whole family. I left my family. I left such a confused and destructive family. I expected the life outside should be better than my family. However, it turned to a dog eat dog world. Everyone was greedy and selfish. Fortunately, I met my boyfriend. He protected me from being bullied by others. He ensured me that he would be a good partner and protector for me in life. We lived together and we loved one another. I expected he would be my husband one day. To get along with him, I took ketamine with him together. Unfortunately, things turned out of my expectation. He fell in love with another beautiful girl. He turned away from me. He abandoned me.

What I left to comfort myself was only drug addiction. At this moment, I could trust nobody. I could rely on no one. I took heavy dosage of ketamine making me feel better. The experience of 'out of body' and 'k hole", tended to help me to be away from unpleasant past memories. However, when I returned to the reality, things were even worse. Everything was out of my expectation. The more I reflected what I had done in the past, the more frustrated I felt. The more I needed to depend on addiction of ketamine to get rid of painful reflection of life meaning.... Oh God, who can save me from this endless torture.

It was clear that Betty suffered greatly from a painful reflective search for meaning in in facing the death of his father, the sex abuse by his step father, and the denial of sex abuse by his mother, the abandonment by his boyfriend and the mental and physical deterioration by drug addiction. To end up this painful life, Betty committed suicide by taking an over dosage of ketamine in a park. Fortunately, she was saved by a police man. She was hospitalized for two weeks and with the help of the medical social worker in the hospital, she was admitted to residential detoxification unit. In this service unit, related welfare workers were very supportive and caring. They encouraged Betty to keep constant contact with her mother. At first, Betty refused to do so. Her hatred feeling towards her mother still prevailed. Her mother visited her several times during her residence in the detoxification center.

What below was Betty's self narration in facing the visit of her mother.

> Betty: I hated my mother, I did not see her. Every time I saw her. I recalled all my details of my traumatic past experiences. It was her that made me to be sexually abused by my stepfather. To preserve her marriage, she sacrificed my virginity, she sacrificed me so to maintain so called a 'cohesive family'. I won't forgive her. I rather preferred to be hungry and mal-nutritious as the days in my childhood after the death of my father. At least, the family environment was warm and supportive. My whole life was spoiled by my bastard stepfather. I could never forget the night he climbed into my bed and raped me. I was so shameful and terrible. My mother never protected me. ....Now she visited me. Her visit was entirely hypocritical. She tried to ask my forgiveness so that she felt better.

In fact, her mother felt deeply regretted about what she had done to Betty's adolescence. She had visited Betty twice when Betty was hospitalization because of her suicidal attempt by taking over dosage ketamine.

> Bettys' mother: 'Indeed, it was very hard to describe my sense of remorse and guilt towards my daughter Betty. She was my beloved one. I had tried my very best to protect her in life. When Betty's father was still there, we worked hard to provide a decent life for her and her younger brother. We were not well educated. To earn a decent life, we needed to work hard. I worked as a cleaner and my husband worked as a construction site worker. We did not want our children to repeat our fate again. Thus, to ensure that we could have some saving for Betty and her younger brother for good education, we worked very hard. Apart from his demanding full time job, he committed several part time jobs, such as a part time taxi driver and a part time waiter in a Chinese restaurant. For years, he only slept for two to three hours every day. That was why he suffered from liver cancer and died when my children were still young.
>
> In the process of medical treatment of her father's liver cancer, we had already used up all our personal saving. We had owed a lot of debt. To live a hand to mouth living and to pay back to the loan shark, I worked many part time and full time jobs. I could only sleep around two to three hours a day. Still, we could not have enough food to eat. Betty and his young brother were mal-nutritious. They were thin and sick. I could not bring them up. At that moment, I was so desperate for help. Fortunately, Betty's step father loved me. His wife died years ago. We loved one another and planned to bring my children and his children up. You knew I had to re-marry so that Betty and her younger brother could have good food, good education and good life in the future. But Betty simply concluded that I re-married simply for the sake of my own comfort.
>
> At first, everything went well, we did share good family life and we treated one another as intimate parent children. Hi, things did not go in my ways. My husband's business went worse in Asian market declined. In fact, he worked very hard to save his

business, but he finally failed. He was very unhappy about that. That was why he committed alcoholic addiction to ease up his pain. To support the family, he worked as manual labor in the container terminal. Very often, he had to work overtime. His life was full of frustration, when he was young, he was abandoned by his mother and his father abused her seriously. So when he was drunk, all these unhappy traumatic memories re-bounced again. That was why he was so angry and abused us. One night he was drunk, he sexually abused Betty. (At that moment, she cried bitterly.) I knew he was wrong. He should not do that. I knew how painful and traumatic for Betty was. But if I put a legal charge on him, the whole family would be ruined. He would properly stay in jail. How could I take care of his and my children? There were four of them. Thus, I persuaded Betty to keep her mouth shut in front of others. I did not mean to hurt her. In fact, I had blamed my husband, and he had said sorry to Betty. He admitted he was drunk and would never do this again. In fact, I was totally heart breaking in the whole process.

All along, I loved Betty deeply. I always hoped that she could have good food, good education and good future. When my husband hurt her, I wanted to die. I had no way out. When Betty ran away from house and lived together with a delinquent male. I began to beware that I was totally wrong. I was not a good mother. I did not recognize that how deep she was hurt in the process of sex abuse by his stepfather. I hoped she could forgive me. But she never did. She hated me deeply. She committed in drug addiction. When her boyfriend left him, she committed suicide. I knew she hated me deeply. She hurt herself so as to hurt me. I could never forgive myself. Frankly speaking I preferred to end up my painful life. The only meaning I still keep myself alive is that I still believe one day my Betty would forgive me. Then I will do everything to compensate my faults in the past. No matter what has happened and what will happen in the future, I am still her beloved mother and she is still my beloved daughter. (In the whole self-narration, Betty's mother cried bitterly and she was overwhelmed with sadness, guilt, emptiness and loneliness.)

Betty did not realize that her mother still loved her and still tried her best to do good thing to her. To help Betty to take a break from all these painful and conflicting and overloading reflective searching for meaning, the social worker tries to facilitate Betty to understand and forgive her mother. In the time Betty staying in the detoxification residential unit, her mother was finally diagnosed to have the second stage lung cancer. The social worker persuaded Betty to visit her mother. After the following counseling, she agreed to do so.

S (social worker): Dear Betty, I had just visited your mum in the hospital. She was seriously sick.

B (Betty): I have no interest to hear that. This woman is not my mother. (Betty harbored deep hatred feeling towards her mother.)

S: The doctor said she suffered from the final stage liver cancer. Her days are numbered……

B: Oh, this should be her punishment for doing such thing to me.

S: I could understand your anger towards your mother. By the end of day, she was still your mum.

B: She was not my mum, if she was my mum, she never let my step father sexually abused me. (She ventilated her unresolved anger towards her mum and her stepfather.)

S: You had told me about this event. I could understand your hurt, your anger and your trauma. It really hurt your whole life.

B: It was my mother's fault. She married a bad guy. She let the bad guy raped me. She did not allow me to put this bad guy to legal sentence. My whole life was totally spoiled by my mother and my bastard stepfather. (B began to cry bitterly.)

S embraced B: I can understand how painful you are in mentioning all these traumatic experiences.

B had cried for 10 minutes and remained silent for a long while. All along, she seemed to absorb in her past memories.

S: Do you feel better now?

B nodded her head.

S: You knew what your mother said when I visited her.

B: I don't want to know. But if you like to say, I would listen. (It seemed that B actually liked to know about what her mother said.)

S: She gave me these things to me (They were a letter written by Betty's mother as well as a small doll.) She told me to give these to you.

B looked at the doll closely.

B: it was my beloved doll, before my father died. My mother brought it to me as my birthday present. Later, I lost it in my step father house.

S: Perhaps, you can also look at your mum's letter. Her days are numbered.

Betty openly the letter and read it word by word. Her tears ran down on her face. She was sad but appeared as warm and being embraced by love and care. For a long while, she said nothing. Suddenly she asked the worker which hospital her mother was staying now. She then said good bye to the worker and rushed to hospital. The social worker picked up her handbag and accompanied her to visit her mother again.

What below was the verbatim recording of Betty's visit to her mother.

At that moment, Betty's mother was lying on bed and related nurses and medical staff was very busy in doing regular medical assessment and test. She looked pale, weak. Around her body, there were different medical apparatus and equipment. She seemed to absorb in bodily pain that she closed her eyes. Betty's voice woke her up. With all her residual energy, she opened her eyes. With a lovable smile, she stretched her arm towards Betty. Betty approached her mother with tears.

Betty's mother (M): You finally came. Mother was wrong, totally wrong. (She was too weak, she simply murmured in front of Betty's ears.)

Betty (B): Mum, you are my mum. (Betty engaged in a highly ambivalent emotion. She failed to articulate it clearly. From her mum's letter, she began to recognize that her mum loved him deeply. But she still clung on how deeply she was hurt by her step-father's sex abuse.)

M: I loved you Betty, I did not understand how deep it hurt you. (Betty's mother used all her residual energy to say this clearly, but was seriously interrupted by coughing and choking.)

B: I knew you love me. But……..

S: Dear Betty, for years, your mum was deeply regretted for what she had done to you. That was why she still kept your doll. Hi, Betty, I think you are now old enough to understand men are not trustworthy just like your boyfriend.

B nodded her head.

M: Dear Betty, I hated your step father, but I needed him at that time to support the whole family, how could bring four children up at that time. (M cried. She could not speak fluently.)

B embraced her mother and cried also.

B: Mum, now I understood your plight and pain in your life. I began to understand how deep you love me and my younger sister.

It was clear that Betty had forgiven her mother after she had seen her mother's letter. She finally knew and felt that her mother loved her. Instead of have a reflective search of discrepancies and pain in life, she felt consistent in life because of the following:

1. Her mother loved her fearing that she and her younger brother could not have good education and good living, she married Betty's stepfather.
2. Her mother loved her and tried to ensure that Betty could have a good family life. As her step father's business was good. Certainly, they could live a good life.
3. Her mother loved her fearing that once her father's sex abuse was put into legal charge, the whole family harmony would be in trouble. At the same time, Betty could not continue her education and good life in the family.
4. Her mother once understood how deeply her daughter was hurt by the sex abuse, she felt deeply regretted. She frequently asked for the forgiveness of her daughter. When she saw that her daughter ran away from home and involved in drug addiction, her heart was broken.
5. Her mother spontaneously asked the forgiveness of Betty. She earnestly hoped that once Betty's anger towards her was released, Betty could abstain from drug and the abuse/control of her boyfriend.
6. When her mother knew that Betty committed suicide, she was sad and depressive that s/he refused to eat for several days. She tried to visit Betty in the hospital or in the detoxification centre but she was refused by Betty. At that moment, she harbored a strong urge to end up her life by jumping off from the window of her flat.
7. The medical practitioner said Betty's mother's health was poor. Even before the discovery of terminal stage of cancer, she was thin, pale and mal-nutritious. She had high blood pressure, diabetes and heart problems. All these chronic illnesses might be deal to prolonged psychological stress and insomnia.

Once Betty recognized that her mother still loved her deeply, she took a break from the continuous discrepancies of reflective search of meaning of life. Instead, she began to feel his life was full continuous and consistent love and concern.

The substitution of Betty's drug addiction to conceal reflective discrepancies in life by meaningful reflection and participation in detoxification programs.

Facing the final days of her mother, Betty began to spend more time in being together of his mother. She actively participated in detoxification programs. What below was her self-narration of her new meaningfulness in her reflection of her life.

Betty said: 'Really thanks for M's intervention. Under her guidance, I embraced a new perspective of my life. In the past, I always complained that everything was out of my expectation. Life for me was totally deprived of love, hope and faith. I hated those who hurt me deeply, including my stepfather and my mother. I also hated my father why he died so early and let me suffered so much in my life. But now I changed my perspective. Despite all these misfortune and sufferings, my mother still loved me. I was deeply loved by her. I began to feel her pains, worries and struggle in life. She struggled very hard for our survival. She knew my pain of being sexually abuse by my step-father. But she tried to ensure I had a stable life in education. She tried to ensure four children could still have a good life. That was why she kept her mouth and my mouth shut. She felt painful. I could imagine how painful and guilty she was in witnessing how I gradually engaged in drug addiction and how I never forgave her. She finally exhausted all her energy and will power to take care of us. That was also why she suffered from terminal stage cancer.

Now her days were numbered. As her only beloved daughter, I should engage my meaning of life in taking good care of her so that we still had a good reunion and affective bond with this short period of time. In a deep self-reflection of my life, I no longer felt that I was lonely, rejected and abandoned. I felt I was deeply connected with love and care.

From that time onward, Betty embraced a new meaning of life. Days and nights, Betty tried to take care of mother, listened to her pain and her final words. Three weeks later, Betty's mother died peacefully. In the funeral, Betty encountered her step-father. As Betty's mother, in her final days demanded him to say sorry to Betty. He did so. Betty could not forgive him immediately, but she felt much better than before. She felt much substantial and meaningful than before.

Good exposure and support for Betty to search new meaning in life in normal relationship, interaction, work, education, social and recreational activities.

After the funeral, Betty engaged in a new meaning of life. As Betty had profound interest in body beauty, she engaged in a body beauty and make up certificate course. She was a bit lagging behind as she had not engaging in learning course for many years. Under the encouragement of her younger brother and the social worker, she regained the confidence to continue the certificate course. She was able to complete the course. Betty's social worker encouraged Betty to teach other residents in the detoxification centre about body beauty and make up. Betty began to beware that life was more meaningful and substantial than before.

Re-establishment of new aspiration in Betty' s whole life or re-connection of unfulfilled needs and life aspiration and Actualization of all these life aspiration and unfulfilled gradually, realistically and substantially.

Gradually, the centre employed Betty as a part time rehabilitation worker. This position gave her a new life to use her own experiences to help other adolescents to abstain from drug addiction. What below was herself narration on this.

Betty: 'I was very happy when I was offered a position as a part time rehabilitation worker for this detoxification centre. It was very important for me. In the past, I always complained that life was so hard for me. I was abandoned by my natural father who died when I was only a little girl. I was abandoned by my mother as she ordered to shut my mother and forget my step-father's sex abuse on me. I was abandoned by my boyfriend. Whenever I reflected my whole life, I just felt it was entirely massive, confused and torturing.

Integrated Recovery of Other Components of Meaning of Life in Persons with Drug Addiction

Apart from sense of ultimate and ontological existence and reflective search of meaning of life, other component of meaning of life in persons with drug addiction can also be recovered in similar direction.

Integrated Recovery of Sense of Continuous Existence

For people with drug addiction, stimulated physical senses from drug addiction replaced the continuous sense of frustration in everyday life with a consequence of further sense of frustration in addictive life. Thus, in the process integrated recovery. It is crucial that:

1. People with drug addiction can develop healthy and good stimulated physical senses from intensive involvement in sports, exercise, good food, enjoyable games and meaningful interaction with others.
2. Once these healthy and good stimulated physical senses can be developed, it can be used by the individual to replace the continuous sense of frustration in everyday life including various frustrations because of prolonged drug addiction.
3. Gradually, regular intensive involvement of sports, exercises, good food, enjoyable games and meaningful interaction with others enable the persons to develop a meaningful sense of continuous existence. S/he has a spontaneous sense of good body (from healthy exercise, good food and sport); a spontaneous sense of good mind (from enjoyable games, reading and learning); a spontaneous sense of good environment (from meaningful interaction with friends); and a spontaneous sense of good self (being accepted, included and even respected by others in good interaction and daily activities.)
4. The continuous good sense existence can be further intensified and by involvement in meaningful activities such as being a volunteer for deprived groups, actualizing one's aspiration in life and being engaged in creative art work. In doing all these, individual properly have a very good sense of continuous existence.

Anna's story clearly showed that how her new born daughter and meaningful creative artwork helped her to build a very good sense of continuous existence.

'Anna said: I had been engaged in addiction to ketamine for ten years. I started taking ketamine when I was only 16. My classmates told me that taking ketamine could help me to ease my feeling of helplessness, worthlessness and meaninglessness. In fact, ever since the death of my father, my whole life was ruined by my mother. She became an alcohol. Day and night, he was totally absorbed by wine. When she was drunk, she even tried to abuse saying that I was just rubbish manufactured by my father when he was driven by sex desires. I knew she hated my father because he was engaged in extra marital relationship. However, he did it merely because my mother tried every mean to humiliate him.

My grandparents were very rich merchants. My mother said that my father married her simply because of money. As far as I know, my father loved my mother deeply. He knew that my mother suffered from bipolar disorder because of abandonment history in her childhood. Thus, he tried to help her to recovery from her fluctuating emotions. In fact, he suffered a lot. When my mum was in depressive mood, he tried every mean to cheer her up. When my mum was in manic episode, he became her victim to humiliate, oppress and abuse so as to release his frustration.

In facing all these, I tried to fight back. When my mother tried to physically abuse us, I fought with her. When he was depressive, I ignored her. The more I did this, the more she hated me. She even cursed me that I was my father's wife rather than her. It really irritated me. I got no hope in my family. Days and nights there were quarrels, yelling and fighting. Every minute in such a family with such a dreadful mum was a painful experience. In fact, every day I did not want to return home after school. Instead, I wandered around street and went to disco and karaoke. My classmates took ketamine with me. The senses of out of body and K holes were really interesting. I gave some a sense of release in my painful and intolerable life.

Gradually, I became more and more addictive to ketamine, as my family atmosphere got worse. Finally, I left my home, and lived with my boyfriend. At first, we had some sharing, I felt being continuously loved and cared. However, as time went by, I realized that his life, similar to mine, harbored a lot of frustration and torture. He had been continuously abused by his alcoholic father. That was why occasionally he also abused me when he was drunk. To resolve all these, we engaged in addiction of ketamine as well as amphetamine together. Once I discovered I was pregnant. He urged me to undergo abortion. I refused to do. We had a severe quarrel. We broke up our togetherness. I went for help for a social worker. She advised me to go to a residential unit for unmarried mother's pregnancy. I went and lived there for ten months and gave birth to a lovely daughter. The social worker, Q in the residential unit was very supportive. She was a kind middle aged woman. She simply treated me as her daughters. She taught me how to take care of myself. I told her about my story and she totally accepted my view. She cared about my physical and mental health so much that I got a feeling of being cared by a lovely mother.

In times of my pregnancy, she introduced me to a creative artist, M, who was a volunteer instructor in this residential unit. She was a very supportive and caring artist. She taught me to draw painting, wood craft and many others. For me, it was very interesting. I concentrated all my effort to learn, to create interesting art piece. I told M my own life story. M encouraged me to express my feelings and my thought in the creative art. I put all my thought in a painting 'a rough sea voyage'. My mother's art, my hatred feeling towards my mother were all released in the rough sea waves. In fact, both M and Q treated me as family members. Q was my substituted mother. She was kind, understanding and supportive. M was my substituted elder sister. She helped me to express my feelings, frustration and anger in a creative way. They accompanied me in my process of giving birth to my baby daughter. They helped me to face the painful laboring and taught me how to take care of my baby. I called my baby daughter Doris. ....

In the past, I was fully frustrated by my mother, my family, my boyfriend and my misfortune in my life. I always kept a feeling that my whole life was ruined by them. I was just the victim of their torture. I myself could not determine my own fate. I did not substantially exist in this world. But after these ten months, my sense of continuous existence changed accordingly. I began to enjoy involving in drawing picture, thinking about my fetus, interacting with my substituted mother, Q and my substituted sister, M. All these gave me a completely new sense of existence. I felt I had a new meaning of life. When I involved in painting, I felt I was free to draw what I want, to express what I want and to create what I want. I got a new sense of autonomy. When I talk with my M and Q, I felt I was respected and integrated. When I thought about my baby girl in my belly, I knew that she was my daughter, the extension of my genes, my thinking and my life. All these gave me a new sense of life. I was no longer a lonely persons being rejected and torture by my family members. Instead, I had my own sense of existence and own meaning of existence.

After my baby girl was born, I learnt to take care of her, including breast feeding and changing nappy. Along, life became very busy but substantial. I lived with a more meaningful life, much more meaningful than before.

Integrated Recovery of the Struggle for Minimal Survival

For people with drug addiction, many of them suffer from painful struggle from past traumas such as abandonment, emotional neglect, oppression, bullying and even abuse by their significant others. This painful struggle is avoided by stimulating effects from addicted drugs. However, the longer the individual addicts to drug, the more difficult s/he needs to struggle for his/her minimal survival within deteriorating physical, social and mental conditions. Thus, an integrated recovery of sense of the struggle for minimal survival should be based on the following:

1. Providing a secure, supportive and empathic psychosocial environment so that the individual does not need to struggle for minimal survival. It can be a safe detoxification residential unit, a secure and supportive vocational setting, or a caring family.
2. Individual's sense of struggle for minimal survival should be well channeled to healthy and constructive challenges in life such as adventure training, sport competition, ball games and/or other challenging activities.
3. All these healthy and constructive challenges in life should be regularized into daily pattern and activities. So that the individual can enjoy regular daily challenges in sports, meaningful enhancement of oneself and others.

All these can be illustrated in the following case. Related parties' consensus in using their stories for academic purpose was sought. For the sake of confidentiality, their personal identity and information is properly disguised.

Alex: The adolescent enjoy the challenge of street dancing competition.

Alex was an adolescent with substance abuse for five year. He was born in low class family. His parents had to work very hard to support a hand to mouth life for Alex and his two sisters. Alex was the eldest brother. When he was only six years old, he was responsible to take care of his two younger sisters when his parents went to work. As her two younger sisters were very naughty and quite rebellious and stirred up a lot of troubles, Alex was always to one to be blamed by her mother. He also had to resolve and settle all troubles created by his younger sisters. Once, when Alex was only 15 years old, his two younger sisters were bullied by a gang of delinquent boys. They threaten Alex's sisters. The whole issue initiated by their criticism of the hair style of one member in the gang. They threatened to kill them. Alex then joined in a group of triad delinquent gang and had a group fighting to settle this matter. From that time onward, Alex became an active member in this triad delinquent gang. Indeed, Alex had to struggle for minimal survival in the gang full of criminal affairs including drug trafficking, drug trade, sex trade and other immoral business. Alex was one of the fighters in the gang. As he was strong, well-built and very brave in fighting, he gradually became the sub-group leader in the gang. Although Alex was well respect by his gang, his life was full of risks of being caught by the police or being murdered by other gangs. He indulged in addiction of amphetamine and cocaine to ease out his tension in a highly risky life. What below was his self-narration showing that how risky his life was and how addiction of amphetamine helped him to ease out all these tension in the struggle for minimal survival.

> Alex: 'It is hard to imagine that life for me is full of risks and unpredictability. I worked as a fighter in the gang. I have to fight for our competitors in our drug dealing business. I have to fight for other opponents in our triad society. I have to fight for our gang when anyone of them is at a risk of being caught by the police. Every day for me is full of risks. While I am courageous enough to enter a gang fight, I should be prepared to be seriously hurt and even died in the gang.
>
> Once, I have a serve fighting with another gang, my lung and my legs were seriously wounded. I could not go into the hospital. I had to hide in some secret place and treated by an illegal doctor for around two weeks. For me, the experiences in these two weeks were really dreadful and intolerable. I dared not to go to anywhere. I was not only afraid of the police who recognized me in the gang fighting and hurt several men in other gangs. I was fully alert that members in other gang would take revenge on me. One day, one member really found me in the street. Fortunately, I was able to escape from his chasing.
>
> Life for me was really hard and frightening for me within this period of time. To ease out my tension, I began to take in amphetamine and cocaine. They helped me to feel that I was full of energy and courage to face difficulties and hardship. With them, I dared to fight the terrible fighting. I dared to face the threatening and risky life.

However, the longer Alex was involved in the addiction of amphetamine and cocaine, the more his mental and physical state deteriorated. The toxic effects made him suffer from continuous insomnia, arousal of delusion and hallucination. Even though he still could be a good fighter in times of gang fight. Deep down in his mind, he knew that sooner or later, amphetamine addiction can take off his own life. He fell in love with a beautiful girl who was his classmate in his primary school. They took drug together. No sooner, his girlfriend left her and dated with his gang master. He was deeply frustrated. He took an over dosage of cocaine and lost his consciousness. His friends took him to the emergency ward and saved his life. He was then referred to a drug detoxification centre. What below was his self-narration about his dreadful sense of total extinction of his life. That means, it was not a sense of struggle for minimal survival, but a total loss of survival.

> Alex: Engaging in addiction of amphetamine and cocaine was, indeed, shortened my life span. But I have no way out. Only amphetamine and cocaine could enlighten my prolonged sense of anxiety, fear and worry of my risky life. It gave me courage to fight and paralyze my fear during fighting. However, addiction of them also weakened my capacity and ability to struggle for survival. My body and my mind became weaker and weaker. When I felt weak, I needed them more. This was an endless vicious circle. My continuous sense to struggle for minimal survival on one hand was elated by amphetamine on one hand but also diminished it on the other hand. As I became weaker and weaker, my girlfriend looked down upon me. She aspired for a hero, a fierce fighter as well as a strong man in sex. She shifted her love to the leader of my gang, John. He was my 'big brother' in our gang. He was strong and did not take amphetamine. When I saw my girlfriend made love with John, I was totally shattered. I felt that my own life was totally ruined by gang fighting, drug and sex. Even though I had tried my best to struggle for a better survival in my life, what ended up was not only a minimal survival but also a sense of nothingness; nothing could be worth to survive. I felt I was dead both mentally and physically. I needed to take a high dosage of amphetamine and cocaine to cheer me up. I knew that was fatal, but I had no other choices……
>
> The feelings of over-dosage amphetamine were very intensive. I felt I was another strong man. I deluded that I was making love with my girlfriend. She was so satisfied and enjoyable. The feeling was so elated. No sooner, I was fainted. When I woke up, I stayed in the hospital. My friends called the emergency and saved my life. After that, I was involved in a severely depressive mood. I had no urge and sense to survive.
>
> My girlfriend was gone. My whole body was weak and I could not be a fighter any more. I was so shameful to return home. I had no face to see my mother, father and my younger sister. …'

It was certain that Alex felt dreadfully meaningless to survive further after the leave of his girlfriend. He committed suicide but he was saved by his friend. In the hospital, he suffered from severely depressive mood. The medical social worker in the hospital referred Alex to psychiatric help. The psychiatrist diagnosed Alex as suffering from substance abuse with major depressive disorder. He was then transferred to a detoxification centre. He stayed there for six months then he was referred to a residential rehabilitation centre. In there, he encountered a good social worker, Ken. Alex enjoyed talking and playing basketball with them. Both of them were experts in Kung Fung fighting. Occasionally, they fought each other for fun. All these stirred up Alex's sense of minimal survival in the past. But it was different now as it was only for fun rather than for immoral criminal actions. Spontaneous exercises strengthened Alex's body and mind. What below was his self-narration of his life.

> Alex: Ken was a very good social worker. He was strong and caring. He regarded me as his own son. He taught me how to express my feeling properly and how to earn a decent living by doing electrical repair. He was also a good Kung Fung fighter. Occasionally, we fought together for fun. Gradually, I did not depend on amphetamine to elate myself from depressive mood and fear of facing risks and frustration in life. However, the current life was relaxed, safe but rather boring. In the past, my life was risky and anxious but it was full of stimulation and challenges. When I was fighting in gang fight, I was highly anxious and fearful. However, when I won the fighting or safely escape, I felt extremely excited and gratified. Deep down in my heart, I seemed to enjoy being a successful fighter and was able to escape from extreme risks and insecurity. I could also discharge my anger through defending myself and hurting others in the gang fighting. But now, secure life and prolonged safety seemed to deprive all these senses of gratification in the hard struggle for minimal survival. Everything was safe, secure, relaxed, predictable, and manageable. I did not need to do any struggle in the secure environment in the residential unit.

Apart from addiction of amphetamine, he was also addictive to risk and exciting and grandiosity that he was a great fighter in the gang fight. To ease Alex from that sort of addiction, his social worker, Ken assisted and encouraged Ken to join in some good adventure training. He had to fulfill many physically exhaustive tasks and duties similar to solider in military exercise and regained a sense of minimal survival in a tough environment. What below is his self-narration.

> Alex: Indeed, deeply thanks for Ken's arrangement. He facilitated me to join the adventure training. In the past, I did not recognize that there was such tough training in Hong Kong. I only recognized that Kung Fu fighting was the most exciting exercise in the world. I thought gang fighting, on one hand, was very risky. On the other hand, it was very exciting and challenging. The risky sense of struggle for minimal survival by diminishing your enemies made you fill of excitement. When your enemies were wounded and lying on the ground, you felt that you were so powerful and unbeatable. You felt you had conquered such a difficult task that no one except you could attain it. That means, following the risky sense of struggling for minimal survival was an intensive sense of grandiosity and excitement. After entering into the detoxification program and learnt to be a normal person again, I thought this should be the end of this addictive and risky excitement. However, the tough adventure training brought me back all these excitement and sense of tough struggle for minimal survival. The only difference from the previous one was that I did not need to hurt other or hurt myself to attain it.

Alex's struggle for minimal survival in gang fighting was gradually replaced by excitement in adventure training. Occasionally, he joined Ken and had Kung Fu practice and training in a famous Kung Fu master training institute. Ken regained his meaning of life in Kung Fu practice, coaching adventure training and helping adolescents to quite from drug addiction.

Integrated Recovery for Ultimate Insight and Wisdom

For people with drug addiction, the integrated recovery of ultimate insight and wisdom should include the following:

1. Provide a normalized environment and insight so that individuals can know that apart from drug addiction, there are other ultimate insight and wisdom in life which is realistic, workable, practical and meaningful. They can be local and indigenized wisdom in resilience from hardship and suffering by clients' significant others. They can be religious ideologies such as Jesus' love, sacrifice and forgiveness in crucifixion. They can be wisdom and knowledge in earning a good living. They can be ultimate happiness in meaningful contribution to family, community and society.
2. Facilitate the individual to actualize all these practical insight and wisdom in life. It can be being a committed Christian, being an enthusiastic volunteer, making a good small business, writing a good book, building up a happy family, and/or actualizing unfulfilled aspirations. In doing all these, individuals begin to believe that life is still full of love, hope, faith, opportunities and care.
3. Regularize all these meaningful activities and consolidate all these practical wisdom by encouraging clients to share their practical life wisdom with others.

All these may be showed in the following case illustration.

The Practical Life Wisdom of Mr. T.

Mr. T was an adult male in Hong Kong. He began to addict to cough medicine when he was only 15 years old. He came from a single parent family in which his mother died when he was only six years old. His father worked as a carpenter in construction site. In the day time, he was taken care by his aunt and his uncle. However, his aunt and uncle were very apathetic to his needs. They only regarded him as a source of extra income from his father. Because of that, their children, T's nephew always bullied him. Even if T told his father about that, his father reminded him to keep quiet and behave properly as no one could take care of T. Under that sort of situation, T had to fight his own battle. He became highly rebellious both at his uncle's house and at school. He was highly sensitive to others' bullying and negative comment. He threw his temperament towards others by fighting. No sooner, T was expelled from one school to another school because of his prevailing aggression. Finally, in Year 9 T could not continue his schooling. He worked as a waiter in a Chinese Restaurant. However, T's hot temper still continued. After a severe quarrel with his colleagues, he used a chopper and hurt three of them. T was caught by the police and send to court with a sentence of 2 years' training in a training institute for juvenile delinquent. In the training institute, T was also bullied by his inmates. The only thing he could do was to fight back. No sooner, years of tough life enabled T to develop his own practical wisdom. What is below was his self-narration on that.

T: Years of bullying and tough life enabled me to develop my own practical wisdom that could be roughly summed in the following:

(i) If you are afraid, you must appear calm and confident in front of your enemies. The more powerful your enemies are and the more confident and calm you needs.

(ii) To survive within tough bullying, you have to be tough also. So you need a strong body, a good marital art training, and a good weapon. You need to fight back suddenly and drastically. So at first, you should appear as timid and obedient or turns yourself into a dead log in facing others' verbal and physical attack. Suddenly, you fight back fiercely likes a deadly machine. You only look at others' weakest point. Use your strongest point to attack your enemies' weakest points.

(iii) You cannot survive alone in tough situation. You need to join with others in a gang. Only shared benefit, shared fear, shared anger and shared desires can join people to others. Once a group of guys are joined. Try your best to be most powerful and apathetic one. Only by doing this, you can be the leader of the games.

When he was discharged from the training institute, he quickly joined in a large delinquent gang and become a sub-team leader and he was responsible for drug trafficking and selling to secondary school students. He became well off materially. He had to fight with other gangs in the competition of drug business. He was frequently wounded and needed to engage in addiction of ketamine so as to ease his pain and fear in gang fighting. As his physical conditions deteriorated, his status in the delinquent gang also declined accordingly. At that moment, interestingly, he developed his own revised practical wisdom in a drug addicted life.

T: In my position, I needed to addict to ketamine. You know there is no way out. Firstly, even though I survived well in my practical wisdom with the delinquent gangs and drug business, however, my body conditions declined in frequent wound in gang fighting. Also, competition among drug business was severe. Every gang wanted to take over others' business. Even within the same delinquent gangs, people are cunning and conflicting. Everyone to destroy one other so that s/he could enjoy all benefit. So, it was highly stressful to keep yourself safe and free from others' covert or overt attack, manipulation and exploitation. To ease out this tension, addiction to ketamine was the quickest and most immediate mean. Gradually, it became a simple formula in my life.

Step 1: I felt tense in my life. It properly came from frustrating events in my life such as anxiety before a gang fighting, being oppressed by my boss, being betrayed by my subordinates, being abandoned by my girlfriend, and being chased by the police. At that moment, fear, anger and helplessness prevailed, if you did not try to avoid such feelings, you properly would beat down by them.

Step 2: Thus, the best way was to take ketamine so that the 'out of body experiences' could give me a sense of total release. After that sort of addictive retreat, I could regain my energy and face the various challenges in life.

Step 3: However, taking ketamine properly deteriorated my physical and mental health. As a consequence, I became weaker and weaker to face the challenges in life. In a sense, I needed to take a heavier dosage of ketamine to rid off my intensified frustration in my deteriorating bodily and physical conditions. It certain became a vicious circle.

Step 4: Life was entirely meaningless without drug addiction. My life became a vacuum of drug, gang fighting and other criminal events with quickly deterioration of body and mind. I knew that one day I certainly committed suicide before I became useless rubbish.

T became meaningless and ontologically empty in his life. He simply had no way to sustain his values and meaning of life. He urgently needed a new practical wisdom of life in adapting the current challenges in life. After a severe gang fighting when he was seriously wounded but he dared not to go to hospital, he took a heavy dosage of ketamine so as to ease his pain of his wound. Unconsciously, he wanted to end up his life in which he found no practical wisdom to survive. Fortunately, he was saved by his friends. He was sent to a nearby hospital. Later, T was transferred to a Christian detoxification centre. A Christian social worker, S approached him. He introduced a new way of practical wisdom in life for S. T had his self-narration of the new practical wisdom of life.

T: 'I have to admit that my wisdom of life in the past, in particular in the period of drug addiction was, in fact, very healthy and abnormal. Deep down my mind, I had a deep urge for love and care. I looked for a life with full security, stability, warmth, genuineness. Nevertheless, I could not get this in my life, in particular in my infancy, childhood and adolescence. That was why I had to struggle for survival within a competitive and risky life. Truly speaking, I was afraid of gang fighting. I always thought that one day I would die in a gang fighting. I felt dreadfully inferior in being bullied, manipulated, abused and oppressed by others. But, to survive, you had to appear as tough, strong, angry, courageous and aggressive. The more I pretended to be strong, tough and aggressive, the more I felt inferior, insecure, risky and empty. I needed addiction of ketamine to resolve this discrepancy and maintain my superficial courage, aggression and strength. But it ended up with further pain and deterioration. In fact, I ought to abstain from drug addiction and trained up my body by vigorous physical exercise. However, I dared not to do so, as stopping drug addiction certainly means facing the endless pain of emptiness and inferiority, insecurity and fear. The vicious circle went on and one until I totally collapse. When I was seriously wound in an illegal gang fighting, the only way to face it was to end up my life by taking over dosage of ketamine.

Fortunately, I was saved by my friends and I was then sent to the hospital. When I woke up, I felt dreadful that I did not die peacefully to end up my problematic life. Why I still had to suffer so much. The medical social worker there sent me to a Christian detoxification centre. In there, there was a very empathetic social worker. He was so good. He listened to my own story with empathy, care, and concern. He told me that he was also a delinquent and drug addict in his adolescence. Interesting, he was also a gang fighter at that time. He told me a completely new wisdom in life.

Up to now, I still remember his words.

"He said: Dear T, life is really short. So we have to live a full life. Someone may think that being full in a life should owe a lot of money, property and fortune. Someone may think it is better to enjoy every moment, having sex with beautiful girl, enjoying stimulating games, taking drug and drinking alcohol with friends are ways to paralyzing our happy moments and totally absorbed in our heightened senses. Someone may think that it is better to enjoy biggest benefit with lowest effort and contribution. Being lazy is clever and being diligent is actually foolish. All these are secular thinking about a full life. Unfortunately, all these secular wisdom of having a full life became highly popular and spontaneously advocated and reflected in advertisement. Unfortunately, we gradually neglect the true wisdom of life. The true wisdom is to serve rather than to be served. The genuine happiness is helping others rather than helped by others. The ultimate meaningfulness in life is to connect with the universe, the infinite God and the nature….."

When he said all that, his face was brilliant and his voice was heightened. He simply became a man of meaning and wisdom. At first, I did not know what he was talking about. I just thought that he just said something irrelevant and high sounding. However, what he continued deeply touched my mind.

"He said: Dear T, I fully understand what you feel now. When I was young, I was like you, I was fully engaged in gang fighting and drug trafficking. I thought when I got money and power; I could do anything I want. This should be the most practical wisdom in my life. However, as times went by, I began to realize that all these were not long lasting. Money, power and social status were all vulnerable and perishable. Everyone worshipped and followed your order when you were the toughest guy in the gang fight or you were the leader of the gang. But when you stepped down from the leadership or you were wounded and could not recover, they looked down upon you, they rejected and bullied you. Money, power, control and social status were only the defense mechanism in a 'dog eats dog' society in which no one really wanted to stay in such environment unless s/he does not have any choice. In fact, deep down in our heart, we aspire for love, hope and faith. We urge for love and being loved. We look for mutual faith and trust among us, in particular our intimate others. We dream for hope in facing hardship and suffering. We depend on hope to ensure we have a better future and a substantial reality in the present. Only love, hope and trust are our ultimate wisdom in life."

His answer really enlightened me making me feel that life was another new dimension. His word really touched me deeply. In the past, I came to a conclusion that in our life we looked for love, hope and trust, but we could never get in the real life. Thus, I thought that in the actual life, I should grasp money, power and position instead. But, after a long life struggle, I began to realize that money, power and position were perishable not endurable. Deep down in my heart, I urged for love, hope and trust. I dared not to speak out. I dared not to ask for it. I dared to expect it. I had no way out.

Fortunately, he gave me clear wisdom that how to attain hope, trust and love through Jesus Christ.

"He said: Truly speaking, though we urge for and we look for love, hope and trust in human being, we can rarely get it. If our parents gave us trust, love and hope, however, if they die, all these will vanish. Thus, the practical wisdom in life should look for eternal and unconditional love, trust, and hope. It can only be obtained in almighty God. Jesus Christ loved us. He died for our sin so that we can come close to God. Only in Him, there is unfailing love, enduring trust and hope for eternality."

At first, what he said was just normal preaching of Christianity. Frankly speaking, in my primary school life, I had heard this for many times from my biblical teachers. However, this time, I heard it again, my feeling was completely different. It just liked fresh water was given to a mind that had long been suffered from thirsty. I had suffered from being betrayed by my fellow gangsters, I had struggled hard to gain money, power and position in my delinquent gang but finally all these vanished suddenly. I trusted no one. I loved no one. I cast no hope on anybody. In fact, in my early life, I was situated in a vacuum of life. I urged for love, I got none and finally I did not trust love. When I heard about Jesus Christ this time, my mind was deeply shocked. He introduced to me how Jesus Christ revitalized his meaning of life again. How Jesus' crucifixion forgave his sins. How God's salvation gave him hope, love and trust again. All these really impressed me. It seemed that I had a new way of life, a brand new form of wisdom in life. He led me to his church where brothers and sisters in Christ did show their endless love, trust and hope to me. They did not regard me as an ex-drug addict or a discharged prisoner. They helped me to find a decent job as an office assistant in a large commercial firm. They included me in the young fellowship in which I made many friends. From them, I could fully acknowledge that only with Christ's love, there were genuine love, hope and faith.

From that time onwards, I had a new way of life. The ultimate wisdom of Christianity such as crucifixion and resurrection of Jesus became my life goal. I started to pray to God to help me to be a good person free from crimes and drug. I aspired to live a normal life. I returned home. In the past, I did not like my deceased mother. She died so early leaving me alone in this world. I did not like my father as he did not care about me. He only worked and worked. When he felt unhappy, he drank heavily. He left me in my uncle's home and I was only regarded as a tool for money in the eyes of my uncle. My nephew bullied me. At that moment, I regarded myself had no relative at all. I hated them. I thought the wisdom of my life to be strong, to be powerful and to be influential so that no one could bully me. If anyone bullied me, I would chop his/her head off. But with Jesus love and forgiveness, I knew I needed to forgive myself as well as others, in particular those who hurt and oppress me. I tried to reconcile with my father. I tried to forgive him and asked for his forgiveness on my past bad deeds. We cried and embraced one another. At that moment, I knew with Jesus' love and forgiveness, I gained my father back. It was really nice and exciting to owe a kind father again in your life. It just liked a ship with a firm anchor in a stormy sea.

In fact, I gained a new way of wisdom in life. I no longer aspire for power and influence. Instead I look for total submission and endurance in God's love. I do not fight for money and gratification of secular desire. Rather, I earnestly strive for love and being love, trust and being trusted, hope and being hope for among my family members, my friends, my peers, my church members. For me, being patient, being endurable, being tolerable and being kind to others are not weak and passive. They are the final and ultimate wisdom in building a world full of kindness, peace and mutual support among one another. Only by doing that, everyone, including ourselves and our significant others can fully enjoy a life with joy, peace, love and hope.

Integrated Recovery of Connection of the Infinite

For people with drug addiction, the connection of the infinite is usually blocked. In rebuilding clients' connection of the infinite in their meaning of life, related professionals should consider the following intervention strategies:

1. Acknowledge and accept clients' anger towards life because of their unfair treatments, sufferings and traumas.
2. Explore clients' knowledge and experience in religious belief and practice within their own cultural and traditional context.
3. Facilitate clients to ease out their frustration within their prolonged suffering, traumas and oppression before and after drug addiction.
4. Enable and encourage clients to connect with certain religious belief and practice.
5. Within this religious belief and practice, clients should be assisted to review their own meaning of life and regain a new perspective towards their own sufferings, traumas and tortures.
6. They should be facilitated to have profound hope, love and faith in this religious belief and practice. Within all these, they should develop their constructive life aspiration, ideal and mission.

All these can be illustrated in the following case. Related parties' consensus in using their stories for academic purpose was sought. Personal identities and information were properly disguised for the sake of confidentiality.

M: The Angry Ice Angel

M was an adult female substance abuser who abused ice (a kind of amphetamine) for many years. She was born in an unhappy family in which her father was a drug dealer and her mother was a sex worker. When she was only five, her mother was died of lung cancer and his father was caught by the police and was sentenced to imprisonment for ten years. M was under the care of her grandmother. However, five years later her grandmother suffered from severe heart disease and were no longer took care of her. M was thus transferred into a girl home and her younger brother was transferred into a boy's home.

Unfortunately, in the girl's home, M was bullied by her roommates, M was so angry with them and one night she took a knife and cut of her roommate's ear off. M was thus sent to the police. As she was only fourteen, she was sentenced for two years' residency in a juvenile correction centre for correctional training. In no way, the training in the correctional training could shape her up. Instead, it only increased her endless anger towards life and others. She had frequent quarrel and fights with her inmates and her instructors. One day, during an outside duty in a nearby country park, she managed to escape.

She wandered around and finally encountered her former classmate, Paul who had already become a key member in a delinquent gang. They got along with one another and finally cohabited together. As Paul was also a drug dealer, M addicted ice (a kind of amphetamine) together with her boyfriend Paul. At first, they supported one another and cooperated very well in their drug dealing. M helped Paul to sell drug to female adolescents. Because of frequent abandonment trauma in early life, M's emotion was highly fluctuated. She demanded a total attention of Paul and was very sensitive to his connection with other girls, especially those young and beautiful ones. All these were out of the toleration limit of Paul. No sooner, they started to have frequent quarrel and fight. Finally, Paul could tolerate no more. He decided to go. M threatened Paul's going by committing suicide in front of him. She took a large dosage of ice and thus she was sent to a nearby hospital.

The police then recognized her as an escaped inmate from the adolescent correctional institute. After a week's hospitalization, she was sent back to the institute for one year correctional training with a diagnosis of depressive disorder with suicidal attempt and substance abuse.

It seemed that Paul's leaving was a deep shock for M. It triggered all her former life traumas of being abandoned by her mother, father and grandmother. She was extremely depressive; she refused to eat anything for several days, and attempted to kill herself by self-cutting. She was thus send to the statutory ward of a mental hospital. In the mental hospital, she was looked after by a medical social worker, Mary was quiet empathic with Paul's situation. She was a very nice Christian and referred M for pastoral counseling in the mental hospital. The pastor in the hospital tried to deliver the gospel of Jesus Christ to her. But M refused this bluntly. After two years hospitalization, M was discharged to a psychiatric half way house for psychiatric rehabilitation in which the writer was the professional consultant there.

M was then under the care of a social worker F. Under the supervision of the writer, F induced the above mentioned intervention to M, hoping to help M in rebuilding a constructive and enduring connection of the infinite in M's meaning of life.

1. Acknowledge and accept M's anger towards life because of unfair treatments, sufferings and traumas.

What below was the verbatim recording from a counseling session in helping M to ventilate and accept M's anger towards her life.

F: Hello, M. how are you, you look very good today.

M: Fine thanks, we have been invited by warden Q for afternoon tea in a nearby fast food restaurant. The food there was fine, and we have just a very good chat.

F: What sort of issues you have shared among yourselves.

M: Oh, it was just casual talk. We all shared why we came here and why we became clients with mental illnesses.

F: Indeed, you have good and interesting. How do you think about that?

M: It was really hard to elaborate our deep feeling. Sometime, I think life is really uncontrollable and things did not happen in the way we want.

F: Life is always out of our control. Do you feel a bit upset about that? (M tried to ventilate F's suppressed anger towards life)

M: A little bit. (M stayed quiet for a long while. She did not murmur a word.)

F: Life is too heavy for us and it is difficult to say.

M nodded her head and F embraced her shoulder for a long while.

M cried bitterly: I don't why I am so miserable in my whole life. I had been spontaneously deserted by my mother, my father, my mother and my boyfriend. I did not manage to hurt anyone, but most of them bullied and oppressed me. That was why I had to fight back. But, I was severely punished by my fighting back. I was imprisoned.... Life is so unfair to me.... (M was finally able to air out all her anger in her life.)

F: You have already been very tough in coping with all that. If I were you, I will be even worse.

From the above verbatim recording, it was clear that M harbored a lot of unresolved anger towards her life, towards her boyfriend and parent's abandonment as well as the bullying by others.

2. Explore M's knowledge and experience in religious belief and practice within their own cultural and traditional context and facilitate clients to ease out their frustration within their prolonged suffering, traumas and oppression before and after drug addiction.

Within the support and encouragement of F, M probably felt much enlightened and respected by others in the half way house. She tuned in the life of the halfway house gradually. In the half way house, there are Christians, Buddhists, and traditional worshippers. They all invited F to join them. What below was F's self-narration about her own religious beliefs and practice in her life.

M: Regarding, religious beliefs and practice, I was quite loose. In fact, my father was a Buddhist. He always worshipped the Buddhist idol at home. He prayed to Buddha, hoping that he could protect him from the caught by the police. My mother was a traditional ancestor worshipper. She tried to burn incenses to our deceased ancestors. None of their worshipped idols impressed me. If their gods were really helpful, how could my father still be imprisoned and my mother still died of lung cancer. I did not believe all these faulty gods. Deep down in my heart, I do want to find a real god, but who is my real god. As god was unreachable, all I could depend on was my own self. That was why I had to struggle and to fight back when others bullied and oppressed me.

However, the more I fought for my own self, the more I felt I was weak and helpless in facing others' challenges, unfair treatment and frustration. Once, I was seriously ill for a few weeks I felt life was really vulnerable. I began to repeat my father's aimless religious worship. I went to several local gods' temples and pray for their protection. But I gained no response from them. There were several occasions that my boyfriends abandoned me. I felt that it my whole life was a just a total failure. I attempted suicide. At that moment, I do felt that life was totally in vain. Every one left and abandoned me. I was angry with my parents and my former boyfriends. If there was any god, certainly, I was angry with God. Why He let me suffer so much. Why my life was so miserable with so many sufferings and abandonment.

From M's self-narration, it was clear that M was confused and puzzled in her life. She had a strong tendency to connect with the infinite in times of frustrations and confusion. However, her parents' worshipping of ancestors and indigenous god in Buddhism could never gain her trust in life. Because of this, she was in a spiritual vacuum in facing her sufferings and tortures in life. Fortunately, F and other residents in the half way house introduced Christianity to F making her have an entirely new perspectives on life. What below was the verbatim recording illustrating how F enabled M to have a new perspective on life.

F: Thanks for M's sharing of her frustration in life. Does anyone encounter similar experiences as M? (F intended to encourage others to share their own view in the group)

C (She was another group member in the sharing group. She was a client recently recovered from psychosis): I was very sympathetic with M. In fact, I have similar experiences as her.

F: It is very kind of you, if you can share your own experiences with us.

C: I was also abandoned by my parents while I was only four years old. They simply left me to my grandmother. They worked overseas leaving me alone with my lonely grandmother in a small village in China. Several years later, my mother divorced with my father, she married an American and stayed in the U.S.A and never returned. My father also married a westerner in Sydney. They never returned. When I was only thirteen years old, my grandmother died of a sudden heart attack. From that time onwards, I was dreadfully lonely in the world. I was taken into an orphanage in which the warden there was cold and apathetic. I ran away and lived with those delinquent boys in the street. I fell in love with one of them and we smuggled to Hong Kong by swimming. Unfortunately, my boyfriend died in the rough sea and I was saved by a fisherman. He married me and later he abandoned me after I had given birth to my second daughter. ..... (At that moment, C cried bitterly.)

F came forward and comforted C.

C: Hi, it really hard to earn a living. I had been a factory worker, a sale girl, a cleaner and ....a sex worker....... (C felt shameful about her past)...I got along with many guys but none of them were trustworthy and good. They all abandoned me.

M: That was life. We struggled hard but life for us was just a nightmare with endless tortures and sufferings. That was why I hated my life, I hated my parents, I hated God.

C: I got similar feelings as you. At first, I hated God, I hated myself. When I was desperately for help with a profound sense of emptiness, loneliness and insecurity, at that moment, some good Christians approached. They did not preach the empty Gospel to me. Instead, they cared about me. When I had an abortion after my boyfriend abandoned me. One sister, Mary took me home and let me lived in her flat for three months until I got a place in the half way house. When I was depressed, she cheered me up. When I was lonely, she accompanied me. When I was empty, she led me to do things meaningful and interesting. Under her encouragement and guidance, I began to read the bible, attended church regularly and prayed to God. In the past, I was angry with God why He let me suffered so much in my life. As I knew that Jesus himself suffered so much, I began to realize that God suffered for our sins and only Him knew my suffering deeply and thoroughly. At that moment, I began to recognize the depth of God's love. Through Jesus, I was totally connected with the almighty loving God. The experiences of being connected with God were really amazing. (At that moment, C sang a song 'Amazing Grace' in a sweet and low voice.)

M: Really thank for your sharing. I was very impressed by your godly experiences. I was a bit jealous about your connection with God. I do hope that one day, God can touch me too.

C: If you have time, you can go with me to the church. I introduce you to Mary. She is such a nice person, I have ever met.

> M: Thank you very much.

From the above self-narration, it was clear that C had a very good connection with the infinite (God) in which she was moved by this and felt being cared, embraced and moved.

3. Enable and encourage clients to connect with certain religious belief and practice.

After the sharing with C, M promised to go to C's church. From that time onwards, M seemed to have stable church life. What below was her narration about how Jesus Christ connected with her.

> M: In the past, I did not believe in God. As I was really painful in my life, I was angry with God why let me suffered so much. I did not believe in ancestor worship or indigenous gods. They did not protect me. They did not care about me. Even my parents worshipped them so much, they still suffered. However, after C's own personal sharing, I began to realize that Christianity was entirely different from others. It was not men seeking God but God seeking man. Jesus died for our sins. He was an infinite God but He turned in a finite human form. He was innocent, but took up our sins. He was eternal but because of our sin, He died in the cross. He was sacred and holy but He died in the most humiliated way in a form of crucifixion. In humane form, He had experienced all sorts of human sufferings, such as being abandoned by others, including His beloved disciples. He was betrayed by His disciples too. His people, at once fully admired Him, but finally abandoned Him and put Him on the cross. I was so moved by Jesus' unfailing and overwhelming love on me. I cried bitterly for my past sins. Once I accept that, I felt totally released. That night, I had a very sound sleep. I got a feeling that Jesus embracing me with love. He never abandoned me. He died for me. He was alive and my sins were totally forgiven. .....

It was clear that M experienced a close connection with the infinite (Jesus Christ). She began to tune in the Christian belief of Jesus' crucifixion and salvation. Once, she did so, she started a new perspective and a new meaning of her life.

4. Within this religious belief and practice, clients should be assisted to review their own meaning of life and regain a new perspective towards their own sufferings, traumas and tortures.

M, after having a good connection with Christianity, she began to embrace a new meaning of life. She engaged back to evening school to finish her secondary school education. In the day time, she committed to a full time worker as an assistant clerk in her church. On week end, she served as a volunteer in a drug rehabilitation centre and introduced God's work and mission on her to those female clients with drug addiction. Three years later, she married to a male member in this church who was an active volunteer in this rehabilitation centre.

> M: 'It is really wonderful to be a Christian. Once, you have invited Jesus Christ as your savior, there was peace and substantiality in your mind. We lived not for the sake of ourselves. Instead, we lived simply to glorify God. That means what we were God centered. He would guide our way and protect our path. Under God's help, I manage to continue my unfinished secondary school education. I managed to find a decent job in the

church. I can contribute myself as a volunteer to serve clients with drug addiction. Indeed, God uses me as a good witness of His power and his work. I am no longer lonely, worthless and shameful in front of other. Within God's power, my whole life became more worthwhile and interesting. From a Christian's point of view, my past life was full of secular temptation (being seduced by substance abuse), fulfillment of desire (sex, courtship), unforgivable anger and hurt towards abandonment by others, meaninglessness and ontological insecurity in life. All these were painful and self-punishment. The only way I could do was to move from one secular sin to another sin, from one temptation to another temptation; and from one abandonment to another. Only with Jesus' salvation, I could free myself from this endless vicious circle of sins. With Jesus, I could liberate myself from secular temptation. Within God's love, I could be healed from traumatic memories of abandonment in lives. With the help of Holy Spirit, I could resist from temptation. Within Jesus' salvation, I could be forgiven from my sins.

5. Clients should be facilitated to have profound hope, love and faith in this religious belief and practice. Within all these, they should develop their constructive life aspiration, ideal and mission.

M, after several years' hard work, was able to finish her secondary school education and managed to have a good result in public examination. She was not able to enter university, but good enough to study in community college. She was thus admitted in a full time Diploma Course in Theological Studies in a Bible College. This was indeed a very well organized course not only giving students a basic but full exposure of biblical knowledge and ways in preaching gospel. It fully equipped M to have good spiritual sharing and support with other school mates. They lived together. They shared their own spiritual experiences and insight towards Jesus' salvation. They embraced one another in facing difficulties and hardship. What below was her own self-narration showing how senses of love, hope and faith in her religious belief.

M: 'when I first came to Jesus, I only felt that He loved me so much that He sacrificed for me and forgave my sins. I felt much enlightened as all my sins in my life were forgiven within Jesus' blood on the cross. I felt I was embraced by Jesus' love and with a hope for a new life. I was no longer an unwanted object being abandoned by my parents and by my former boyfriends. When I first engaged in the fellowship of my church, I really felt I was beloved by brother and sister in Christ. There was genuine warmth, care and love.

As time went by, the sense of being loved by Jesus and being cared by brothers and sisters in Christ seemed to be diffused and diluted. There were a lot of burden in life. I remembered once there was a severe quarrel between my boyfriend (my present husband) and me. At that time, he was the small group leader in the youth fellowship in our church. I was really frustrated by the apathetic attitude of the chairman of our fellowship. He engaged in a dirty politics in the church by allying with the elders and kick out the former chairman in this fellowship. I was really angry with him and tried to start a 'fight' with him by group other members in the fellowship to reject him to be the chairman. My boyfriend said all my action was secular and with no faith in God's words. He insisted we should do nothing but prayed to God and let his justice be done. I was furious to his answer saying that he was only a foolish coward. After this quarrel, we had been separated for three months.

In this period of time, our whole fellowship was broken into two parties, one supporting the current chairman and one being against him. While the fighting was furious, one strange thing happened. One night, I got a dream. In the dream, I heard a clear voce from Jesus saying that the fighting made Him feel sad and He was crying bitterly for our sins. The next day, I received a phone call from the leader of party who supported the current chairman. She said she had a similar dream. Both of us were shocked. Without delay we prayed together and repented in front of God. We stopped our fighting and submitted ourselves to God's views. One month later, the current chairman of the fellowship had a severe car accident with bone fracture and bleeding in his liver. He needed to be hospitalized for two months. He repented his own misdeed in front of God and resigned from his chairman position.

From that time onwards, I knew God really cared. He was really in control of everything. What we needed to do was only submission to His view and had patience to let God reveal His plan. Also, I began to realize my boyfriend had much stronger faith towards God than me. From that time onwards, I began to learn from him how to have profound but simple faith towards Him believing His almighty power as well as unfailing love to us. Christianity was not only religious belief but practical day to day wisdom in facing difficulties in life.

Integrated Recovery of the Will to Meaning

The Will of Meaning in Addiction

Persons with drug addiction have a strong will for meaning in life. However, their will to meaning is entirely blocked by frustration, hardship, unpleasant events and even traumas and abuses in life and developmental process. Life for them is really boring, empty and meaningless. They camouflage their will of meaning by addiction and/ or use addiction to resolve their inner conflict. They depend on drug addiction to ease out the intolerable tension in noogenic neurosis. It also serves an immediate gratification for existential frustration and vacuum. Finally, drug addiction becomes the quickest and most easily available way to fill up the existential vacuum with a result of endless dependence on drug addiction.

Recovery of Will of Meaning in Persons with Drug Addiction

The recovery persons with drug addiction should be a restoration of individuals' normal noo-dynamic, inner psychic energy in searching for will of meaning through constructive and healthy means. Related interventions include the following:

1. Recognizing and accepting one's existential vacuum, noogenic neurosis in drug addiction.
2. Restoration of individual's noo-dynamics in searching for a better meaning in life.
3. Facilitate the individual to have better and constructive means in filling up his/her existential vacuum.

4. Resolving and ventilation of one's hardship, suffering and traumas in drug addiction as well as in life before addiction.
5. Channeling one's will of meaning to life with good significance to oneself and others.

All these can be demonstrated in the following case illustration.

John was a male Chinese with drug addiction. He had been addicted to ketamine for 10 years already. He was born in a drug addiction family. His father was a drug dealer of heroine. His mother was an assistant in this drug dealing business. When John was only three years old, his mother was caught by the police and was sentenced for ten years imprisonment. Thus, both John and his elder sister were brought up by his grandmother who was very strict and rigid in child rearing. Whenever they committed any misbehavior, she would impose bodily punishment on them. John's father rarely returned home to look after them. Apart from taking heroine himself, he was also an alcoholic. Whenever he returned home, he was drunk and physically abused John and his elder sister. Thus, when John was only 13 years old, one night after he was seriously physically abused by his father, he ran away. He stayed in his peer's home and never returned home. To survive, he worked as an illegal child labor in a local factory. To protect himself from being bullied by others, he joined a delinquent gang. Three years later, he also became a drug dealer selling drug to other adolescents in schools and in parks. As a victim from a drug addiction family, John did have unresolved emotional complex in facing his own drug dealing. What is below is his self-narration on this.

John: I came from a drug dealing family; I was really a victim of drug addiction. Both my parents were drug addicts. My mother was imprisoned when I was only three years old. My father was a drug dealer and an alcoholic. Whenever he was drunk and returned home, he beat us fiercely. I knew more than anyone about the harmful effects of drug addiction to the whole family.

I hated drug dealers including my parents. However, I committed the indecent act as my parents. I sold drugs to innocents students in primary and secondary schools. In some cases, I seduced them to do so. All these create an unresolved dilemma in my mind. I hated both my parents and myself. Whenever I thought of this, I was deeply frustrated. I was really in a state of existential vacuum (it was interesting term taught by my social worker saying that what I had done in my whole life was nothing and empty). I was deeply hurt by drug but now I hurt other also deeply by drug. There was no way out. I always asked myself why I had to commit the same hatred error as my parents. May be deep down, I wanted to take revenge on my parents by hurting others.

Very often, at night I woke up by continuous nightmares in which I was swollen by a monster of drug. At the same time, I became another monster of drug to swallow others.

All these were unbearable for me. I felt extremely empty and meaningless in my life. The only way to get rid of these unbearable frustrations were to take drug, taking a large dosage of ketamine help me to release from all these frustration and pain. However, the more I engaged in taking ketamine, the more frustrated I became and the more I hate myself… I had attempted suicide to end up my life by taking over dosage ketamine. Fortunately, my neighbor saved my life. For me, life at that time was just an endless circle of heavy addiction to punish myself, selling drug to hurt other, deep hate towards my addicted parents and deep regret and endless emptiness.

John's will of meaning was deeply demolished by the endless circle of heavy addiction to punish himself, selling drug to hurt others, deep hate towards his parents and deep regret and endless emptiness. It trapped John within an intensive existential vacuum and noogenic neurosis. Thus, John had to recognize and accept his existential vacuum and noogenic neurosis before he could restore his will of meaning in life.

1. Recognizing and accepting one's existential vacuum, noogenic neurosis in drug addiction.

'John became a drug dealer as well as an addict in the delinquent gang. On one hand, he sold psychotropic drugs such as ketamine, amphetamine, and hallucinogens to young people in schools. On the other hand, he took ketamine whenever he felt frustrated and bored in his life. He did earn a good sum of money from selling drug and he got along well with his girlfriend who came from a broken family. They took ketamine together. Occasionally, John needed involved in gang fighting to protect his and his gang's territory in drug dealing. Gradually, John's body was deeply weakened by the destructive effect of prolonged intake of ketamine. His social functioning and ability to carry out his drug dealing business were also deeply affected. Coupled with the separation of his girl and the death of his grandmother, John was mentally collapsed. He committed suicide by taking a large dosage of ketamine. Fortunately, he was saved by his close friend. He was thus admitted in a mental hospital with a diagnosis of substance abuse, major depressive disorder and suicide. He stayed there for three weeks and then was transferred to a drug rehabilitation center.

In this center, John was taken care by an empathic social worker, Michal. He was a recovered drug addict before he received formal social work training. He was also a committed Christian. He was able to understand John's existential vacuum and noogenic neurosis in the process of drug addiction. What below was the verbatim recording showing that how Michal helped John to recognize and accept his existential vacuum and noogenic neurosis in life.

John: Dear Michal, really thank for your care in these two months.

Michal: You are welcome. You know, I had been a drug addict in my adolescence. Frankly speaking, I understood how a drug addict feel.

John: Life for me was really massive and meaningless. I was angry with my parents as drug dealer, but I was drug dealer again. I hated drug addiction but I involved in drug addiction myself. Life was entirely meaningless and just an endless circle again.

Michal: I can really understand your feeling. You know I have a beloved brother, Tim. We came from a poor family in which my father worked too hard to earn a decent living for our family. He died of lung cancer when I was only ten and my younger brother was only five. Before he died, he reminded me to take care of Tim.

John: So as me, I was deserted by my father emotionally as he rarely returned home. When he came back, he was drunk and abused us. My mother was imprisoned for ten years. I was brought up by my grandmother but she was really hot tempered and hit me frequently.

Michael: So as my mother. After my father died, my mother had to take care for the whole family. She needed work day and night so as to earn a hand to mouth living. I had to do all the household chores including taking care of my brother. But he was very naughty. He went outside and joined a delinquent gang. He sold drug to others and always involved in gang fighting.

John: He must in deep trouble. You saved him from troubles.

Michal: Indeed, you are so clever. You know well. Whenever he involved in gang fighting, I told him not to do so. He never listened. I had to follow him secretly and saved him in time of risk and emergency. Once, he was chased by a gang with sharp choppers. I came out and fought with them to protect him. Both Tim and me were seriously hurt. Three of our enemies were died in the fighting. In the hospital, Time was died. I stayed there for three months. I was charged with murder and homicide. As I was less than sixteen year old, I was only sentenced for two years imprisonment in a correctional institute.

John: It is the first time you tell me your own story. It was so sad, you could not save your brother and you were charged with murder and homicide.

Michal: You know it so sad for me. At that time, my mind was blank and my life was just like an empty vessel. I did not know what sort of thing I have done. I just had a strong urge to end my life so that I could accompany my deceased brother. My mother cursed me I should responsible for the death of my younger brother. In the corrective institution, I tried to suicide twice but I was saved by my inmates. My mother cursed me, my beloved brother was dead. What was the meaning of life? It should be nothing but rubbish in my family. You know that was a state of existential vacuum. ... (Michal was so involved in his sharing and he wiped.)

John: Dear Michal. I can understand how difficult your life was. In the past, I always thought that I was the most unlucky man in the whole world. My parents were drug dealers and drug addicts. My father abused me and I was also a bad guy in the world. My whole life was just a tragedy. I hated myself. I hated God and I hated my parents. My whole life was ruined by my prevailing hate and anger. Hi, after hearing your own story, I began to recognize that your sufferings were much deeper than mine. ..... (John also cried. It seemed that his tears began to wash his anger behind his prevailing existential vacuum and noogenic neurosis in his whole life.)

Michal and John embraced one another. They did not say any word. In their mind, they fully understood how painful they were in their own life.

John began to recognize and accept his own existential vacuum and noogenic neurosis in life. He did not need prolonged and deep drug addiction to conceal his deep seated existential vacuum and noongenic neurosis.

2. Restoration of the client's noo-dynamics in searching for a better meaning in life.

With the continuous support from Michal, John seemed to regain his will to meaning. Michael successfully helped John to restore his noo-dynamics in searching for a better meaning in life. What below was Michael's self-narration.

Michael: Indeed it is my pleasure to serve as a social worker for John. We really have a very good sharing. We both suffered from drug addiction. His parents were drug dealer and drug addiction. So as my deceased younger brother, he was also a drug dealer and drug addict. Both of us did not want to be drug addicts. We were simply the victims of our family members. In the past, we felt were lonely victims. But now, we felt we were good companions. Even I had got over all these sufferings in life. I felt John's response was a good support to me. John was no longer my client. He was my friend, or just my 'young brother'. I needed to restore his will to meaning in life.

With that in mind, I was determined to try all my means to help him. First, I accompanied John to visit his parents. At first, John did not want to do so. He said, he would not forgive them who made his childhood and adolescence so massive and confused. Later, he promised me to do so. Actually, his mother was released from the prisoner five years ago. She lived with John's father in a small wooden hut. When they saw John, they were so happy. They never dreamt that John could visit them. Under my encouragement, they started to talk and share their current situation. In fact, John's father suffered from liver cancer for one year already. John's mother also suffered from diabetes. Their health was deteriorating and they were poor and dependent on public assistant. After seeing all that, it seemed that John's anger with his parents were partially resolved. We brought them out for tea and dim sum in a nearby Chinese restaurant. John's parents were very excited by this. They told John about their own situation within these years. They also said sorry to John for what they had done to John. Under this condition, John was deeply impressed. He began to forgive his parents on what they had done to him in his childhood. From that time onwards, John seemed to regain his will of meaning to life..........

John's unresolved emotional complex towards his parents in his childhood was resolved. He began to regain his inner psychic on noo-dynamics, a strong urge to will of meaning in life.

3. Facilitate the client to have a better and constructive means in filling up his/her existential vacuum

John regained her noo-dynamics to will of meaning in his life and showed the following actions in consolidating his will meaning of life.

a. He served as a volunteer in the community education team in the drug rehabilitation center. He shared his own experiences in recovery from drug addiction with adolescents.
b. Under the encouragement from Michal, he was converted into a Christian with a full dedication of his life to spiritual recovery of drug addiction.
c. He rented a flat and lived with his parents and tried to take care of them.

For John, he regained his inner psychic energy to re-orientate his own situation to a better meaning of life to suit his own aspiration.

John: Indeed, I deeply thank for Michael's support and changes. I really regain the inner urge to search for a more meaningful life. Michael invited me to join in the community education in our drug rehabilitation center. Indeed, I enjoy sharing my experiences with adolescents giving them a valid witness that how drug addiction ruins our life and our family. In doing so, I get a deep feeling that even my darkest side in my life can be used by God to serve as a valid tool to glorify Him and benefit the society. I feel energetic, substantial and confident. That is really good to become a Christian. In the past, I hated Christians. I thought they were hypocrites. In my childhood, I lived in a small dirty flat. The flat owner claimed that they were Christians. They did not allow us to put some Buddhist idols in the flat. They said this was not acceptable for Christians. They appeared to be sacred and holy in doing so. However, they were so cold and apathetic in pushing us to pay our rent or increase the rent drastically. In the past, they did not know that my parents were drug dealers. Once the police came and charged my mum for drug trafficking. They approached us again and threatened us either to leave immediately or increase the rent for thirty percentages. They were indeed hypocrites. I hated them and I hated what so call Christians from that time onwards.

Michael changed my attitude entirely. He was so nice to me. Besides, he was frank and supportive. He led me to a good church in which the pastor and related brother and sister in Christ were so supportive and caring. They did not mind my drug addiction and drug dealing background. They did not look down upon us. Instead, they extended a warmest welcome to us. They were also frank and empathic. They listened to our stories carefully. They showed deep appreciation to God's work on us and regarded us as the angels from God to teach them about repentance from secular temptation. With that sort of support and recognition, I regained my confidence to relate to persons in a genuine and warm manner. I no longer needed to be highly defensive and anxious to protect myself from being hurt by others. I also restored my hope, faith and love in relating to God and others. That was so wonderful. God's grace changed me totally. I was no longer lonely and desperate with life. I began to harbor hope that I could live a life more fully than before. Under God's grace, I could glorify Him and serve others in His ways.

With all these, I was no longer angry with my parents. I forgave them as Jesus forgave my sins. I rented a flat and lived with them so that I could take care of them. They changed accordingly. They also cared about my daily living. Despite they had chronic illness, they became caring parents. I regained a good feeling of a united family.

John's noo-dynamism was restored with a full engagement of meaningful activities such as being a committed Christian, serving as a volunteer in anti-drug education and care and attention home. He felt substantial in family life with the togetherness of his parents. He felt meaningful and self-actualized by using his own experiences to educate adolescents to avoid drug addiction. He felt spiritually connected with God in Christianity.

4. Resolving and ventilation of one's hardship, suffering and traumas in drug addiction as well as in life before addiction.

With all these, John was substantial in life. His past hardship, suffering and traumas in drug addiction and in life before addiction were totally resolved. What is below is his own self-narration about this.

John: In the past, I was fully occupied by anger towards my parents, myself and life. I hate my parents they were drug dealers and were unable to take care of me. I hated my

> father as he physically abused me. I hated myself as I was drug dealer and addict. I hated my life. I hated God why I had to suffer so much. Why I was born in such a bad family. It was totally unfair to me. However, under Michal's guidance, I became a committed Christian. With the love and forgiveness from Christ, all these anger and hates could no long ruin my life. Instead, I fully trusted that God was in total control of everything. With Jesus' love, I forgave my parents. Indeed, the feeling of being forgiven by God and forgiving those who hurt you deeply was wonderful. In the past, I frequently had some 'angry dreams' in which I tried to chop my drug addicted parents, my delinquent gang leader. However, after I had killed them, I felt dreadfully guilt and I also became a monster of drug dealers. Very often, I committed suicide in my dream. Interestingly, after I forgave my parents because of God's love and I knew I was totally forgiven by Jesus, all these dreams vanished. I got a feeling of being free from past traumas, hate and anger in life.

John's anger towards himself was dissolved by Jesus' crucifixion and resurrection. His anger towards his parents was resolved by his forgiveness and reunion of his parents. His anger towards life was replaced by God's love, parental care and encouragement from his social worker, Michel. His emptiness in life was filled up by meaningful work with adolescents in preventing them to become drug addicts.

5. Channeling one's will of meaning to life with good significance to oneself and others.

John's life was fully engaged in activities with good significance to himself and others. What below was Michal's self-narration.

> Michel: 'Indeed, John started a new life. In the past, he was full unresolved anger and frustration in his life. He held up intense anger towards his parents, himself and his life. Now, he appeared happy and joyful in his new life. He was very eager to spread the gospel to others. Whenever, he gave his own testimonial to adolescents in schools. He assertively proclaimed how God changed his life and how God forgave him and thus he could forgive his parents. All these were very moving, many secondary school students even cried. They said John established a very good example, how could come out from his love and hate dilemma with his parents. In fact, John became a very influential person. He became an active leader in the church fellowship. He found a job as a sale person in the church bookstore. He suggested many good strategies to promote Christian book sales. One year later he was promoted to be an assistant manager in this bookstore. In this home, John was caring son for his parents. In church, he was so supportive to young members in his fellowship. In the bookstore, he was empathic and insightful for his colleagues. In schools, his own testimonials were highly welcomed by secondary students. He was no longer a lonely guy being trapped within his own anger and frustration in life, in drug dealing and drug addiction. He was a man full of dynamic and psychic energy that was so influential and significance to people around him.

Integrated Recovery of Meaning of Love in Drug Addiction

For people with drug addiction, their urge for deepest love is still there but in their lives they can never get it. They replace it by erotic love and compensatory love in terms of drug addiction. Integrated recovery for meaning of love of persons with drug addiction should mean the following:

1. Love is the only media/way for persons with addiction to reconnect their essence with others
2. By love, they are able to see the genuineness with others.
3. Through love they can actualize their potentiality despite addiction.
4. Help them to recognize and re-actualize love rather than sex, concern rather than stimulation, support instead of addictive isolation.
5. Transcend them from one levels of love to another.

All these can be illustrated in the following case.

H: A Woman Who Search for Love but cannot Get It

H was a female around 24 years. She was good looking and appeared as mature and attractive to males. She worked as a waitress in a Chinese restaurant for three years. Before that she was a drug addict and she had taken ketamine and amphetamine for eight years. In her whole life, she searched for love but she could hardly get it.

H was born in a single parent's family in which her father died when she was only two years old. To support a decent living, H's mother worked as a prostitute in the city area. H felt highly shameful about her mother's job. She left home when she was only fifteen year old and joined a delinquent gang. No sooner, she fell in love with the leader of this group. At first, they loved one another and got along well. However, one year later, her boyfriend fell in love with another girl and deserted her. She was pregnant at that moment. She was deeply frustrated and underwent an illegal abortion immediately. Later, she committed suicide by trying to jump over in a tall building. Fortunately, she was saved by a security guard there and she was sent to a nearby hospital for treatment.

One year later, H got along with another boyfriend, Q who was a drug dealer as well as a drug addict. To escape from previous life trauma, H took ketamine and amphetamine with Q together. H casted her hope on Q, hoping that she could love and attach to Q deeply or vice versa. However, things did not happen in H's expectation. Q left H one day and got along with another girl whom he met in a disco. H was furious; she went to this disco and tried to kill that girl in the disco. To save his new girlfriend, Q knocked down H. She was sent to hospital for treatment. She was also charged with suspected homicide and was imprisoned for two years. When she was discharged, she worked as a waitress in a Chinese restaurant. She fell in love again with another waiter in the same restaurant. They cohabitated for two years, H gave birth to a lovely baby boy, Tom. When H thought she could have a completed and warm family with supportive husband and lovely baby, she discovered that her boyfriend engaged in sexual relationship with another woman during her period of pregnancy. She was so depressive about that. All her search for love in her whole life was in vain. She felt empty and meaningless and had no urge to continue her life. She swallowed many sleeping pills and committed suicide. Fortunately, she was rescued by her close friends. She was then sent to a nearby mental hospital. She was diagnosed as suffering from major depressive disorder with suicidal risk and substance abuse. Within the mental hospital, H was totally engaged in her depressive mood. She did not murmur any word. She refused to eat and drink for one or two days. At that moment, a medical social worker, Mary approached H. She was very caring and empathic to H. Under her caring, H gradually regained her urge to live. What below was H's self-narration showing that how she searched for love but she could never get life.

H: Frankly speaking, I was deprived for love for my whole life. My father was died when I was only two years old. My mother was a sex worker. She cared about his 'customers' but she did not care about me. I was looked down by my neighbors, my classmates as well as relatives and friends. They teased me as the 'hen's baby' (in Chinese Cantonese culture, 'hen' meant 'prostitute'). I was so shameful about that. I urged for love and respect from my significant others including my mother, my neighbors and my schoolmates but I could get none. All I had in my childhood was merely stigma, bullying, gossip and ignorance by others. In many occasion, to put an end to all these, I needed to fight back. I needed to yell and curse anyone who put into such oppression. However, the more I defended myself, the more others labeled me as target to be excluded and bullying. That was why I had to leave this dreadful social environment when I was only fifteen year old.

I harbored a strong desire to be loved and cared by other when I first encounter my first boyfriend. I fully recognized that he was a gangster, a delinquent and a criminal. But I could feel his love and care to me, especially when I was being bullied by my neighbors and schoolmates, he was the only one who stood up and fight for me. Apart from him, who cared about me? That was why I followed him. I hoped I could be his girlfriend and even his wife for my whole life. I dreamt that I could have a happy family with him. But one year later, he got along with another girl. At that moment, I was pregnant and dreaming to have a happy family with him. I was furious about that. I went for an illegal abortion in Shenzhen. I killed not only my baby but killed my own dream and aspiration. There was no love, no hope and no trust in the whole world. I went to the top floor of a tall building and wanted to climb over the window and jumped down to end my empty life. The security guard there saved my life. They sent me to a hospital.

When I went out of the hospital, I felt deeply depressed. What was the aim of my whole life? I worked as a causal worker in fast food shop. One day, one of my former neighbors visited the food shop and discovered me. She teased me again as the 'hen baby'. I was so angry and threw a glass cup to her. She was hurt and I was immediately sacked by my boss. I cursed my boss and he sent a security guard and sent me to the police. At that moment, a strong man, Q, suddenly came forward and pushed away the security guard and helped me to escape. He was one of my familiar customers in the fast food shop. I could feel how he loved and cared about me for this moment. No sooner, we lived together. I dreamt again that I finally discovered true love and sooner or later, I should have a happy family.

One month later, he frankly told me that he was a drug dealer, selling drugs to adolescents. It surprised me at all. My first boyfriend was a delinquent too. As far as he loved me, everything was not important at all. To show that I accepted him, I took ketamine and cocaine with him. Apart from selling drug, he was also a good cook and very skillful in bakery. I encouraged him to open a bakery or a small fast food shop so that we could work together and construct our future. When we planned all these and decided to proceed our good future, I discovered Q engaged with another young girl. One day, when I returned home, I found they were making love in our bed. I was so angry and threw bottle on that girl. However, my boyfriend protected her. He even cursed me as crazy woman and hit me on my face. The nasty girl ran away. To preserve my dream of a happy family, I urged my boyfriend to desert this nasty girl and stay with me and continue our dream of a happy family and opening a nice fast food shop. At first, my boyfriend agreed to do so. He said this girl met him in the disco and seduced him. He promised to leave this girl. However, three days later, he left me in the early morning without saying any words. I was so furious on his leaving. I took up a chopper and went to the disco and intended to kill this nasty girl.

My boyfriend even protected this nasty girl and knocked me down. My heart was totally shattered. How could I tolerate the fact that Q loved this nasty girl far more than me.

I was sent to a mental hospital for psychiatric treatment. For two days, I was totally tied up in a hospital bed. When I was recovered from my diffusion of mental confusion, I was charged as homicide and later was sentenced to two years' imprisonment. In the prison, I really thought that my whole life was merely a massive confusion. I urged for love. But by the end of the day, I could get nothing. Instead, in the prison, I had to face maltreatment and bullying from inmates and workers. I searched for love in my whole life. But what I could get was only suffering, hate and abandonment.

When I was discharged from the prison, the probation office helped me to find a job as a waitress in a Chinese restaurant. I met another handsome man. He was also a waiter in this restaurant. We liked each other and we co-habited for two years. Within these two years, I gave birth to a lovely baby boy, Tom. He was so lovely and my aspiration to have a happy family was actualized. I planned to marry my boyfriend so that my baby could have a good family. However, he showed no interest on that. He became more and more distant to me and Tom. One of his colleagues told me that he got along with another young girl during my pregnancy. They had continuous sex relationship. I was so depressed in hearing that. One day, I sent my baby boy to my close friend and I return home and swallow a whole bottle of sleeping bill to commit suicide. I was saved by my close friend Mary and the police sent me to a nearby mental hospital for urgent treatment.

As my depressive mood prevails and I still harbored intense urge to commit suicide, I was thus diagnosed as suffering from major depressive disorder and required involuntary admission in a mental hospital. I was totally trapped within my depressive mood. For me, my whole life was nothing but a complete confusion. I searched for love earnestly. I urged for a happy and completed family with good husband and lovely children. This was only the normal aspiration for every human being. Why others could get it but I could not. Every time, when I was getting near to this happy dream, God shattered it. I was angry with God, with myself, with my former boyfriends, my shameful mother and my deceased father. For me, life was nothing but only torture. It was entirely meaningless, aimless and worthless. Apart from death, I could see no way to escape from

> my lifelong misfortune. I refused to eat or drink for a week. They restrained me in my bed and inject related medication to save my life.

From H's self-narration, it was clear that in her whole life, she searched for love but she could never get it. She urged for mutually dependent love hoping that her boyfriend and her could depend or support one another and establish a happy family. She also urged for reciprocal love. She thought that as she had tried her best to care about her boyfriend, he should also love her for return. She lost her love from her parents. Thus, in the whole life, she looked for compensatory love from her boyfriend. When the first boyfriend deserted her, she looked for compensation from the second boyfriend. When the second boyfriend deserted her, she looked for compensation from the third boyfriend. The more she lost for love, the more she was deserted by her boyfriends, and the more she felt helpless, hopeless, meaningless and worthless in life. Finally, what she could look for was merely erotic love. The only way to paralyze herself or escape from the pain of life-long abandonment was drug addiction.

> H: Whenever my boyfriends abandoned me. The first thing I wanted was ketamine and/or amphetamine. Ketamine really gave me a sense of being separated from this cold and apathetic world. After I had taken it, it seemed that I was gone away from my troubled body and frustrating reality. My soul was flowing among things. I felt extremely free. Taking amphetamine was another enlightening experience. It gave me a sense of excitement. It was a great sense of extreme excitement. No matter how depressed I was, this sense of extreme excitement pushed me up. I felt extremely competent to do anything including to attract handsome boy, to get a good job, to earn a good sum of money and to have a happy family. Sometimes, I took ketamine and amphetamine together. It was really amazing to get rid of all my traumatic memories and abandonment by others. I could get love from my parents, from my boyfriends and from son. All I could get it was just erotic love from ketamine and amphetamine. They were all erotic substitute for my lifelong abandonment from human beings.

First Encounter of Genuine Love in Life

In H's life, she searched for love but she was in vain, leaving her with more and more abandonment trauma. The encounter of a genuine social worker, Mary, made her feel the meaning of genuine love. What below was Mary's narration of this.

> H: Indeed, it was hard imagine how depressive H was when I first met her in the hospital ward. She harbored a strong urge to end up her life. She cried bitterly for a while and remained quiet for most of the time. Within three days, she refused to eat or drink so she could die slowly. To pretend her to end up her life, she was injected with various kind of nutritious solution and was kept restrained in her bed.
>
> I approached her and told her about my name and my purpose of visiting her. She did not murmur a word. I stayed with her quietly for half an hour. Then I told her I had to leave her as I had another appointment with a client. Three hours later, I came back with some snacks for her. I gave her some snacks but she refused to eat. I told her that I felt her pain in her mind. I said it was really painful to be abandoned by parents, boyfriends. When I said these, she cried bitterly. I embraced her and told her that I was also been

abandoned by my father as he committed adultery when I was a small child. Fortunately, my mother loved me deeply. I really understood the feeling of being abandoned. I embraced her and we cried together.... At that moment, I felt I was really connected with her with love.

Even though H did not show any response in the first and second encounter, Mary still kept on. She cared and respected H deeply. Indeed, it was the first time for H in life to have such a deep and genuine encounter. What below was H's self-narration on that.

H: Frankly speaking, it was the first time in my life in knowing what is real genuine love. Mary was such a caring worker. In fact, I had encountered many workers before. Most of them were good professionals. However, none of them behaved like Mary. If she I was fully absorbed in my severely depressive mood and gave no response to them, they usually labeled me as unmotivated and irresponsive client. They would send me for medical treatment or further restrain. She was the only worker who visited me consistently several times. She was the only worker who was willing to stay with me for so long. She was the only worker who was willing to share her own frustration in life. At that moment, I did not feel that she was a social worker. I just felt that she was actually my close friend or even my elder sister. She was so frank, so caring and so genuine. Frankly speaking, this was the first time in my life that I was cared for and loved by others. The feelings of being loved, cared and concerned were so good....'

From H's self-narration, it was clear that H was deeply cared by Mary. This was the first time in her life to be loved by others. She regained her urge to be recovered.

From Genuine Love to an Intense Urge to Recover and be Independent

Within the support, care and love from Mary, H agreed to participate in a rehabilitation program for drug addiction. She needed to live there for half and year so that she could be fully recovered. Within these six months, H was taken also by a caring and genuine social worker, Rose. Under the encouragement of Rose and Mary, her urge for recovery and living normal life was regained.

H: Mary encouraged me to live in the rehabilitation centre. At first, I refused to do so. I did not think all such services and intervention worth anything. I had witnessed many friends who had substance abuse entered in such program. Within six months inside the rehabilitation centre, their substance abuse was diminished not because of the effectiveness of such program but simply because they did not able to get any drug to use. Once they left the centre, their drug addiction resumed. Many of them told me that apart from drug addiction, they did not have any one to love or to be loved, what is the meaning of life without drug. Truly speaking, I thought the rehabilitation effects of such centers and programs were minimal provided that we still felt meaningless and aimless in life. One friend told me that staff and professionals there were apathetic and social control oriented. They only took care of their own needs. They did not care about the feelings and needs of clients.

Nevertheless, Mary understood that I did not have a good impression of drug rehabilitation center. She brought me to this center and had a short chat with residents and workers there before I decided to live there. This visit was vital for me. The workers there were very caring. They listened to my story carefully. They were good and committed Christians. They prayed for me. One of the worker, Rose, even cried for me. She really understood the pain and sufferings in my whole life. After that, I determined to join in the rehabilitation program there.

Once I joined in, related workers, in particular Rose was very caring. They simply regarded me as their younger sister. They listened to my stories carefully. They cried with me for my pain in life. They embraced me when I felt lonely and helpless. They helped me to forgive my mother. In fact, my mum was pretty old. She was no longer an attractive sex worker. Instead, she appeared as dump woman with heart problems. He also helped me to visit my son in the boy's home. Within all these, I regained my meaning of life and I really felt, love was still surrounding me. I restore my will power to recover. Life was still full of hope and aspiration. I could look for a happy family in the future with my son and my mother....

It was really clear that H's sense of being and meaning of life was restored by the care and concern of Rose and Mary together with the re-establishment of bonding with his son and his mother. Rose also tried her best to facilitate H to forgive her mother.

Rose: Ms. M, thanks for your visit. It was really a remote place. You had to walk a long way to come here.

M: I spent around an hour to walk to hit. I had not exercised for a long time and I have heart problem, so a ten minute walk take me an hour. I walked for a short while, and then I had to take a rest, and walked again.

Rose: Hi, H sees how your mother cared about you.

H did not look at her mother. She still harbored a deep seated anger towards her mother.

M: I owed her really a lot. I had heart problem and I did not get the money to do the surgery. The doctor in the public hospital told me that I had to wait for two years to undergo the operation. Within these two years, any heart attack, if not being properly treated immediately can be fatal.

Rose: So you actually take your life at risk to visit H. What a great mother you are?

M: Thank for your appreciation. In fact, I am so shameful to be a poor mother for H. I had been a sex worker to earn a hand to mouth living ever since the death of H's father. It was really shameful? (M began to wipe sadly.)

Rose: I could understand your shame and frustration. In fact, you do think you are indebted for H and asked for her forgiveness.... (Rose tried to air out M's deep seated frustration and unresolved emotional complex towards H.)

M: (with tears in her eyes) I am getting old. I have heart problems and other chronic illness. I don't know when I will die. It should be sooner or later. I really wanted to ask for H's forgiveness before I died. (At that moment, M was so sad that she could not speak clearly. She simply murmured her words sadly.)

Rose: I know you love H deeply. It was really hard to earn a living in the past, especially if you have a little daughter with you.

M: I was lazy. I had tried to work as a factory worker, but the wages there was low. The workload was great. People there bullied me. I could not stay there. At that time, this was the only job I could do to support our living.....

Rose: Being a sex worker was also a difficult life for a woman, in particular with your baby daughter H.

At that moment, H was also crying. She suddenly came into the discussion.

H: Mum, I hated you; you did not worth to be my mum. For the whole life, you only make feel shameful and nothing else.

Rose: Dear H, I could understand your hatred feeling towards your mother. She really broke your heart when you were young (Rose tried to ventilate H's negative feeling out.)

H: I hated you; I have no such mother in life.

M: I knew I was a bad mother in all my life. But I don't know when I died. So..........I should not or I should dare to ask for your forgiveness. (M packed up her things and ready to leave the rehabilitation centre.)

At that moment, Rose embraced H and pushed her to get close to her mother.

H suddenly broke into tears and embraced her mother closely. In fact, this was the first time in his life that her mother asked for her forgiveness.

They embraced for a long while without saying a word. Tears ran down from their eyes and washed away years of shame, hate, anger and frustration in their whole lives.

Time seemed be frozen by their embracement. H no longer felt that she was abandoned and ashamed by others. Instead, an intensive inherent urge of mutual co-dependence between mother and daughter, being loved and love together was restored.

With that sort of genuine love and an intensive sense of forgiveness, it seemed that H restored her urge for recovery. What below was herself narration.

H: I could not say how I felt in meeting my mother. I really hated her so deeply that I would never forgive her in my whole life. I was so ashamed by her being a prostitute. I felt that she not only ashamed me but also my deceased my father. She in fact, spoiled my whole life. She was worth to die in terminal illness as quickly as possible so that she could disappear in my whole life. I never treated her as my mother. However, as she appeared in front of me, especially, when she appeared so old, so sick and so regrettable, a deep feeling of motherhood returned to me again. My slim and suppressed memories of being embraced by her, being carried by her suddenly retained. All these feelings are so good and so encouraging. With all these, my urge to recover, to have a full and meaningful recovery came back. Why should I spoil my life by drug addiction?

As my mother suffered from heart attack and other chronic illness, I thought I need to have a full recovery before she died. Time was short and we needed to treasure it once we knew that there was someone we love. I should not let someone I love down. Beside my mum, I still had my son. Rose and Mary were also genuine and supportive social workers. They were not only social workers, they liked my elder sisters. In fact, I had a good family. With their support, I had to be recovered.

From Recovery to Transcendence of Love

H finally forgave her mother and she took home leave and lived with her mother. She also took back her son Tom from the boy house. She was totally abstained from drug so to have a full recovery in front of her mother. They lived happily together. One month later, her mother died in a severe heart attack. H cried bitterly for two days. Rose and Mary helped H to settle the funeral. After that, H returned to the drug rehabilitation centre. H finished the rehabilitation program in six months. Within this period, H also learnt the skill of book keeping and tried her best to improve her language ability in English and Putongha. Rose helped H to get a job as a junior book keeper in a large commercial firm. H worked very hard, she was appreciated by her supervisor. One year later, she was promoted to be a book keeper. Two years later, she was promoted to be a senior clerk in this agency. With a stable job and stable income, H was able to rent a flat and lived with her son Tom. She hired a maid to take care of his son Tom in the day time. In the evening, she tried her very best to fulfill her role as a mother. On week end, apart from taking care of her son, H also actively involved in volunteer work with clients with substance abuse. She acted as a peer mentor for clients in the rehabilitation center. She loved with them all her heart.

Integrated Recovery of Meaning of Suffering in Addiction

The integrated recovery of meaning of suffering for people with drug addiction should focus on the following:

1. Enable persons with substance abuse and addiction to ventilate and elaborate their meaninglessness in suffering in life and suffering in addiction.
2. Empathic listening and acknowledgement of the ontological pain for people with substance abuse and addiction in search for super meaning of suffering in life.
3. Facilitate people with substance abuse and addiction to find new meaning of love of being loved.
4. The new meaning of love and being loved should enable people with substance abuse and addiction to formulate new meaning in suffering in life.
5. All these can be illustrated in the following case.

The Rough Bottom of R: The Tragedy of an Old Man with Drug Addiction

R was an old man around 70 years. He had been engaged in drug addiction ever since he was 30 years old. R was born in a rural village in the mainland China. His parents were a poor farmer. Even though under the Communist China, poor farmers were respected by in the political ladder, the government was too poor to support numerous farmers who struggled extremely hard for their minimal survival. R parents worked very hard and little R could never have enough food to eat. The whole family including R, his parents, grandparents and his younger sister lived within a small hut of the mountain. Their farmland was cultivated from slope of a huge mountain. The mountain was very remote and isolated from nearby towns.

No sooner, R's parents died of terminal illness, leaving R and his grandparents and younger sisters. At that time, R was only 12 years old. To support the whole family, R needed to work a child labor in a large city. He worked very hard so as to support a hand to mouth life for his family. His life was boring, full of endless work and fatigue. To cheer up, he took up amphetamine with his friends. No sooner, he involved in drug trafficking so as to earn more money for his family. In one drug trafficking, he was caught by the police, as he was only 14 years old, he was sentenced to a two years' detention in a correction service institution.

After that, he managed to sneak into Hong Kong. He worked as a manual labor in a large factory. He tried his very best to work, to save money and to support his own family. Several years later, his grandparents died and his younger sister also managed to sneak into Hong Kong. At first, he and his younger sister supported one another and lived together in a small flat. Later, his younger sister married with a young man in the same factory and they migrated to Canada three years later leaving R lonely in Hong Kong.

Despite R was only 30 years old, he looked old, depressed and fatigue in facing his whole life. No sooner he engaged in taking heroin. Gradually, he craved for drug and lost his job. To get enough money for drug addiction, he engaged in criminal affairs such as drug trafficking, robbery and gang fight. His leg and arm were severely hurt in a gang fight. To save his life, his left arm was amputated and his right leg was crippled. He went on his illegal affairs to get enough money for basic survival and taking heroin. One day, in drug trafficking, he was caught by the police. In the detention centre, he tried to commit suicide by hanging himself with his belt. He was saved but the hanging hurt his neck seriously. From that time onward, his neck was twisted, he could never have his head straight.

Physically, R was crippled, with only one arm left and twisted neck. Psychologically, he was lonely, helpless and addicted to heroin. Spiritually, he was empty, aimless and meaningless in life. He had nowhere to go and no meaning in life. For him, every day was an endless repetition of trying all his best to get enough money to take heroin. Only within heroin addiction, he could temporarily escape from all these endless torture. In his mind, he fully acknowledged that apart from endless torture and suffering, he had no way to go until one day he died of over dosage of heroin and/or other physical illness because of deteriorating bodily conditions.

Enable R to ventilate and elaborate their meaninglessness in suffering in life and suffering in addiction as well as empathic listening and acknowledgement of R's ontological pain

One day, after he had taken heroin, he went up to the top floor of a tall building and ready to jump down and ended up his own life. Fortunately, a security guard discovered him and called the police. Then, he was sent to a mental hospital. R was diagnosed as suffering from major depressive disorder with a high risk of suicide. He was then hospitalized for one year. Within this year, R was detoxified. He was no longer dependent on heroin. R was sent to a rehabilitation center for follow up. In this centre, he encountered a very empathic social worker, Amy. In front of her, R felt being understood and very earnestly to tell his own stories. Amy felt sad about R's sufferings in life. What below was the verbatim recording of R's narration and Amy's empathic response.

R: My whole life is entirely empty and meaningless. My parents died, my sister left me alone. My leg was crippled and my arm was amputated. My neck was twisted. I was totally deteriorated by prolonged heroin intake. There was no way out, nothing for me is worth to be mentioned. I am nothing. …. (R seemed to fully be absorbed in his painful recall and memories.)

Amy: R, I could understand your pain in life. Indeed, you are already very tough. I cannot imagine if my parents and grandparents died as well as I was disabled… (Amy's tears ran down on her face.)

R: Thank very much for your empathic understanding. You are the first professional that cries for such a poor and useless man like me.

Amy cleaned the tears on her face and smiled kindly: It was painful to see your younger sister migrated to Canada. Did she contact you often?

R: At first we did maintain some regular contact. But after I had committed illegal affairs and re-engaged in heavy addiction of heroin, I felt shameful to contact my younger sister. I was afraid my criminal offence might influence her family. I lost contact with her for four years already.

Amy: So, despite she left you, you still cared about her. Did she marry?

R: By the time she migrated to Canada, she had already married a Chinese Canadian. I think she must have a happy family. Hi…………..(R signed deeply in thinking about her sister.)

Amy: Your younger sister is the only relative of you. Isn't it?

R: I think yes, I get an uncle and a cousin in Hong Kong, but ... when I craved for drug; I had borrowed money from them. They knew that I was a drug addict. They looked down upon me.

Amy: So, you feel shameful in contacting them. That means, you feel guilty about your drug addiction and your criminal affairs.

R: Certainly, I feel shameful for all I have done in my life. I did not have any courage to face them.

Amy: I can understand how you feel. Life is sometimes out of our control. Anyway you have tried your very best to struggle but thing did not turn out in your preferred way.

R: Thanks for your kind words. Indeed, you are the most kind-hearted professional I have ever met. I can feel your love and concern and empathy deeply.

Facilitate R to find new meaning of love of being loved

Amy facilitated R to find new meaning of love and being loved. Firstly, Amy helped R to connect with his sister. After several years' time, R had lost contact with his sister. She no longer lived in the previous address. Amy had to pose an advertisement in a famous Chinese newspaper. Fortunately, after three months' time, she sister, S wrote a letter to Amy telling her new address, and phone number. What below was the verbatim recording of Amy and S in the phone.

Amy: Hi, S really liked to hear from you.

S: Thanks a lot for your phone. I missed my brother for a number of years.

Amy: He missed you too.

S: Why he didn't contact me?

Amy: He was too shameful to contact you?

S: Oh, why? Forever, he was my beloved brother?

Amy: He committed illegal offence and drug addiction. He was afraid of making troubles to your family.

S: Oh, my poor brother, he really suffered a lot. When our parents died of terminal illness, he worked very hard as a child labor in a large city to support our family. It was really too hard for him. At that time, he was only 12 years old. He had to work 12 hours each day and his boss oppressed him very much. Every day for him was endless work and fatigue and bullying from his boss and his colleagues. Only drug could help him to escape from such frustration in life. To earn more money and to protect him from being oppressed by others, he needed to join a delinquent gang and involved in drug trafficking. He never told us how hard his life was. He only tolerated all this by himself. (S began to wipe in the phone.)

Amy: It is very good that you care your eldest brother so much. By the way, do you realize that he lost his left arm and his right leg was crippled in a gang fight? His neck was twisted in a hanging suicide…. Despite he was too shameful to meet you; I think he really needed you and your comfort at this moment.

S: Did he hurt seriously, does he still alive? I must see him as soon as possible. Right now I was totally caught up by my two kids. I had to discuss with my husband and I will make a trip to Hong Kong as soon as possible. (S showed deep concern for R.)

Amy: He was fine in our drug detoxification and rehabilitation centre. He felt regret with what he had done in the past. He felt shameful to contact any relatives and friends.

S: I will arrange the thing immediately. Kindly don't tell my elder brother. I am afraid when he knows about that, he tries to avoid seeing me.

Amy: I know that. I will keep our conservation confidential. Let us give R a great surprise on your arrival.

Finally, S arrived the drug detoxification centre. It really caught R by surprise. He tried to run out of the centre. But Amy stopped him. At last S, R and Amy met together. They sat on the sitting room and had the following verbatim recording.

Amy: Welcome S. It is really nice to see your arrival.

S: I loved to see you. Dear brother R. How are you? I missed you so much?

R: S……long time on see……. (R was very reluctant to speak; tears ran down on his face. He could not speak anything. …)

S came forward and embraced R. At first, he tended to struggle away but he finally embraced tightly with S. For a long while, both S and R could not say anything…..

Amy: Thanks God… (Amy was so impressed. She cried also…)

After 15 minutes silence, they were ready to share.

R: Dear S. Thanks for your visit. I did not worth to be your brother. You better forgot that you had such a shameful brother. Your children felt shameful to have an uncle as a criminal and chronic drug addict.

S: Dearest S. please does not say such painful words. You are my only beloved. I missed you much. All my children urged to see you. They urged me to see you but they have to continue their schooling. My husband did not have holiday. That was why I came alone.

R: I was so bad, I committed illegal offence. I had borrowed a lot of money from relatives. I was too shameful to see them all. I was too shameful to see you. Leave me alone. I am now crippled and disabled. I deserved a life of pain and shame.

S: Dearest S, without you, I had already died of hunger in my life. Without you, I would never be able to come to Hong Kong. Without you, I could never migrate to Canada. Without you, I could not marry my husband and could not have my children.

Without you, my life was empty and meaninglessness. I loved you deeply my brother. No matter how crippled, disabled and illegal you are, you are still my most beloved brother forever. My beloved brother, I love you so much. ....(S poured out her love towards her brother fully)

S's powerful narration of her love towards her brother deeply impressed both Amy and R. They kept silence in a long while. Finally, Amy stood up and led R's hand to S. They hold their hands tightly. It seemed that S' deepest love towards her brother really dissolved R's ambivalence senses of inferiority, meaninglessness, shame and loneliness in his whole life.

From above mentioned verbatim recording, it was clear that S' deepest sense of love towards his brother was very powerful. Apart from dissolving R's prolonged senses of inferiority, loneliness, anger towards himself, and chronic meaninglessness and emptiness, it gave R an intensive sense of love and being loved. Despite all his sufferings in life, he was still deeply loved by his sister. It triggered his age old memories. When he was young, he played with her sister in their farmland. In their children, they faced numerous hardships. They were poor, they starved together, and they felt sad and lonely about the death of their parents. With a sense of love, he struggled for life. He worked as child labor in a large city in China. He was bullied by other. He could tolerate and survive all these simply because he loved her young sister deeply. Later, he joined in a delinquent gang; he committed illegal offence and took drug. In doing so, he fully recognized that he was illegal as well as immoral on one hand. He had to do so, as it was the only way for him to earn more money as well as to protect himself for supporting his sister on the other hand. Later on, he supported his sister and his family to live a decent living. He supported her to have good secondary school and university education which is very rare in his village. He also supported her to sneak into Hong Kong. He loved her deeply. For her, he could sacrifice everything. All these feeling and memories came back. His feeling of love, hope and trust to his sister returned. Once it returned, his meaning of suffering was restored.

Enable R to Develop New Meaning of Suffering in His Life

After R has regained the sense of love and being loved from the reunion of his younger sister, R found new meaning of suffering in his life. With the encouragement and support from his sister, he tried to pay back all the loans from bank and his relatives. Despite he was crippled and disable he worked a messenger in a social welfare organization. The social worker, Amy helped him to apply for compassionate housing from the Housing Authority. Finally, he was able have a small cubicle in a public estate. He was able to earn enough money to support a minimal daily life. His sister stayed in Hong Kong for one month and went back to Canada. Two months later, she, her husband (Mic) and two sons (Tom and Jack) came to Hong Kong for two weeks in summer holiday. They had a happy vacation time. In their happy reunion, R did find new meaning in his sufferings in life. What below is the verbatim recording of this happy reunion in a Chinese restaurant.

S: Dear brother, it is really nice we can have a dinner together.

Tom: I am so hungry. Mum, can I eat something. I like big Mac. (Tom was a lovely two years old child)

Jack: Mum said big Mac was no good for our health. Be a good boy and well behaved yourself. (Jack was the eldest brother of Tom. He was five years old.)

Mic: I think we all feel hungry. Let order some good food. Dear brother R, what sort of food you like or does not like.

R: I do not have any preference. Any food you like I like too. It is really wonderful to have dinner with Tom, Jack, S, Mic and Amy. I think that should my happiest moment in life. (R was very impressive. He certainly felt love and being loved. He was no longer a lonely, empty and disabled man. He still had his own family to care and be cared.)

Tom: Dear Uncle R, I like to eat dim sum and spring roll.

Jack: Tom, don't be impolite, let the adult decided first.

Tom; I know that brother Tom like to eat spring roll too. He also like to eat fire rice. We all like to eat fire rice.

R: Let us have dim sum, fire rice and spring roll. (R smiled happily and enjoyed the togetherness of Tom and Jack very much.)

S; Tom and Jack, see how Uncle R loved you so much.

Tom and Jack: We loved you too, Uncle R.

R: Dear Tom and Jack, remember to be a good boy, study hard and be kind to your mother. Never behave like Uncle R.

Tom: Why? Are you a bad buy and we should not behave like you.

Jack: Uncle R should not a bad guy.

R: Uncle R did not behave well in life. So never behave like me. (With tears, R whispered his words)

S: Dear Tom and Jack, you are too small to understand our adult world. You must know that Uncle R tried his very best to take care of your mother. So you must tried your very best to show due respect to Uncle R.

Tom and Jack surrounded R and tried to embrace him with love.

R kept quietly for a long while. He seemed to deeply enjoy the lovable embracing from Tom and Jack.

Mic: Our family is grateful to Uncle R forever. Without Uncle R, there would never be S, and without S, there would never be our family.

R: Thanks God, I finally have a such as a lovely and wonderful family.

Mic: Uncle R, we all welcomed you to visit us in Canada.

R: I am too old and disabled to take a long flight.

S: Dear brother R, when we get everything well prepared. We would move back to Hong Kong to accompany you.

R: It was too much change for your whole family. I do not worth enough to sacrifice your life in Canada to come back to Hong Kong. In particular Tom and Jack was accustomed to life there.

Mic: Fine, Tom and Jack was still small, when they come to Hong Kong they can have more education in Chinese. I am going to find a job in Hong Kong. If I can do so, I properly move back to Hong Kong. So don't worry about us. You have done too much for S and us. It should be the time we do something for you. Dear Brother R.

S: Yes, we should do something for you…..

Amy: It is really nice to witness such a wonderful family reunion. Dear R, I can really sense how much you are being loved and cared.

R was totally embraced by the love from his sister, brother in law and two nephews. With that sort of profound love, indeed, R developed new meaning in sufferings in life. What below was his self narration on the meaning of suffering of his life.

R: Indeed, this should be my happiest moment in our life. I never dream that I can unite with my sister and her family. Tom and Jack were so lovely. Mic was such a nice guy. He was so understanding and supportive. He was so genuine. I am so happy to witness that my sister was full of blessing in life. She had such a nice family. When I looked at them, I deeply felt that all my suffering was meaningful and worthwhile. In the past, I was so painful. I worked doubly hard when I was only 14. I was bullied by others. I had to commit illegal offence so as to earn more money for my family. I joined the delinquent groups. I was so stressful, anxious and frustrated that I had to take drug to ease my nerves. In my whole life, I only have one simple mission. I had to make my family a warm, caring and sufficient. Even I sacrificed my life to make my sister have a good life. It was worthwhile and meaningful. Despite, I was imprisoned, crippled and lost my left arm and my whole life was nothing but a confused mess. Finally, my sister got a happy family. She was well educated and married to a very nice husband. She got two lovely kids. Thank God, my whole life's struggle was worthwhile and meaningful.

Profound Love and Meaning of Life Enable R to a Full Recovery

Within the profound love of her young sister, R was fully abstained from drug addiction. In addition to that he found a job as a part time cleaner in a Chinese restaurant. He also joined a Christian church and finally became a committed Christian. He then served as a volunteer in a Christian Detoxification and Rehabilitation Centre. Two years later, his younger sister came to Hong Kong and lived with him together. He had a clear mission that God sent him to protect his younger sister and his family. He also had a clear vision that he would try his best to serve as a part time volunteer missionary to lead people with drug addiction back to God's hand. What below was R' self-narration.

R: Thank God, I finally understand why God put me such a difficult situation in life. Why God let me suffer so much. I am an angel sent from God to protect, to nurture and care my younger sister. I engaged in prolonged drug addiction so that I can use my own experiences to counsel, to help and to supervise youngsters to quite their substance abuse. I am a lively witness showing that God's deep and profound love shaped me thoroughly from a useless drug addict, a crippled and disabled old man to become a torch to sparkle the will to life and recovery of adolescent drug addict. I told them my own stories how I engaged in substance abuse, drug trafficking, gang fight and other immoral and illegal offence. I told them how my left arm was lost and how my leg was crippled. I affirmed that if I could change myself, they could change themselves too. There is never too late to abstain from drug addiction and substance abuse. Thank God, I really started a new life again. God gives me such a great chance to start a new life. ....

Integrated Recovery of Life Transitoriness and Wholeness in Addiction

As mentioned above, for persons with drug addiction, they usually harbor many discrepancies among their past, present and future. Thus, integrated recovery in life transitoriness and sense of wholeness should include the following:

1. Encourage them to create and develop a meaningful and healthy present.
2. Enable them to recall happy memories in the past.

3. Integrate their current meaningful and healthy present with their happy past memories.
4. Facilitate them to develop meaning in their past suffering trauma.
5. Help them to construct a meaningful and hopeful future.
6. Encourage them to develop integrated and meaningful life transitoriness in the past, present and future.
7. Facilitate them to establish a positive sense of wholeness and whereness in actual reality.

All these can be illustrated in the following case.

The Lonely Life of P

P was born with an eye deformation. Because of that, her parents abandon her and she was thus taken to a children home. In there, there were around 30 homeless children. As the house parents there were quite egocentric and did not care much about them. They engaged in frequent quarrel, bullying and oppression among one another. Under that circumstance, P had to defend herself by being highly aggressive towards others' attack and bullying. No sooner, P was regarded as a subgroup leader in the one of the gang within the residents. All along, P demonstrated good leadership in mastering her small gang of six girls. As united together, no one dared enough to bully them. Instead, they bullied others. Once, they involved in a fight with another gang in the children home. One girl in another gang was seriously hurt by P. Thus, P was transferred to a corrective juvenile training centre. Within the corrective institution, P was thus bullied and oppressed by both inmates and staff. Within this spontaneous oppression, P became depressive, inferior and helpless. She harbor intensive depressive mood and always broke into tears. Fortunately, one inmate, Q came out and protected P from abuse and oppression. She was in fact the girlfriend of the leader, Y of a famous delinquent gang. When P and Q were discharged from the corrective centre, P was a faithful follower of Q. One year later, P also became the girlfriend of Y. It made Q become furious towards P. She hired someone to murder P. Fortunately, this was discovered by Y. From that onward, P was totally attached to Y and became his most intimate girlfriend. Y was caring at first and he hired a famous doctor to make an artificial eye for P. With them, no one could discover P was deformed in her left eye. Instead, she appeared as young, beautiful and lovely. As Y was a drug dealer involved in drug trafficking. P inhaled cocaine with Y and engaged actively in drug dealing and trafficking. Unfortunately, she was caught by the police and was sentenced to three year imprisonment. Within these three year imprisonment, Y was humiliated by others. When she left the prison, she harbored both anger and frustration towards the oppressive world. As she could not find a good job, she worked as a sex worker in a night club. She was young, beautiful and assertive with sufficient sex and courtship experiences to attract and seduce his customers. No sooner, she became one of the most attractive ladies in this night club. Everything went well as she could attract quite a number of rich customers. However, some of them were abnormal and with a tendency to abuse P physically and sexually and gave her a good deal of money as reward. Because of money, P had to tolerate this quietly. However, she felt deeply hurt emotionally, physically and mentally. To get rid of all these frustration, P restored her habit of cocaine addiction. At the same time, she also engaged in compulsive gambling, heavy drinking as well as one night stance with other handsome guy in the nightclub. No sooner, P's physical, mental and financial conditions were deeply disturbed by all these unhealthy addiction and confused life pattern. Despite she was well dressed and make up, she still looked pale, unhealthy and even depressive. She could no longer be attractive to those rich and choosy customers. Her status and position in the night club deteriorated accordingly. Finally, after a severe quarrel with her manager in the nightclub, she was sacked. Later she worked in a much lower class night club. She felt sad and inferior and she needed to involve in even heavier compulsive gambling, drinking and addiction of cocaine. Even worse off, because of compulsive gambling, she was heavily indebted to a loan shark who was actually controlled by underground society. They used various illegal and immoral means to humiliate P. They even disturbed P's customers in the night club. Finally, P was also sacked by this night club. P was deeply disturbed. She had no way out except suicide. She climbed up in a top building and jumped down to end up her life. Fortunately, when she jumped down a tent in the building slow down her falling and she was saved but with a broken leg and rib. She was thus sent to a nearby mental hospital with a diagnosis of severe depression, chronic substance abuse and suicide. She stayed there for three months. Within these three months, she had attempted suicide three times. She was thus restrained in her bed for a long while and heavy dosage of psychiatric drug was induced. Finally, she appeared as inert, dull and withdrawn from the reality. When she was discharged from the mental hospital, her medical social worker transferred her to a psychiatric half way house for treatment. In there, a genuine social worker, K was responsible to take care of P. What below is K's narration describing how inert, empty and meaningless P was when she was first sent to the halfway house.

> K: Indeed, K was extremely inert, withdrawn and passive when she first admitted into our half way house. She refused to say any words in first few days. She simply ate, drunk and sitting still on the sofa of the sitting room. Some residents and workers approach her to talk with her but she simply kept in a dead silence. Sometimes, she stared at the ceiling. Sometimes, she focused her attention fully on street outside the window. It seemed that she harbored too many traumatic memories in her life that all her struggle in life was in vain. She was young but looked pale and old. Once, in the mid night I saw her in her bed crying bitterly. When I approached her to comfort her, she stopped crying immediately and refused my comfort. She did not approach to anyone in the half way house. For her rehabilitation, I referred her to work in a shelter workshop nearby. She was willing to work, but worked very slowly as a chronic schizophrenic client. It was really hard for us to understand what exactly she was thinking in every moment.'

From K's narration, it was clear that P suffered from ontological emptiness in which the traumatic past, the meaningless present and the hopeless future was just an existential vacuum. Because of that, her sense of being and existence was thus deeply hindered. She did not feel any meaning to continue her life and she did not beware anything in the outside world that worth her engagement and involvement.

Encourage P to Acknowledge, Create and Develop a Meaningful and Healthy Present

P had been idling in the half way for two months. Within these two months, many residents tried to connect with her but failed. K was very empathic with P and she tried to sit near to P and accompany her for a long while every day. Gradually, P began to initiate short conversation with K. What below is K's self-narration demonstrating how patient, caring and empathic was in relating to P's intensive feeling of emptiness.

K: P was so inert and passive for a whole month in the half way house. I tried to contact with her previous social workers in life, including her medical social worker in the mental hospital. From her, I knew that she came from a children home and had worked as a sex worker in night club. She did not tell much more about further details. Then I contacted the social worker in her former children home. Related social worker had only worked there for a couple of year. He did not know much about P. Finally, I visited the children home and a welfare worker, L, there who had been a client in this children home in her childhood knew P well. She was a good friend of P during their childhood in the children home. She had frequent contact with p before P committed suicide and was admitted in the mental hospital. From her, I knew that P suffered much from her life. She was born with a deformed left eye. She was deserted by her parents and grew up in a children home. She survived toughly in her early life by involving in frequent gang fight, illegal acts, imprisonment, and sex trade. Her life was full of misfortune, being deserted, betrayed and degraded by others. Indeed, she needed to live a tough life and fight of her own survival. But by the end of life, what end up were just endless suffering, torture, and traumas. That was why she was so frustrated, upset and inert in life. When I realized all these, I began to have a deep empathy with her. With that deep empathy, I am able to tolerate his inertness, withdrawal and passivity. Once, she sat quietly in the sofa of the sitting room, she stared at the television for two hours. Instead of regarding her as unmotivated client, I sat closely to her and also stared at the television. Occasionally, I embraced her shoulder for a short while and continued to look at the television. At first, she felt strange about my action and did not look at me. I stayed with her for half hour and then do my own clerical work in a table near her. The next day, she also stared at the television. I repeated my action as before. I continued to do so for several days.

Gradually, she looked at me when I embraced her but did not say any words. In the tenth day, she seemed to enjoy my embracement and lay her head on my shoulder just like a child laying her head on her mother. For a long while, she did not say a word but I fully knew that she was fully absorbed in her own traumas in life in which she dreamed for a good mother and father to care her, to support her and to love her so that she could be protected from related traumas in life. She lay on my shoulder for more than fifteen minutes. I embraced her and told her that it was very safe in our half way house. Everybody in the house loved her and cared about.

From that time onwards, she was no so inert and passive in our house. When I was there, she occasionally hold my hand and sometimes when I sat on the sofa of the sitting room she came forward and say hello with me. She seemed to be quite attached to me. But when I tried to chat with her, she only said some short answers such as 'yes' or 'no'. She began to have good eye contact with me and with other residents. It was quite clear that P's sense of reality has improved a lot.

Once, there was a phone call for P in the house. It was strange as P has never received phone call before. In the phone call, P was very excited for a while and then she cried. She put down the phone and rushed to my office. In her eyes, there was joy as well as confusion. She told me that her lost mother tried to contact her. She had deserted her since P was born. She could not believe her ear that the phone call really came from her mother.

One week later, P's mother, F was accompanied by a social worker from social welfare department came and visit P. She was a woman around fifty, well dressed and seemed to be quite regretted to what she had done to P. She cried in front of P and asked for her forgiveness. P was quite confused. On one hand, she was really angry with her mother's abandonment. On the other hand, she was really excited to see her mother. She did not say any word but her eyes were full of tears showing that how much she suffered in her life ever since she was deserted by her mother. For a long while, they hugged together. Her mother than brought her out for dinner. The social worker told me that F was a rich woman. She deserted P when she was only a girlfriend of P's father, B who was a married billionaire. B did not want the appearance of P to destruct his family life. Twenty years later, B's wife died of terminal cancer. From that time onward, F formally married P and they started to search for the whereabouts of P. Recently, F also suffered from terminal illness, he aspired to see P before he died.

After the visit of her mother, P's mental state was much improved. She no longer idling in the half way house. Instead, she visited her father house and stayed there for a couple of weeks. Her father died peacefully with the togetherness of P and F. After the funeral, F urged P to stay with her at home. P refused, she still harbored a hidden anger that F deserted her and makes her suffered so much in her life. Instead, she moved back to the halfway house. From that time onward, P was no longer inert, passive and withdrawal. She became active and helpful in doing related duties in the house. She was also very initiative in searching for a decent job for herself.

P: 'Indeed, it was really hard to tell my feeling after seeing my mother. When I was small living in the children I also dreamed that one day my mother would suddenly appeared and rescue me from the dreadful children home that was full of oppression, abuse and bullying. However, every morning when I woke up, I desperately knew that it was merely a dream but nothing else. When I grew older, I began to hate my mum. It was her who abandoned me and made me suffer so much in my whole life. I cursed God why others could enjoy a happy family with caring parents but I had suffered so much. As I was imprisoned, being a prostitute, and being sexually abused by customers, I found my whole life was just an entirely endless suffering, torture and abandonment. That was why I had to use various addictive means such as drug addiction, compulsive gambling to paralyze my inner pain. However, life did not allow me to take a rest from my sufferings. Instead, it increased my loan shark chased me everywhere and they even broke my own way to earn a living. I had nowhere to go except committing suicide. Even I was saved from my suicide, but from that time onward, my whole life was deadly frozen. In the half way house, my mind and spirit was already dead. I did not harbor any will power or energy to do anything, to say any word and to interact with anyone. Life for me was a dead lock.

Fortunately, K was still empathic with me. Despite I was so inert, passive and withdrawn, she did not abandon me. Instead, she still played attention to me. She still respected me. She accompanied me patiently and waiting for my response. Also, she helped me to restore my confidence that I still got somebody regarded me as a holistic person even I did not respond to them.

I was totally surprised by the incoming phone call from my mother. I never thought that she could find me and say sorry to me. For me, it was just the great gift of God for me. It just liked my childhood dream came true. She abandoned me when I was a baby simply because she dared not to admit my presence so to avoid disturbance of my father's family. That was I was born to be a nuisance of my family. I was so sad to hear that. Apart from my disability of my eye, I was born to be a trouble maker. That was why I needed to be a sex worker. Facing the presence of my mother, I did have an unresolved love and hate complex towards her. On one hand, I hated her deeply on why she abandoned me. On the other hand, I was so glad that she finally admitted her fault and took courage to find me and repent for what she had done to me.

From that time onward, my life was no longer alone and with endless torture, abandonment and suffering. At least, I had two people in the whole world really care about no matter who I was and what I had done. They were my mother and my social worker. The feeling of being loved and cared was fantastic and interesting. Once you were cared and loved by others, you also loved yourself. I knew that I should not let my mother and my respectable social worker down. I needed to recover so that their hope and love towards me was realistic and worthwhile. Every day I got up, I began to embrace some substantial work and task that I needed to do. I needed to cheer myself up. I needed to forget my painful past and cast my hope on the future and engaged in my present substantially......

After the enduring companionship of the social worker and the appearance of her mother, P's sense of meaning of life was retained. She retained hope in the future. As there were still two persons in the world that still loved and respected P, she regained her own self-respect and self-confidence that she should do something good for herself and for others. She had a substantial present and hopeful future she had to work hard for all of that. It was a meaningful present to found for a good job so that she would not let her mother and her social worker down.

Enable P to Recall Happy Memories in the Past

Despite P had already engaged in a meaningful present, she still absorbed in her unhappy and traumatic past memories. To have a complete healing, it was important that P could recall her happy past memories. Her social worker, K, under the supervision of the writer, tried to perform the following intervention for K so to help P to recall her happy past.

K: How is your job interview?

P: I don't know. I hope it was successful. This should be a good job. I liked to be a clerk in a large shipping company.

K: Do you have confidence in it.

P: I don't know, within three years in prison, I learnt book keeping and some basic clerical work. I actually had a certificate in book keeping and clerical work. In the night club, I helped my boss to some basic documentary work.

K: That is good, do you tell you past history to them. (K purposefully led P to tell her past history)

P: Of course not. I think they should hire me according to my ability not according to my past history. Indeed, it was too shameful to tell other about my traumatic past.

K: Do you mean your life in children home and other developments in life?

P: Everyone looked down about a night club sex worker; in particular I had been imprisoned for three years and with a horrible history of compulsive gambling, drug addiction and committing suicide. Who dare to hire such a bad worker in your company?

K: Despite all this, you still look young, nice manner and dress beautiful. Everyone would admire you as a young and lovely lady. (Once, P's mother appeared, she regained self-confidence and meaning of life and began to dress properly and meaningfully.)

P: That is the talent of night club worker. (Both P and K laughed.)

K: I think I am not qualified to be a night club worker.

P: That is why you are such a good social worker. (P and K laughed again. K purposefully be humorous and let the atmosphere be enlightening so that K could be in better mood to recall some happy experiences in the past.)

K: By the way, in your past, apart from your customers in the night club, any one in your life really appreciated your beauty as well as your genuineness and warmth in facing others. (K intended to go into P's happy past experiences.)

P: Oh, regardless of my eye deformation, people around me in the children home, my previous boyfriends, and even the nurse in the mental hospital said that I looked young and beautiful. I remembered that one young psychiatric nurse approached me when I was first admitted in the mental hospital saying that why I had to commit suicide even I looked young and beautiful.

K: So the young and beautiful liked to commit suicide leaving us such ugly and old ones still alive. (K tried to be humorous so that she could recall happy memories in the past)

P laughed: Dear K you are the kindest and also noble lady I have ever met in my life. You are so respectable. You are such a good social worker.

K: Thanks for your hearty appreciation. I am a Christian. I tried to share God's love with my clients including you. By the way, your beauty must attracted many friends around in your childhood and adolescence.

P: Don't talk about my childhood and adolescence; there were far too many fight, confusion, bullying and oppression. (P began to recall traumatic experiences and memories in childhood and adolescence.)

K: Despite all that, you were still though and strong in facing all these challenges and difficulties. You had told me that you were the leader of a small gang in your children home. (K helped P to recall her coping and resilience in childhood and adolescence.)

P: Yes, at that moment, I was at the children's home. There was bullying and oppression or even fights among children there. We needed to defend ourselves among us. I was the leader of a small subgroup of five girls. We called ourselves the Girl Fighters. Whenever other bullied us, we fought back fiercely.

K: So you were the best fighter. Did you know Kung Fu fighting? (Chinese marital art)

P laughed: Of course not, but I knew how to defend myself.

K: That was good, can you demonstrate some of your favorable marital art technique. (K purposefully encouraged P to demonstrate this so to help P to have a vivid recall of her good memories)

P: In here. Oh no.

K called along some residents in the half way house and let they practice P's skills of marital art. They practiced it in a funny way making P laughed.

P: I was too old now to practice all these. We are now the old women group.

Other residents said that P was still young and beautiful.

K: Where are other members of your Girl Fighters? Are there still in Hong Kong/

P: I don't know their whereabouts? Five years ago, I met one of them, G on the street, she was a sale girl. She said another member M was a policewoman. I thought they were far better than me. At least, they had not committed any criminal offence. I was too shame to tell her my conditions. I just said I was married and then I went away quickly.

K: Would you think it should be a good idea if I had their whereabouts from your previous children home and let us gather together for your birthday party in the coming month. I am pretty sure that your mother should celebrate your birthday for you. She was too glad to find you. (K did this so that K could have both a good memories of the past as well as formulating a good present with her close friends and her mother.)

P kept quiet for a long while. It seemed that many memories came to her mind.

P: I don't know whether you can find them or not. ......

K: If you don't oppose my suggestion, I would put on it. I am sure that I can find them out.

K took her promise seriously. She visited the children home and tried all means to search for the where about of members of 'Girl Fighters'. Finally, she was able to find G and M. G was a sale girl in a large department store. M was an inspector in the police force. They felt empathetic with P's conditions and tried their best to contact all members of the Girl Fighters. They were G, M, A, D and E. A was a teacher in a primary school. D also married to a man with drug addiction. Similar to P, she committed drug addiction and drug dealing and was imprisoned for three years. She was rehabilitated in a Christian rehabilitation centre and was successfully recovered. They all treasured the time of being together again. One month later, there was a great birthday party for P. At first, P's mother wanted to organize this party in her house, in which there were plenty of space and beautiful meadow, however, P affirmed that she wanted this to be organized in their previous children home. What below was the verbatim recording of some interesting dialogue in the birthday party in which P was helped to recall her wonderful past memories.

K: Indeed, it is a great occasion that we all gather together to celebrate P's birthday. Another great thing to celebrate is that P had met her mother. These two events really deserve our great celebration. Isn't it?

They all said yes. They were very excited.

P: Thanks for your participation. Indeed, it is my great honor and glory to have you all. I never dream that I can have such a great day.

G: What a great event, P, our 'Girl Fighters' really have a great day.

M: Yes, when we were in our children home, no one dared to threaten us. Now we came together again. There should not be anything can separate us. We are still the Girl Fighters.

D: Let us have a great day. Indeed, I have not met G, M, A and P for a long time. G was a sale girl, M was a police inspector, and A was a teacher. All of them are good girls leaving me and P were bad ones. We had done many bad things in our lives, but thanked God we were back now. We should also celebrate for P and my recovery.

A: I really remembered the days in our children home. We were bullied by other older and stronger children in the home. All of us were victims in their oppression and bulling. We needed to unite together and formulate our Girl fighters. From that time onwards, we were strong, we were tough and no one dared to oppress us again.

P's mother: I am so glad you are all here to celebrate P's 27 years birthday. It was the honor of P and me. Twenty seven years ago, I made a serious mistake in my whole life that I abandoned P at the door of the children home. I was not a good mother at all. I do not deserve to reunion with P, but God's grace is so great that He let me find P. She was so good that she forgave me..... (P's mother was so very excited, she broke into tears and K and A came along and embraced her)

P: In the past, I always complained God that why my whole life suffered so much hardship and torture in life. But now, I began to thank God, within my traumatic past, I still had a mother and a group of close friends still loved me, cared me and treasured me. Today should be my unforgettable day in my own life......'

(The birthday party went on with happiness and celebrations. Everyone was so impressed by P and the 'Girl Fighters' and P's mother. It was not only a great day for P, but also a great day for P's mother, P's friend, K and all participants in the children home.)

Integration of a Meaningful Past, Present and Future for P and a Sense of Wholeness

After the birthday party, P was very excited, she really forgave her mother. She was very glad that she could meet her friends in the children home. From that time onward, they had frequent contact among them. As G was a sale girl in a large departmental store, she invited P to work within this store as a sale girl too. They helped one another. At the same time, D invited P to come her church and became volunteers in the Christian rehabilitation centre. One year later, P was converted into a Christian. With all these, P life was very meaningful and substantial. In looking back to her whole life, P had the following self-narration.

P: Really thank for the kind work of social worker K, and the support of my former close friends G, A and D. They were really supportive and kind. Before I reunited with them, I think my past, present and future was all suffering, abandonment, unfair treatment and even traumas in life. I was angry with people around, no one treat me well.

However, after I had encountered K, my whole life changed drastically. She was so supportive and caring. The meeting of my mother was really caught us by surprise. The union of my former members in the Girl Fighters, really agitated me. I thought all of them brought me back to my life. Because of getting union of them, my whole life changed. I began to take a new view on my life.

My past was not only full of sufferings, sadness and hardships. Instead, it also had friendship, happiness and mutual support among friends, inmates in childhood and adolescence. My past was not only full of abandonment by my mother and my father as well as my boyfriend but also my mother's worries, regret and guilt in abandoning as well as her eagerness and hopefulness in endless search for me.

My present was not only endless suffering such as imprisonment, being bullied or abandonment by others but also amazing love, care and acceptance from professional, friends and parent. Because of them, I was sure that my future was bright and clear. I had tremendous values in my life. I am a good supervisor and well appreciated by my customers and my boss. I am a good Christian, I devoted my life to serve God and those with chronic drug addiction. I think God does not forget me. He gives me all things I did not get before, including love and support from parent, friends and workers as well as success in career. In my past, when I looked forward, I knew I had no future apart from imprisonment, abandonment and drug addiction. I needed to wait to die sooner or later in pain and in suffering. That was why I wanted to end up my painful life by suicide. But now, as I have already anchored in a meaningful and substantial present, I know my future is a hopeful togetherness with my beloved mother and friends with substantial contribution to the society, church and clients with drug addiction.

CONCLUSION

As a conclusion, this chapter is a comprehensive articulation about meaning of life and drug addiction. Based on related concepts, the writer describes various components of meaning of life including, sense of ultimate and ontological existence, constant search for meaning, sense of continuous existence, a struggle for minimal survival, ultimate insight and wisdom, and connection for the infinite. All these are well connected with one's meaning of love, meaning of suffering and will to meaning in life. It is clear that substance abuse and drug addiction are closely related to meaning of life. People with drug addiction usually suffer from intolerable frustration in life in which they feel empty and meaningless. Thus, drug addiction becomes the only available way to escape from intolerable sense of frustration. In extreme case, drug addiction and substance abuse finally become clients' sole meaning of life and sense of existence. The more they involve in drug addiction, the more frustrated they becomes as drug addiction gradually deteriorate their physical health, mental health as well as financial and social condition and the more they depend on drug addiction. Thus, for integrated recovery, persons with drug addiction need to reconstruct a meaningful life.

REFERENCES

Aristotle (1962) Man and state' in the *Politics*, translated by T. A. Sinclair. London: Penguin Books Ltd.

Cottingham, J. (2003) *On Meaning of Life*. New York: Routledge.

Frankl, V. (1997). *Man's Search for Ultimate Meaning*. New York: Plenum.

Frankl, V. (1984) Man's Search for Meaning: An Introduction to Logotherapy, New York: A Touchstone Book.

Kierkegaard, S. (1991) *Practice in Christianity.* Translated by H.V. Hong & E. H. Hong, Princeton: Princeton University Press.

Peele S. (1985) The Meaning of Addiction: Lexington Books

Schlick, M. (1979) On the meaning of life', in Schlick, A. M., Barbard F. B. V.

Schlick (Eds) Philosophical Paper II, pp. 112-128, London: R. Reidel Publishing Company.

Taylor, R. (1970) *Good and Evil,* London: Macmillian.

Waisburg, J., & Porter, J. (1994). Purpose in life and outcomes of treatment for alcohol dependence. *British Journal of Clinical Psychology*, 33:49-63.

Wohlgennant, R. (1988) Has the question about the meaning of life any meaning. In Hanfling, O. (Edited) *Life and Meaning*, pp. 20-33. Oxford: Blackwell.

Wright, S. (2013) *An Existential view of Alcohol Dependence and the Search for Meaning*.

Wurm, C. (2003). Is 'Addiction' a helpful concept? An existential view. *Europrean Psychotherapy*, 4(1): 175-182.

Yip, K.S. (2012) *Clinical Practice with Chinese Persons with Severe Depression: A Normalized, Integrated, Communicative, Holistic and Evolving Hope (NICHE) Recovery*, New York: Nova Sciences Publisher.

INDEX

A

B

D

E

F

G

H

I

J

K

L

M

N

R

S

T

U

V

W

Y